State Fragility and Resilience in sub-Saharan Africa

This book focuses on the indicators of fragility and the resilience of state-led interventions to address them in sub-Saharan Africa. It analyzes the 'figure' of fragile states as the unit of analysis and situates the study of fragility, governance and political adaptation within contemporary global and local political, economic and socio-cultural contexts.

The chapters offer an indispensable, econometrically informed guide to better understanding issues that have an impact on fragility in governance and nation-building and affect policy-making and program design targeting institutions in various circumstances. These issues, as they relate to the indicators of fragility, are the contexts and correlates of armed conflicts on statehood and state fragility, the poverty-trap, pandemics and household food insecurity, and child labor. Case studies from across 46 sub-Saharan African (SSA) countries are assessed to offer clear, broad and multidisciplinary views of what the future holds for them and the international donor communities at large. Regarding state-led interventions, the authors utilize insightful statistical methods and epistemologies to explain the correlates of behavioral language frames and conflict de-escalation on battle-related deaths across the conflict zones within the sub-region, the regional and country-level interventions to end child labor, the institutional frameworks and interventions in the advancement of food security and health.

This book will be of interest to scholars of economics, development, politics in developing countries, Area and African Studies, peace, conflict and security studies.

John Idriss Lahai is a Research Fellow at the University of New England, Australia.

Isaac Koomson is a PhD candidate at the UNE Business School at the University of New England, Australia.

Routledge Contemporary Africa Series

The International Criminal Court and the Lord's Resistance Army
Enduring Dilemmas of Transitional Justice
Joseph Otieno Wasonga

African Intellectuals in the Post-colonial World
Fetson A. Kalua

National Healing, Integration and Reconciliation in Zimbabwe
Ezra Chitando, Kelvin Chikonzo and Nehemiah Chivandikwa

Africa's Elite Football
Structure, Politics, and Everyday Challenges
Chuka Onwumechili

Social Licensing and Mining in South Africa
Sethulego Matebesi

The Everyday Life of the Poor in Cameroon
The Role of Social Networks in Meeting Needs
Nathanael Ojong

Introduction to Rwandan Law
Jean-Marie Kamatali

State Fragility and Resilience in sub-Saharan Africa
Indicators and Interventions
John Idriss Lahai and Isaac Koomson

For more information about this series, please visit: www.routledge.com/Routledge-Contemporary-Africa/book-series/RCAFR

State Fragility and Resilience in sub-Saharan Africa

Indicators and Interventions

John Idriss Lahai and Isaac Koomson

Routledge
Taylor & Francis Group
LONDON AND NEW YORK

First published 2020 by Routledge

2 Park Square, Milton Park, Abingdon, Oxon OX14 4RN

605 Third Avenue, New York, NY 10017

Routledge is an imprint of the Taylor & Francis Group, an informa business

First issued in paperback 2021

Publisher's Note

The publisher has gone to great lengths to ensure the quality of this reprint but points out that some imperfections in the original copies may be apparent.

British Library Cataloguing-in-Publication Data
A catalogue record for this book is available from the British Library

Library of Congress Cataloging-in-Publication Data
Names: Lahai, John Idriss, author. | Koomson, Isaac, author.
Title: State fragility and resilience in sub-Saharan Africa : indicators and interventions / John Idriss Lahai and Isaac Koomson.
Description: Abingdon, Oxon ; New York, NY : Routledge, 2020. | Series: Routledge contemporary Africa | Includes bibliographical references and index. | Identifiers: LCCN 2019044841 | ISBN 9780367410797 (hardback) | ISBN 9780367853846 (ebook)
Subjects: LCSH: Political stability–Africa, Sub-Saharan. | Nation-building–Africa, Sub-Saharan. | Conflict management–Africa, Sub-Saharan. | Child labor–Africa, Sub-Saharan. | Food security–Africa, Sub-Saharan. | Africa, Sub-Saharan–Social conditions–21st century.
Classification: LCC JQ1875 .L35 2020 | DDC 320.967–dc23
LC record available at https://lccn.loc.gov/2019044841

ISBN: 978-0-367-41079-7 (hbk)
ISBN: 978-1-03-217418-1 (pbk)
DOI: 10.4324/9780367853846

Typeset in Times New Roman
by Wearset Ltd, Boldon, Tyne and Wear

Contents

Figures

Tables

1 Introduction

National harmonies, the needs of an internationalized economy, group interests, classes and legal structures did not prevent conflict coming, did not ameliorate it when it did come, did not fight it and did not win it. It was *governments* [used interchangeably with the *state*] that fought it and did win it, by intricate calculations as to strategy and tactics, by mobilizing the political, material and psychological resources of nations, through appeal to the national interest (Hans J. Morgenthau, in *Politics Among Nations* (published in 1948) quoted in Navari 1991, 4). In this book we argue that the postcolonial state in sub-Saharan Africa cannot be trivialized, given its role in the making of the indicators of fragility: such as conflict, political instability, poverty, pandemics, corruption, food insecurity, gender inequality and child labor. Despite—or because of—this role, however, the postcolonial state should be seen as a resilient actor; one with a central role in managing economic, social and political fragility. Building on empirical discussions and statistical models of fragility and the role of the state, we propose two theoretical frameworks to understand, first (in Part I of this book), the critical indicators of fragility; and, second (in Part II), using the 'fragility-as-resilience' discourse as an 'affective analytical tool,' the character of state resilience and interventions, with particular emphasis on the state-centric approaches.

Why a state-centric approach? We believe this framework enables us to describe, predict and understand the meaning of the 'state,' and to challenge the existing knowledge about it within the limits of relevant epistemological and practical assumptions. Having said that, we recognize—and, in fact, problematize—the existential crisis the concept of 'state' (including its place and power) is currently undergoing. We also note that the increase in political interventions in the region is not driven solely by altruistic motives. The routinization of governmental interventions to end fragility is also driven by a power-seeking desire not just to control the resilience spaces at all levels of the state, but also to transform them into platforms for experimentation either with externally framed neoliberal peace and development policies or with indigenous policies that would guarantee these governments' political survival—at all costs, and by whatever means possible.

In view of the historical pre-eminence of such self-serving intervention, some would argue against the use of a state-centric approach. The question thus arises:

why is the re-centering of the state relevant to our study of fragility and state resilience in the region? On the one hand, we believe a state-centric approach challenges, to use the words of Marta Iniguez de Heredia and Zubairu Wai, "the dominant and hegemonic notion that Africa is peripheral, exceptionally outside world politics [and the international political economy, or IPE], and marginal." This aim provides legitimacy to approaches (including that proposed here) that "constitute an elegant epistemological critique of [the IPE] and how it relates to Africa, painting a complex picture of the dynamics of [the global economy], the larger structures within which is produced, and Africa's place in it" (de Heredia and Wai 2018, *jacket*). On the other hand, the centering of the state is also about explaining the functions that only the state can perform. It was Hans J. Morgenthau (in *Politics Among Nations*, published in 1948) who reminded us that

> national harmonies, the needs of an internationalized economy, group interests, classes and legal structures did not prevent conflict coming, did not ameliorate it when it did come, did not fight it and did not win it. It was *governments* [used interchangeably with the *state*] which fought it and did win it, by intricate calculations as to strategy and tactics, by mobilizing the political, material and psychological resources of nations, through appeal to the national interest.
>
> (Quoted in Navari 1991, 4)

Morgenthau was seeking to draw our attention to that which we should not lose sight of, namely, the relevance and resilience of the state. His call, though he was speaking on behalf of Western countries at a time when they were struggling for world domination against another contender, the Soviet Union, has relevance today and can be applied in the context of state fragility. The turn of events following the end of the Cold War in 1989 had unwanted consequences for sub-Saharan Africa. There was an upsurge in civil conflicts (as reactions against the regimes created by and for the Cold War powers) and other indicators of fragility. But, with the world becoming a global village, the turmoil of the region can no longer be characterized as 'problems of Africa,' for its people and governments to deal with alone.

In the place of indifference, what can best be described as an interdisciplinary social science and humanistic inquiry into Africa's state/hood, fragility crises and societal resilience has emerged. Political scientists have turned their attention to what constitutes 'political behavior' in situations of fragility. These 'fragile' situations are "[p]eriods when states or institutions lack the capacity, accountability, or legitimacy to mediate relations between citizen groups and between citizens and the state, making them vulnerable to violence" (World Bank 2011a, xvi, 2011b). 'Fragile situations' have either (a) a harmonized average Country Policy and Institutional Assessment (CPIA) rating of 3.2 or less, or (b) the presence of a UN and/or regional peace-keeping or peace-building mission within the past three years (World Bank 2003, cited in Ferreira 2015, 34). Sociologists of the functionalist school understand that sub-Saharan African countries are becoming increasingly complex and differentiated due to globalization (see Shizha and Diallo 2016). Globalization has brought socialized forms of political mobilities (Urry 2000), civilizational ideas of justice and power (Sriram 2004, 2005) and other forms of network activities (Pieterse 1994) into societies hitherto resistant to the influences of Western modernity (Gill 2003; Taylor and Nel 2002; Gelb and Floyd 1999). As such, there is growing sociological inquiry into the forces shaping people's lived experiences, and the consequences of such experiences, within the structures and functions of these dysfunctional societies. Gender studies scholars also have something to say: that structural gender inequality should be considered in the explanations of the causes and consequences of fragility (Caprioli 2005; Kevane 2004). Ethnologists and anthropologists, who were among the first to embrace the idea of societal resilience in the fragile spaces of sub-Saharan Africa (see Moore 1994; Nyamnjoh 2012; Herskovits 1959), have also begun to look at the biological and physiological aspects of societies in the making and unmaking of fragility (Comaroff and Comaroff 1993; Bryceson 2006). Empiricist peace studies scholars (Bertocchi and Guerzoni 2012; Boege et al. 2008, 2009; Renders and Terlinden 2010) and journalists (Somerville 2016) have also embraced the idea that not all histories of fragility fall into the *category* of fragility; some forms of fragility may equally be understood as episodic events shaping the evolving hybrid political orders.

Meanwhile, economists studying the rise and fall of market forces in the IPE have begun to draw correlations between relative deprivation, greed and grievances, and conflicts (Collier and Hoeffler 2004; Collier and Sambanis 2005; Collier, Hoeffler and Rohner 2009), the arms-industrial complex (Tan 2014; Dunne and Tian 2013) and the volatility of markets in the capitalist North and political instability in Africa (Berdal and Malone 2000; Moore 2000). They have realized that there would be an adverse impact on consumption patterns in Paris, New York, London, Sydney and Toronto, among other major consumer economies, were there to be an international rights-based outcry against child labor in the cocoa bean plantations of, say, the Ivory Coast (Amanor 2012; Squicciarini and Swinnen 2016); they have realized that the outbreak of, say, Ebola, in any sub-Saharan African country would impact the global tourism industries and, hence, the livelihood of millions employed by this sector in Western Europe, the Asia-Pacific and North America (Lahai 2017). With patterns of consumer behaviors and the trends of demand and supply in the developed economies inextricably tied, to an extent, to what happens in the volatile spaces of sub-Saharan Africa, IPE has expanded to accommodate a sub-discipline of 'the political economy of development in Africa.'

Of course, one should not forget the role played by scholars of postcolonial theory. They challenged the peripherality of Africa in the IPE and its marginal status in the development of policies that would affect the governments and peoples of the postcolonial African states (de Heredia and Wai 2018; Wai 2014). For them, the inclusion of Africa as a region in the theoretical evolution of the IPE discipline is Orwellian; a discipline that has historically encouraged theories situating Africa as a space on the margins of the broader international system, even when this space owes its fragility to European economic inventions, to imperialism and liberalism, with little room for alternative paths. While 'Africans' are recognized, the hegemonic nature of liberalism has clearly rendered the African state subservient to the power of the hegemon; a hegemon that seeks to invalidate the global relevance of Africa in order to sustain its geopolitical power. Thus, despite a recognition that would supposedly take Africa 'out of the global shadows' in a neoliberal world order' (Ferguson 2006), the invalidation of the relevance of the African states—so the postcolonialist theorists tell us—makes it all but impossible to end fragility. And where this marginality persists, the people of these spaces will continue to wear, stoically and with a sense of inferiority, the stereotypes and stigma associated with their being and knowing. Made to think that they are responsible for their backwardness, both their efforts to bring back Africa into mainstream international relations and IPE scholarship and their ability to help their states out of the fragility trap are predicated on a reading in which they are dependent on externally formulated policies. These theorists have re-created narratives in which the 'who' that created the conditions for fragility mitigation was, at some point in the histories of Sub-Saharan Africa, also responsible for the militarized desertification of 'what' would have enabled their successor-states to break free of neo-colonial conditioning of their development and governance. Against this backdrop, they question the assumption that the fragile sub-Saharan states had a 'comparative advantage' that should have enabled them to develop on the basis of agricultural and natural resource products exported to the west. For them, sub-Saharan Africa cannot benefit from any such advantage as long as Africa remains on the margins of the international political and economic landscape. If anything, sub-Saharan Africa's marginality, which was not of its own making, has reinforced economic and political fragility in the region.

That said, how the fundamentals of fragility and the roles of the state, both in the making of fragility and in building resilient communities, are understood also depends on discourses of 'place' and 'power.' The spatial theorists Robert W. Preucel and Lynn Meskell (2004, 215) define 'place' as the "outcome of the social process of valuing space; a product of the imaginary, of desire, and the primary means by which we articulate with space and transform it into a humanized landscape." Place, they tell us, is about space—"the physical setting in which everything occurs" (ibid.). While recognizing the postmodern argument that space is a 'relative' term, for the purposes of this book we understand it as a passive 'container' that encapsulates the (1) physical enclosures of territoriality, and (2) "civil inclusionary exclusivity" (Halfmann 1998, quoted in Mau 2012, 8)—which basically means, "how the nation-state is still able to control the inclusion—and by extension, the exclusion—of people in various functional systems." Thus, "regardless of their close connections to the geographical space known as the nation-state, diverse groups of people can be treated differently" according to whether they are viewed as legitimate members of the space (Ndhlovu 2018, 5); and, as an addendum, those who reside outside their legitimate spaces can be viewed as outsiders by the people of that place, based on what they make of such sojourners' place of origin. Thus, for example, an African living in the United States of America can be viewed and subjected to increased security surveillance if the U.S. government and people see his region and country of origin as a space that represents an existential threat to their national security. To this end, the study of space has undergone considerable advances (or, rather, taken a 'spatial turn') since it was first theorized in 1974 by the French Marxist philosopher and sociologist Henri Lefebvre in *La production de l'espace* (see Gottdiener 1993; Lefebvre 1991; Goonewardena et al. 2008). This 'spatial turn' constitutes our understanding (for the purpose of this book) of place as a platform that is not static but, instead, a projected space where the struggles over ideas, beliefs, principles and bodies take place.

In the circumstances, then, it is not surprising that the tensions and contradictions of place, have led some to go as far as to hold that what constitutes place has a correlation to power—the operational definition of which, Robert Alan Dahl tells us, is the "successful attempt by A to get B to do something he would not otherwise do" (Dahl 1957, 202). In Dahl's view, the polyarchic descriptor, 'appropriateness' (i.e., the political actions of governments), and the impact of power, as it relates to legitimate governance policies, procedures, and actions of the state, should be assessed with regard to governmental performance in preventing and managing the indicators of fragility in sub-Saharan Africa. If we are to examine the indicators of fragility and political resilience based on government performance, then the need to re-center the African state becomes all the more critical. A noteworthy observation, however, is that our attempt to bring the African state 'back' into the center is not premised on the belief that it is a unitary actor. In a globalizing world with many centers of powers and actors, the state is a component of the whole. Adding to this observation, we also accept that, notwithstanding the presence of existential threats to its survival, the state is the actor that provides the space for all other things to occur and acts as the regulator, whether directly or indirectly, of the activities of those within its political space (territory).

In relation to the second framework, 'fragility-as-resilience,' we employ (and expand on) Nicolas Lemay-Hébert's (2018) working definition of the term, and his differentiation of the 'old' approaches to fragility (that see fragility as a place of no return) from the 'new' empirical positioning of the word 'fragility' (as it relates to state-building and as 'risk-mitigation') with resilience-building as the fundamental premise of its normative possibilities (Lemay-Hébert 2018). For Lemay-Hébert, the problem with 'fragility' is not solely its dangers, but the validity of the knowledge that is resistant to the shift from the old to the new. He believes—and we agree—that

> general retreat in the [epistemic] community from the labelling of fragile states towards a more complex understanding of 'states of fragility' is a way of recognising the growing resistance to the concept—thus the retreat—but in doing so, this move also opens up new governmentality opportunities for policy actors, re-engaging on the familiar field of securitisation.
>
> (Ibid., 3)

This shift or rather, 'retreat,' he contends, exposes the ways in which one can look at the operational aspects of the words 'resilience' and 'fragility.' These words, according to Lemay-Hébert, operate through the dualist conception of securitization: "*securitization of the other*" (i.e., pathologizing specific states and societies while legitimizing international intervention) and "*securitization of the self*," or moving towards new risk mitigation strategies. This is what we rely on for our empirical analyses of the issues covered in Part II of this book, on state resilience and intervention. These issues (with each discussed in individual chapters) are: (1) Behavioral language frames, conflict de-escalation words and the reduction of battle-related deaths; (2) Regional and country-level interventions to end child labor; and (3) Institutional interventions in the advancement of food security and health. However, a point of departure from Lemay-Hébert's conceptualization—which should be seen as our contribution to this emerging, expanding concept—is our attention to the state. It is our belief that, despite the characterization of the 'state' as fragile and, therefore, a problem to be excised, its resilience in the face of the odds against it should not be dismissed. To do so would only reinforce the problem of indifference to the state of fragility in sub-Saharan Africa.

The significance of the book

This book focuses on core issues of relevance to the political economy of sub-Saharan African countries. These issues, as they relate to the indicators of fragility, are the 'contexts and correlates of armed conflicts on statehood and state fragility'; the poverty trap; pandemics and household food insecurity; and child labor and poverty. Regarding the interventions, we developed insightful empirical methods and theories to explain the correlate of behavioral language frames and conflict de-escalation on battle-related deaths across the zones of conflicts; regional and country-level interventions to end child labor; institutional frameworks and interventions in the advancement of food security and health. Taken together, these are issues that have thus far received limited systematic, multidisciplinary and empirically informed critical analysis that may help to understand fragility and resilience better.

Against this backdrop, this book makes a major contribution to the literature in the following ways. First, since the 1980s scholars of the applied social sciences and humanities have discussed a range of state fragility and failure trends in sub-Saharan Africa. The current literature on these trends mostly falls within single sub-disciplines, such as econometrics or political science or anthropology, it is also characterized by inconclusive normative assumptions that were either not tested across countries in sub-Saharan Africa, or were not designed to confront the new realities of state resilience in this sub-region, or by sweeping generalizations from non-empirically tested studies built on a small number of practical cases. In the course of researching this book, we conducted a literature review of over 270 scholarly works (journal articles, chapter contributions in edited volumes and books) on statehood, fragility and resilience in sub-Saharan

Africa, and found only a small number (around 50) based on original empirical data that covers the whole region. Further, none of these 270 scholarly works employed methodological frameworks (within a single study) that drew from mathematical and applied linguistics, securitization theory, political theory, legal theory (and international labor law), applied child development theories and applied econometric techniques in the analyses of statehood, fragility and resilience in the political economy of sub-Saharan Africa. The research in this book employs all these methodologies and theories—as well as contributing a new theory, which we call the "theory of conflict de-escalating words (CDWs)"—in examining, in Part II, the critical indicators of fragility and, in Part III, the institutional frameworks and interventions to reverse the incidences of fragility in sub-Saharan African.

Second, as of the time of writing this book, there are few critical works that comparatively analyze the impact of the contexts and correlates of internal and internationalized armed conflicts on state fragility. The few authoritative works on these are located mostly in the global North and build on the ground-breaking work of Paul Collier and Anke Hoeffler on vertical inequality (2004), Frances Stewart on horizontal inequality (2006), the World Bank on institutional trust (2011a) and Mary Caprioli on gender structural inequalities (2000, 2005). Even where these works form the core of the empirical leanings of the literature, our literature review reveals that they are limited to the shorter pieces of book reviews published in the supplementary sections of refereed journals. What we do, in Chapter 3 of this book, is use the theoretical directions and tools and indices of these ground-breaking works to understand how the context-specific 'lived experiences' of peoples are imagined, understood and theorized, on the one hand; and, on the other, how definitional variations in their representations of conflicts—including those presented by the Uppsala Conflict Data Program[1] (1997–2013)—enable us to understand the convergences and divergences in theorization and the causal effects of armed conflicts and the indicators of state fragility (as listed by the Fund for Peace (2017)) on the measurement of the adaptive resilience of states. It is this observation that makes this book, to the best of our knowledge, one of the first (if not the first) to systematically engage these works and indices to explain the context-specific representations of conflict-induced state fragility. As of the time of writing this book, there is no literature that looks at the impact of conflict de-escalating words (in peace accords signed between 1989 and 2002 across 13 sub-Saharan African) in the reduction of battle-related deaths. At the time of writing this book, and to the best of our knowledge, there is no study that employs frame analysis to comparatively scrutinize the national anti-child-labor policies of countries across the five subregional economic blocs of sub-Saharan Africa, with the aim of understanding the impact of legal norms (international and regional labor law, international human rights law) and institutional regimes in eliminating the worst forms of child labor. The existing studies that have attempted to cover the other issues presented in our book are neither pluri-disciplinary nor empirically extensive. Thus, this book is an important scholarly contribution that not only studies the indicators of state fragility but also suggests the relevance of having 'child labor' as a stand-alone indicator of state fragility. As of today, the category 'child' is missing in the indexes of state fragility in sub-Saharan Africa; and, in tandem, what we suggest, with regards to our theory of conflict de-escalation words, has just opened up the field of securitization theory (of the Copenhagen school).

Finally, we recognize the existence of several outstanding books, journal articles, book chapters and policy papers that have broadened our understanding of the indicators of, and interventions to resolve, state fragility in sub-Saharan Africa. There are also many scholarly works that have treated the problem of fragility and pathways of resolving the drivers of state fragility through narrow theoretical frames, which, in turn, makes their methodologies problematic. Our book unifies these thematic topics into one volume and employs insightful methodological approaches to understand these issues. Thus, institutions and people with an interest state fragility need look no further for a work that contains all the indicators of, and interventions against, state fragility in sub-Saharan Africa. This book makes a significant contribution to multiple sub-fields of state fragility studies. We say "multiple sub-fields" because our book will be of interest to various disciplines: Area and African studies, political science, development studies, micro/macroeconomics, gender and women's studies, peace, security and conflict studies, childhood studies, critical postcolonial studies, sociology, anthropology, applied linguistics, quantitative research methods and international relations. As such, it contains everything that would be relevant to policy-makers and academic institutions. We cannot assume that this is the only book that will tell the story of state resilience in sub-Saharan Africa. As we shall see below, there are other texts that address one or more of the thematic issues we cover. In fact, the eras of the Millennium Development Goals (MDGs) (2002–2016) and the SDGs (2016 to date) have contributed to a rapid shift of attention to the role of governments in sub-Saharan Africa—from a unit (of analysis) posing a danger to global peace and security in a mostly neoliberal world order (and hence, a problem to be excised and contained (Amin 2006)), to a partner in the global–local (*glo-cal*) pursuits of sustainable political stability, and social and economic development (Sachs 2012; Nilsson et al. 2016; World Health Organization 2015).

Summary of the chapters

In this book, readers are provided with some insights into how we got involved in the project and some anecdotes on the data collection. We introduce the reader to the topics of the book, and the central questions it addresses. It discusses the significance of the book; and, finally, discusses the outline of the book.

The first chapter gives the reader an understanding that the fundamental issues underlying the problem of state fragility in sub-Saharan Africa are not as straightforward as they may appear. This is, in part, due to the way the roles of African governments are understood and theorized. Some authors have gone so far as to hold that the triggers of fragility in the region are mere reoccurrences of what life has always been in its habitable spaces; and, hence, of little cause for global concern. Others, while recognizing the global dimensions to the woes of this crisis-ridden region, have, nonetheless, pointed to the contestations surrounding the 'state': what it is, and what has been its role in the making/unmaking of fragility. They have questioned whether the African state should be regarded as a proactive agent in the building of resilient communities that can cope with the impact of fragility. They would like to know more about the ways in which the 'state,' whose leadership is responsible for creating some of the structures that foster fragility, can also be the driver for the unmaking of the fragile spaces in the region. To others, the issues go beyond the wrongs of the state. It should also be about its resilience in the face of the odds. That said, this introductory chapter argues that the postcolonial state in Africa cannot be dismissed because of its role in the making of some of the fragility indicators: conflicts, political instability, poverty, pandemics, corruption, household food insecurity, gender inequality and [child labor]. It should also be seen as a resilient actor, with a central role in the case management of the incidences of economic, social and political fragility. Building on empirical discussions and statistical models of fragility and the role of the state, we propose two theoretical frameworks to understand, in Part I of this book, the critical indicators of fragility, and, in Part II, the character of state resilience and interventions, with emphasis on the state-centric approach and the 'fragility-as-resilience' discourse.

In the second chapter, we observe that despite the existence of many theories of conflict escalation and de-escalation; and the methods and datasets that are guiding the multi-dimensional framing of the correlation between conflicts and fragility, the lack of consensus on what causes conflicts has had far-reaching consequences. Attempts to synchronize the context-specific agendas of professionals in the field (individuals, agencies and governments) into these multi-layered academic positions (be they dominant or peripheral), and their definitions of the various forms of conflicts, have had an impact on the measurement of indicators of conflicts. We recognize that, despite the existence of definitions, datasets and databases, the literature on the intersection between conflict and state fragility in SSA is not conclusive. Against this backdrop, our intention in the first half of this chapter is to present (a) the tools and adaptive indices that have been used to measure the causes and causal effect of conflicts, (b) summaries of the definitions and typologies of conflicts, and (c) the key theoretical perspectives (and their methodological frameworks) on the causes of conflict in sub-Saharan Africa. In the second half, we scrutinize the ways in which the proponents of those perspectives have imagined, understood and theorized the context-specific variations of the impact of conflict on state fragility. In addition, our aim is to contribute to the existing studies on conflict by focusing on attempts to centralize the experiences of states—that is, as actors representing the collective emotions (and knowledge) of the people within them. Through this, we are able to reveal the convergences and divergences in the theoretical (and practical) underpinnings of conflict as a critical indicator of state fragility and a tool for measuring the resilience of states in SSA.

The third chapter deals with the contexts and correlates of conflict. We problematize the various perspectives that have been presented to understand the political economy of war and peace; greed and grievance; and needs and wants, and their correlation to the making and unmaking of wars in Africa. The fourth chapter begins with the questions: Would the mainstreaming of conflict de-escalation words (CDWs) in the outcome documents—Peace Accords (PAs)—of state-led political settlements of conflicts lead to a reduction of battle-related deaths in a year or two following the conclusions of peace negotiations? We infer that the more CDWs are found in PAs the lesser the incidences of battle-related deaths; and the higher the number of words of stalemate (such as sanctions and criminal prosecution of faction leaders) the higher the incidences of battle-related deaths. Our findings show that the effect of reconciliatory words on battle-related deaths depicts an inverted-U relationship. This therefore called for a rigorous statistically verified threshold analysis to discover the number of words that can trigger this relationship. We focus on 49 Peace Accords (with emphasis on 145 key semantic and syntactical observations) across countries in sub-Saharan Africa (from 1990 to 2003) to count not just the number of times conflict de-escalation words were used, but also to de-construct their meanings and connections to state-led efforts to resolve conflicts and reduce battle-related deaths. Our empirical threshold analysis pegs the number of conflict de-escalating words at 35. What this means is that, increasing the amount of reconciliatory words in a peace accord beyond 35 can reduce the number of battle-related deaths. To count these reconciliatory words in these peace accords, we used Nvivo to run a text search and validated the outcome with a manual Hand Tally Counter. We also de-construct frame meanings and their connections to state-led efforts to reduce battle-related deaths. In the first section, we explore the literature on the relevance of (non-)linearity of the semantic and syntactic aspects of language framing in the study of conflict escalation/de-escalation. Linguistically speaking, they are two different frames; but in the discourse of securitization, they are opposed to each other. Whereas CDWs have effects that depict a peaceful end: the reversal of existential threats in political speech acts on incidences that deserve special securitized executive action. In the second section, we introduce our theory of CDWs. We situate this theory in Walter J. Ong's theorization of literate and oracy countries, with recognition of the Afrocentric readings of peace in the decolonized platforms of alternative dispute resolution at the sub-regional levels. In the third section, using scatter plots, pooled OLS and random effect models, we show why and how these words or frames of conflict de-escalation contribute to a reduction in battle-related deaths. Our findings reveal that the lesser the amount of reconciliatory words included in a peace accord, the higher the number of battle-related deaths—per any additional non-reconciliatory word; but the number of deaths begins to decline with the mainstreaming of higher amounts of reconciliatory words. In this context, we suggest the choice to project CDWs is to get parties in a conflict to think less about warfare and more about ways of getting out of what the Hirshleifer-Skaperdas game theory of conflict has referred to as adversarial traps, with the rent-seeking soundbites for resource (for war) appropriation.

The fifth chapter paints a realistic image of the African child laborer—the omitted category in the measurement indicators of state fragility. We observe that there is a decreasing rate in the incidence of child labor in major regions of the world but the situation in sub-Saharan Africa is experiencing an upward trend despite governments' improved efforts with the objective of curbing the menace within the sub-region. This chapter extends the existing child labor–poverty nexus to state fragility by drawing on theoretical and empirical evidence using survey data from two countries: Ghana and Tanzania. Our synthesis of empirical findings with the extant literature shows that poor and low-income parents subject their children to relatively more hours of child labor, thereby putting their economic and social prospects in jeopardy. We also find that some of the children engaged in worst forms of child labor are entrapped in commercial sex exploitation, are forcibly recruited into non-state armed groups while others deal in illicit drugs. The negative implication of this outcome is that child labor activities perpetually impoverish the children, their immediate societies and their countries due to the vicious cycle of poverty or largely owing to economic failures on the part of the state. Victims of these economic and political failures who begin to feel disenfranchised become the source of uprisings and upheavals, leaving the country(s) branded as a fragile state. Accordingly, studies have found that poverty is one key driver of child labor, along with a poorly developed agricultural sector, high population growth/fertility rates and low levels of educational attainment and participation. This chapter draws the linkages between poverty, child labor and state fragility by drawing on theoretical and empirical evidence from Ghana, and Tanzania. SSA is the focus given that it has the highest incidence of child labor in the world; the International Labour Organization (ILO) has also indicated that a breakthrough in Africa would be critical to ending child labor worldwide. The relevance of the child labor discourse is reflected in the pledges by governments in SSA to take pragmatic steps in achieving the United Nations Sustainable Development Goals (SDGs). The rest of this chapter proceeds as follows. Section two deals with child labor activities in SSA and is followed by a section on definitions of child labor. Section four discusses the child labor–poverty nexus, while section five provides a discussion on the cycle of poverty in fragile states. Section six examines the prospects of child labor and its implications for society while section seven outlines the methodology used in the data analyses. Here, we talk about the theories, the data source, the cross-sectional data and Logit estimation technique employed in the data analyses. The analysis is done for the estimations because they both seek to provide empirical evidence for the effect of household wealth on child labor outcomes. Post-estimation tests such as the link test is used to ensure that the models are correctly specified while the variance inflation factor (VIF) is also employed to avoid the usage of models that suffer from multicollinearity.

The sixth chapter traces, in part one, the political and legal histories of the anti-child labor regimes in sub-Saharan Africa. This is to demonstrate that the discourse on the need for a robust national plan or policy to combat the worst forms of child labor is supported by regional institutional and legal advancements, which fall within a broader, multidimensional international human rights regime. It is this argument that provides the basis for the second section, which addresses the politics of re-affirmation of the global child protection regime brought by the African Charter on the Rights and Welfare of the Child (ACRWC). We examine, using frame theory, the country-level advances in the elimination of the worst forms of child labor. We scrutinize the national plans of five sub-Saharan African countries—selected from an extensive poll of countries within the five sub-regional economic blocs in the region: Cameroon (from the Economic Community of Central African States (ECCAS) sub-region); Kenya (the Intergovernmental Authority for Development, IGAD); Ghana (the Economic Community of West African States, ECOWAS); Tanzania (the East African Community, EAC); and Zimbabwe (the Southern African Development Community, SADC). We examine how the construct of 'intervention' (which seeks to fulfil the fundamental aspects of international human rights law and the emergent doctrine of an international responsibility to protect: prevent, react and rebuild) is structured through 15 sub-frames of the themes of (1) social programming, (2) legal proactivity and (3) institutional interventions, monitoring and evaluation. We look at the similarities in the framing of risk management as it relates to medical, social, nutrition, criminal prosecution and compulsory schooling interventions. Whereas frame theory was the umbrella scheme we used to understand subject matter similarities, for the legal proactivity section, we employed French and Raven's (1959) "The Basis of Social Power Theory," to ascertain the impact of the national laws on child labor on the society. On the issue of institutional intervention, we also draw from the various behavioral and child development theories of Sigmund Freud, Erik Erikson, Jean Piaget, John Bowlby and Lev Vygotsky.

In the seventh chapter, we contend that since the onset of the Ebola Virus Diseases (EVD) in Guinea in 2013, the estimated number of resultant deaths for all three affected countries was more than 11,000 out of 27,000 reported cases by June 2015. Of all the affected countries, Sierra Leone reported the highest number of cases of 12,901 with 3,915 deaths. The nature of the pandemic and the resultant deaths have socioeconomic and food insecurity implications for affected households. The chapter examines socio-economic determinants of food insecurity at the household level in Sierra Leone using six indicators of food insecurity. Data for the chapter are the three rounds of the High Frequency Cell Phone Survey data that were jointly collected by Statistics Sierra Leone (SSL) and Innovations for Poverty Action (IPA). Empirical techniques include Random-effects Poisson and population-averaged Poisson models. We generate an index of food insecurity from six household coping strategies that indicate food insecurity, using principal component analysis, and employ the household unitary model since the data used for the analyses was generated by focusing on the household head. Findings indicate that households that engage in agriculture only are more have a higher risk of being food insecure. On the contrary, households that have diversified their income portfolios experience a reduction in their levels of food insecurity as incomes from their non-farm enterprises experience boost. We also find that households in

Freetown are less food insecure compared to their counterparts in other urban areas. In specific terms, we find that incomes from non-farm enterprises significantly reduce the intensity at which households restrict adult consumption for small children to eat. Similar reductions in food insecurity intensities can be said for households that rely on less preferred or expensive food as well as those that reduce number of meals eaten in a day. This is the grounds on which we stand to recommend that households in fragile states engage in income diversification to mitigate the harsh conditions of food insecurity in times of an Ebola pandemic.

The eighth chapter sets out to show that, while the increasing incidences of food insecurity impose enormous pressure on what governments can do at the national levels to mitigate against health shocks, it has not prevented them from developing innovative policies to increase crop yield and increase their per capita dietary energy supply (DES) in line with FAO's aggregated estimates of household energy (kcal) consumption per day. The primary objectives of this chapter are, first, to evaluate the goals, policy directives and guiding principles of the national food and nutrition policies of sub-Saharan African countries that received a country ranking and overall score in the 2017 Global Food Security Index. Second, the identified goals are our baseline in exploring some of the key strategies and interventions to contain food insecurity. That said, we begin this chapter with an overview of the causes of food insecurity. In the second section, we examine the various strategies states have used to end food insecurity; using the Ghana model on buffer food stock as a guide, we examine the magnitude of the transfers between the agricultural sector and the health sector. The aim here is to determine whether this model (attending especially to its best practices and lessons) can be replicated in countries that were affected by the Ebola Virus Disease of 2014 and 2016. We seek to ascertain how this Ghana model can be used to transform the food and nutrition security regimes of these countries. Finally, the concluding chapter discusses the role of research in the contemporary theorization of state interventions to address the incidence of state fragility in sub-Saharan Africa.

Note

1 https://ucdp.uu.se/

References

Amanor, Kojo Sebastian. 2012. "Global Resource Grabs, Agribusiness Concentration and the Smallholder: Two West African Case Studies." *The Journal of Peasant Studies* 39 (3–4): 731–749.

Amin, Samir. 2006. "The Millennium Development Goals: A Critique from the South." *Monthly Review* 57 (10): 1.

Berdal, Mats R. and David Malone. 2000. *Greed & Grievance: Economic Agendas in Civil Wars*. Boulder, CO: Lynne Rienner Publishers.

Bertocchi, Graziella, and Andrea Guerzoni. 2012. "Growth, History, or Institutions: What Explains State Fragility in Sub-Saharan Africa?" *Journal of Peace Research* 49 (6): 769–783.

Boege, Volker, Anne Brown, Kevin Clements, and Anna Nolan. 2008. *On Hybrid Political Orders and Emerging States: State Formation in the Context of 'Fragility.'* Berlin, Germany: Berghof Center for Constructive Conflict Management. http://berghof-handbook.net/documents/publications/boege_etal_handbook.pdf.

Boege, Volker, M. Anne Brown, and Kevin P. Clements. 2009. "Hybrid Political Orders, Not Fragile States." *Peace Review* 21 (1): 13–21.

Bryceson, Deborah Fahy. 2006. "Fragile Cities: Fundamentals of Urban Life in East and Southern Africa." In *African Urban Economies: Viability, Vitality or Vitiation?*, edited by Deborah Fahy Bryceson and Deborah Potts, 3–38. New York, NY: Palgrave Macmillan.

Caprioli, Mary. 2000. "Gendered Conflict." *Journal of Peace Research* 37 (1): 51–68.

Caprioli, Mary. 2005. "Primed for Violence: The Role of Gender Inequality in Predicting Internal Conflict." *International Studies Quarterly* 49 (2): 161–178.

Collier, Paul, and Anke Hoeffler. 2004. "Greed and Grievance in Civil War." *Oxford Economic Papers* 56 (4): 563–595.

Collier, Paul, Anke Hoeffler, and Dominic Rohner. 2009. "Beyond Greed and Grievance: Feasibility and Civil War." *Oxford Economic Papers* 61 (1): 1–27.

Collier, Paul, and Nicholas Sambanis. 2005. *Understanding Civil War: Africa*. Vol. 1. Washington, DC: World Bank Publications.

Comaroff, Jean, and John L. Comaroff, eds. 1993. *Modernity and Its Malcontents: Ritual and Power in Postcolonial Africa*. Chicago, IL: University of Chicago Press.

Dahl, Robert A. 1957. "The Concept of Power." *Systems Research and Behavioral Science* 2 (3): 201–215.

Dunne, J. Paul, and Nan Tian. 2013. "Military Expenditure and Economic Growth: A Survey." *The Economics of Peace and Security Journal* 8 (1): 5–11.

Ferguson, James. 2006. *Global Shadows: Africa in the Neoliberal World Order*. Durham, NC: Duke University Press.

Ferreira, Ines Afonso Roque. 2015. "Defining and Measuring State Fragility: A New Proposal." In, 39. Berkeley, CA. http://cega.berkeley.edu/assets/miscellaneous_files/109_-_ABCA_2015_Ines_Ferreira_Defining_and_measuring_state_fragility__A_new_proposal_May15.pdf.

Gelb, Alan, and Rob Floyd. 1999. "The Challenge of Globalisation for Africa." *South African Journal of International Affairs* 6 (2): 1–17.

Gill, Stephen. 2003. "Globalisation, Market Civilisation and Disciplinary Neoliberalism." In *Globalization: Critical Concepts in Sociology*, edited by Roland Robertson and Kathleen White, 256–81. London, UK: Routledge.

Goonewardena, Kanishka, Stefan Kipfer, Richard Milgrom, and Christian Schmid, eds. 2008. *Space, Difference, Everyday Life: Reading Henri Lefebvre*. New York, NY: Routledge.

Gottdiener, Mark. 1993. "A Marx for Our Time: Henri Lefebvre and the Production of Space." *Sociological Theory* 11 (1): 129–134.

Heredia, Marta Iñiguez de, and Zubairu Wai, eds. 2018. *Recentering Africa in International Relations: Beyond Lack, Peripherality, and Failure*. New York, NY: Palgrave Macmillan.

Herskovits, Melville J. 1959. "Anthropology and Africa—a Wider Perspective." *Africa* 29 (3): 225–238.

Kevane, Michael. 2004. *Women and Development in Africa: How Gender Works*. Boulder, CO: Lynne Rienner Publishers.

Lahai, John Idriss. 2017. *The Ebola Pandemic in Sierra Leone: Representations, Actors, Interventions and the Path to Recovery*. Basingstoke, Hampshire: Palgrave Macmillan.

Lefebvre, Henri. 1991. *The Production of Space (Translated by Donald Nicholson-Smith)*. Oxford, UK: Blackwell Publishing.

Lemay-Hébert, Nicolas. 2018. "From Saving Failed States to Managing Risks: Reinterpreting Fragility through Resilience." In *Governance and Political Adaptation in Fragile States*, edited by John Idriss Lahai, Karin von Strokirch, Howard Brasted, and Helen Ware. New York, NY: Palgrave Macmillan.

Mau, Steffen. 2012. *Social Transnationalism: Lifeworlds Beyond the Nation-State*. New York, NY: Routledge.

Moore, David. 2000. "Levelling the Playing Fields & Embedding Illusions: 'Post-Conflict' Discourse & Neo-Liberal 'Development' in War-Torn Africa." *Review of African Political Economy* 27 (83): 11–28.

Moore, Sally Falk. 1994. *Anthropology and Africa: Changing Perspectives on a Changing Scene*. Charlottesville, Virginia: University of Virginia Press.

Navari, Cornelia. 1991. "Introduction: The State as a Contested Concept in International Relations." In *The Condition of States: A Study in International Political Theory*, edited by Cornelia Navari, 1–18. Buckingham, UK: Open University Press.

Ndhlovu, Finex. 2018. *Language, Vernacular Discourse and Nationalisms: Uncovering the Myths of Transnational Worlds*. New York, NY: Palgrave Macmillan.

Nilsson, Maans, Dave Griggs, and Martin Visbeck. 2016. "Policy: Map the Interactions between Sustainable Development Goals." *Nature News* 534 (7607): 320.

Nyamnjoh, Francis B. 2012. "Blinded by Sight: Divining the Future of Anthropology in Africa." *Africa Spectrum*, 63–92.

Pieterse, Jan Nederveen. 1994. "Globalisation as Hybridisation." *International Sociology* 9 (2): 161–184.

Preucel, Robert W., and Lynn Meskell. 2004. "Places." In *A Companion to Social Archaeology*, edited by Lynn Meskell and Robert W. Preucel, 215–229. Malden, Massachusetts: Blackwell Publishing.

Renders, Marleen, and Ulf Terlinden. 2010. "Negotiating Statehood in a Hybrid Political Order: The Case of Somaliland." *Development and Change* 41 (4): 723–746.

Sachs, Jeffrey D. 2012. "From Millennium Development Goals to Sustainable Development Goals." *The Lancet* 379 (9832): 2206–2211.

Shizha, Edward, and Lamine Diallo. 2016. *Africa in the Age of Globalisation: Perceptions, Misperceptions and Realities*. Abingdon, UK: Routledge.

Somerville, Keith. 2016. *Africa's Long Road since Independence: The Many Histories of a Continent*. London, UK: Hurst Publishers.

Squicciarini, Mara P. and Johan Swinnen, eds. 2016. *The Economics of Chocolate*. Oxford, UK: Oxford University Press.

Sriram, Chandra Lekha. 2004. "Globalising Justice: From Universal Jurisdiction to Mixed Tribunals." *Netherlands Quarterly of Human Rights* 22 (1): 7–32.

Sriram, Chandra Lekha. 2005. *Globalizing Justice for Mass Atrocities: A Revolution in Accountability*. Abingdon, UK: Routledge.

Stewart, Frances. 2006. "The Implications of Horizontal Inequality for Aid." CRISE Working Paper, No. 36. Oxford: CRISE, University of Oxford.

Tan, Andrew T. H., ed. 2014. *The Global Arms Trade: A Handbook*. Abingdon, UK: Routledge.

Taylor, Ian, and Philip Nel. 2002. " 'New Africa', Globalisation and the Confines of Elite Reformism: 'Getting the Rhetoric Right', Getting the Strategy Wrong." *Third World Quarterly* 23 (1): 163–180.

Urry, John. 2000. *Sociology beyond Societies: Mobilities for the Twenty-First Century*. London, UK: Routledge.

Wai, Zubairu. 2014. "The Empire's New Clothes: Africa, Liberal Interventionism and Contemporary World Order." *Review of African Political Economy* 41 (142): 483–499.

World Bank. 2011a. "Operationalizing the 2011 World Development Report: Conflict, Security, and Development." (Development Committee's Joint Ministerial Committee of the Borad of Governors of the Bank and the Fund on the Transfer of Real Resources to Developing Countries; DC2011-0003 (April 4). Washington, DC: World Bank. http://siteresources.worldbank.org/DEVCOMMINT/Documentation/22884392/DC2011-0003%28E%29WDR2011.pdf.

World Bank. 2011b. "World Development Report 2011: Conflict, Security and Development." Washington, DC: World Bank. http://documents.worldbank.org/curated/en/806531468161369474/pdf/622550PUB0WDR0000public00BOX361476B.pdf.

World Health Organization. 2015. "Health in 2015: From MDGs, Millennium Development Goals to SDGs, Sustainable Development Goals." Geneva: World Health Organization. http://apps.who.int/iris/bitstream/handle/10665/200009/9789241?sequence=1.

Part I

Statehood and conflicts

Contextual indicators and interventions

2 Conceptualizing the state, state fragility and resilience in the political economy of sub-Saharan Africa

The fundamental issues underlying the problem of state fragility in sub-Saharan Africa are not as straightforward as they may appear. This is, in part, due to the way the roles of African governments are understood and theorized. Some authors have gone as far as to hold that the triggers of fragility in the region are mere reoccurrences of what life has always been in its habitable spaces; and, hence, of little cause for global concern. Other authors, while recognizing the global dimensions to the woes of this crisis-ridden region, have, nonetheless, pointed to the contestations surrounding the 'state': what it is, and what has been its role in the making/unmaking of fragility. They have questioned whether the African state should be regarded as a proactive agent in the building of resilient communities that can cope with the impact of fragility; they would like to know more about the ways in which the 'state,' whose leadership is responsible for creating some of the structures that foster fragility, can also be the driver for the unmaking of the fragile spaces in the region. To others, the issues go beyond the wrongs of the state. It should also be about its resilience in the face of the odds. As a follow-up to the introduction, in this chapter, we explore two key issues in the study of contemporary state fragility in sub-Saharan Africa: the concepts of the 'state' and the emergent theorization of 'resilience' as a concept of 'self-securitization' out of which state interventions to protect, prevent and react to the incidences of state fragility.

The persistence of fragile states (understood, prior to 2014, as collapsed, failing and failed states) in sub-Saharan Africa is, to borrow, and put into context the words of Oliver P. Richmond (whose concern was on 'ills of the neoliberal peacebuilding agendas' of the West in Africa), a triumph—to some degree at least—of "process, technology, bureaucracy, and ideology over substance, and more directly, over the lives of millions of ordinary people for a generation or more in politically unstable parts of the world" (Richmond 2010, 1). That notwithstanding, inquiry into the lives and socio-cultural, political and economic circumstances of the states and people in Africa has increased significantly in recent decades, following the publication in 1994 of Robert D. Kaplan's influential article 'The Coming Anarchy.' What followed Kaplan's piece was the emergence of a 'social science' discipline that focuses exclusively on Africa's problems. In keeping with the motivation to understand the crisis-ridden postcolonial spaces of sub-Saharan Africa, the practices, and theories associated with (1) 'statehood,' (2) 'fragility' (and its association with the concept of securitization), and (3) 'resilience' are now undergoing significant reflective and critical evaluation. This has touched on almost all disciplines: from history to economics; and from political science to cultural anthropology. At the policy level, the evolving focus of inquiry into these concepts is spearheaded by the research departments of the United Nations and the Bretton Woods system (the World Bank and the International Monetary Fund, IMF). What have they made of these concepts, whose theorization has been confined mainly to the Global North? Through a multidisciplinary approach, we present comprehensive, but short definitions of these concepts, with sub-Saharan Africa as a focus.

Theorizing the 'state' in sub-Saharan Africa

In 1987, Patrick Dunleavy and Brendan O'Leary published their reflections on the meaning, and controversies, of statehood and how it was understood by several schools of international relations: pluralism and neo-pluralism, realism, the new rights and Marxism. Their reflection is worth quoting here at length.

> The state is a word on everybody's lips. Technocrats claim they can steer it, judges that they can discern its interests, and politicians that they know how to run it. Liberals have seemed to believe that the state should be an 'umpire,' a 'referee,' a regulator and an arbiter—even a 'cash register—of conflicting interests in society. By contrast, Marxists have condemned the state as an 'instrument' or 'executive committee' of a dominant class. Cynical realists have seen the state as an elitist organization of manipulators and/or parasites, using 'political formulas' to fool the masses of ordinary citizens. Some intellectuals conceptualize the state as the condensation of all power relations in society, as a surveillance system, or as an autonomous machine which energizes whole societies with patriotic or nationalist ideologies. Others [the new rights; the anarchist movements] want to 'smash' the state or cause it to wither away into a historical memory ... But most political thinkers [including Thomas Hobbes, Edmund Burke, Jeremy Bentham, Georg Wilhelm Friedrich Hegel, Jungen Habermas, Antonio Gramsci, Friedrich Hayek, Marx Weber, and Mikhail Bakunin, among others] have regarded the state as an ineluctable feature of modernity, part of the landscape of all societies other than those based on kinship or feudal patronage.
>
> (Dunleavy and O'Leary 1987, 6)

The phrase "rather than those based on 'kinship or feudal patronage'" presupposes the elimination of the prime markers of sub-nationalisms and identities (e.g., markers of ethnic-nationalism), with the potential of compromising statehood. With this in mind, we ask (and answer): What then is a state? The 'state' (and what statehood denotes) is a "coercion-wielding" organization that is, as already stated above, different "from households and kinship groups" and "exercise[s] clear priority in some respects over all other organizations within substantial territories" (Charles Tilly 1990, quoted in Hampel 2015, 1629). Its coercive, organizational and 'priority-setting' characterization, it has been argued, derives from its etymological basis in the Latin word 'status.' It was used mainly when citizens of the Roman Empire talked about the '*status rei publicae*' or the condition of 'public matters' (Dowdall 1923). As such, the concept of the state was all-encompassing, claiming the right to manage public matters on behalf of the people; and these matters, having been legitimately defined by the state, included the socio-cultural, economic and political affairs of the public/citizenry.

Beyond the dialectics of words, there are several angles—the bureaucratic/institutional, the legal (customary international law) and the political—from which one can approach the origins and performative functions of the state. The first angle was presented by Max Weber's bureaucratic theory, which addressed the institutional foundation of the state. Weber refers to the state as a compulsory political entity whose central political authority, the government, should have successfully claimed the monopoly of the legitimate use of force within a given territory. In the exercise of its legitimate powers, the hermeneutic of the state, Weber contends, demands that things should not be left to chance; that, as a condition for the successful implementation of its political functions, 'reason' (rational knowledge, which implies 'professionalism') and 'ethics' (the law of legitimation) should guide the bureaucratic structures charged with the maintenance of law and order (through the use of legitimate force—in its 'Dahl-ian' sense) (see Anter 2014; Giddens 1985). According to Harry Redner, Weber's definition(s) of the state "held up well until after the second world war." Since then, however, new circumstances have required that they be altered. Through these alterations, "total expropriation of all powers did not take place. Instead, a fusion of state and society ensued" (Redner 1990, 638).

These developments, which bring us to the second angle (the legal) of the origins of the states, resulted from the shortcomings of the constitutive approach of state creation and recognition, on the one hand; and, on the other, the rise of autonomous entities, whose recognition would require minimum criteria developed to manage the crises of expropriation and militarization, and the development of law to back customary international law that regulates inter-state relations. It is believed that the constitutive approach to state formation and recognition may have started immediately after the signing of the Treaty of Westphalia in 1648 (which, in ending the Thirty-Year War among the major European powers, brought about the separation of church and state). This theory continued to be of legal and political relevance even after the 1884/1885 Berlin conferences for the partition of Africa by European powers. In the main, this theory of state/hood reiterates that states exist exclusively through their recognition by other states, either in the form of 'diplomatic recognition' or 'recognition of existence' of an entity in need of a formal status in the international system. In both cases, state recognition requires fulfilling the general rules or principles of customary international law, and, where such rules apply, the discretion of state (in need of recognition) to declare itself sovereign may come from *circulus in probando* (or the circle of proving; or circular logic: which implies that 'voluntary silence means consent') (see, Krasner 1999; MacGibbon 1957).

The question of the acceptability of sovereignty through 'diplomatic recognition' and 'recognition of existence,' amid the dilemma produced by the practice of *circulus in probando*, contributed to the expansion of European imperial state power into Africa and beyond. It has also resulted in imperial tensions in Western (and on the fringes of Western) Europe. These tensions would ultimately feed into the narratives and actions that sparked the powder kegs of World War I (1914–1918). Subsequently, with the belligerent state (Germany) dissatisfied with the outcome of the Treaty of Versailles and seeking territorial expansion (into Czechoslovakia, Poland, etc.), there was a need for a shift from a constitutive to a declarative path to statehood, a set of criteria that entities must fulfill before their statehood could be recognized. It was under these circumstances that the Montevideo Convention on the Rights and Duties of States was called, and a treaty signed on December 26, 1933. In practice, this treaty created the principle of 'reasonability' in the threshold of permanence: that is, states must have reasonable prospects of persisting under any condition, including situations of state decay, collapse and failure. Predicated on the belief that the actions of states toward one another should be legitimated by the general, uncoercive domestic support of the sending and the receiving states, both of which must be in control of (that is, have a monopoly over the use of force within) their territories, the 'new,' law-abiding state was born into a global community (Grant 1999; Krasner 1999). To reaffirm this commitment, at least on paper, that they (the states) will 'abide' by the law, Article 8 ('the prohibition of aggression clause' that reassures state of their protection from the dangers of conflicts from other member states (Rabel 1941); and from the consequences of the 'politics of difference' (see Otto 1996)) was included in the Montevideo Convention. As envisaged by the attendees of the Montevideo meetings and drafters of the convention, state recognition (be it de facto or otherwise) does not imply

> merely that [a] government is deemed to have satisfied the required considerations, but also that the recognizing state will deal with the government as the governing authority of the state and accept the usual legal consequences of such status in terms of privileges and immunities within the domestic legal order.
>
> (Shaw 2017, 337)

But was this de facto recognition extended to the polities of sub-Saharan Africa? The answer is a resounding 'no'! At the time of the Montevideo Convention, the whole of Africa (excepting Ethiopia and Liberia) were European—Belgian, British, French, German, Italian, Portuguese and Spanish—colonies. With this, we turn our attention to the other, yet marginal, history of the state and statehood in sub-Saharan Africa; a history that projected a cultural outlook onto the interconnectedness between people and land. The decision to strip Africans of the foremost requirement of statehood—the land (which defines one's territorial boundary; and sub-national identity of 'place')—was taken at the Berlin Conferences of 1884 and 1885, which were organized to resolve the crises brewing over the 'scramble for territory' in Africa between European powers:

> particularly between the British and French in West Africa [and] Egypt; the Portuguese and British in East Africa; and the French and King Leopold II [the notorious ruler of Belgium who 'founded,' as a 'private venture,' what can best be described as a 'concentration camp' cloaked, by name, as a 'Congo Free State'] in central Africa.
>
> (Heath 2010, 177)

It should be emphasized here that the loss of land meant, first, the rise of the politics of the co-option and de-legitimation of the entitlement of the peoples of the colonized spaces to determine their future without external dictates and coercion; and, second, the setting in motion of political systems, such as the indirect rule model, that contributed to the weakening of the pre-colonial political institutions. Unlike India and China, which were able to draw upon their untouched traditional institutions to escape the fragility trap, the dysfunctional institutions the colonial powers bequeathed to the sub-Saharan successor-states at independence only reinforced the structures of state fragility—and eventual failure (Clapham 2000; Lahai and Lahai 2018). It is against this backdrop that Mamoud Mamdani refers to the British Government's colonial model of indirect rule as "decentralized despotism" (1996, 8); and to subsequent Eurocentric postcolonial reinventions as bifurcated forms of oppressive "power that mediated racial domination through tribal organized local authority" (ibid., 16), reproducing racial identity in citizens and ethnic identity in subjects (ibid., 25).

Theorizing state fragility

Fragility can assume any of the following dysfunctions: a country's inability to provide essential services to its people; the existence of persistent and extreme poverty; unstable and weak governance structures; lack of territorial control; and high propensity to conflict and civil conflicts (Bertocchi and Guerzoni 2012, 1). Lemay-Hébert observes that these dysfunctions carry the "image of a flawed comparison between developed, successful western states and the periphery, as well as the image of a … societal failure [that] can be attributed *in toto* to local communities" (2018, 45). Interestingly, there are those who understand the problem associated with trying to conceptualize fragility based on the inconclusive list of country-level indicators. Using a large dataset that included a comprehensive list of definitions of fragile states, with consideration of donor agencies' priority areas (fragile states' political authority and legitimacy, and economic capacity), David Carment and Yiagadeesen Samy observe that:

> Fragility measures the extent to which the actual characteristics of a state differ from their ideal situation; states are constrained by both internal and

> external forces that are [continually] changing over time. Consequently, all states are, to some extent, fragile; weakness in one or more of the ALC [authority, legitimacy and capacity] dimensions will negatively impact the fragility of a particular country. In that sense, we need to consider not only the extreme cases of failing, failed and collapsed states but also the ones that have the potential to fail.
>
> (Carment and Samy 2012, 4)

Influenced, perhaps, by Carment and Samy's observation that 'all states are, to some extent, fragile,' the Fund for Peace, which produces a Fragile State Index annually, abandoned the concept of 'failed states' in favor of the concept of 'fragile states,' notwithstanding the fact that their methodological approach (which includes content analysis, quantitative datasets, integration and triangulation datasets, and qualitative research) remains unchanged (Lemay-Hébert 2018, 45).

Thus, the definition of 'fragility' is as contentious as its history. Conceptually, the term, with circumstantial nuances, means different things to different people, institutions and states. To the epistemic communities, there are three main nexuses in the evolving attempts to define the term: the fragility–security nexus, the fragility–economic development nexus, and the fragility–social nexus. To the security studies community, the preferred definition of fragility rests on the highly problematic "failed state" dialectic. Proponents of the fragility–security nexus, especially Gerald Helman and Steven Ratner (1992), are unconvinced that the mutation of the state fragility agenda—the rise of varying degrees of political correctness that call for a shift from narratives of fragility as a permanent crisis to those that see it as situational and non-static—should make the continued use of the term 'failed' state untenable (see Wilde 2002, 425; Lemay-Hébert 2018).

Writing on the fragility–security nexus, with a focus on the conditions under which politicians in sub-Saharan African countries can assume complete control of the security apparatus of their states, Robert H. Bates (2008) concludes that the 'political disorder' that accompanies the political attempts at control should be the starting point in defining fragility and failed states in late-twentieth century sub-Saharan Africa. Critical of this 'conflict-breaks-state' perspective, Karl Adalbert Hampel contends that, while political disorder may explain the unmaking of states in the region, this view's historiological conclusions on the instrumentalization of conflicts is problematic. It relies on a dichotomized approach that does not take into consideration the socio-political variations that are "linked to the historical sociology of state formation [and failure]" (2015, 1629). For Hampel, the processes of state-making in sub-Saharan Africa are also responsible for the *un*making of state infrastructures, for political instability, and for state deformation. Against the backdrop of this observation, he suggests that the definition of state fragility should include the changes to the horizontalization of fragility. Emphatically, the focus should be, as Klute and Trotha (2004) observe, on the impact that the emergence of parastates and para-sovereignties has on the making of fragility in countries like Somalia, where clan- and religion-based sub-nationalisms are incredibly potent. That said, Leonardo Figueroa

Helland and Stefan Borg define fragility (in 'failed' states) as the "fierce struggles among elites competing in the use and legitimation of physical violence in order to successfully claim to monopolize it" (Helland and Borg 2014, 878).

Those approaching the concept of fragility from economics and development studies are of the view that the "failed state approach [of the fragility–security nexus] is flawed because it cannot grasp a crucial factor—legitimacy—except in a narrow normative and prescriptive sense" (Hampel 2015, 1629). This normative position, it has been argued, is concerned with the political legitimacy of a given political authority (Levitov 2016, 2). As a corrective measure, Graziella Bertocchi and Andrea Guerzoni argue that, of the conventional definitions of fragility, it is those presented by the economic development institutions that better explain the economic severity of fragility (Bertocchi and Guerzoni 2012). These institutions include, among others, the Organisation for Economic Co-operation and Development (OECD), the World Bank, the Asian Development Bank (ADB), and the European Commission. Below are examples of their definitions of fragility.

World Bank's (WB) Country Policy and Institutional Assessment (CPIA) of low-income countries under stress (LICUS):

> State policies and institutions are weak in these countries: making them vulnerable in their capacity to deliver services to their citizens, to control corruption, or to provide for sufficient voice and accountability. They face risks of conflict and political instability.
>
> (World Bank 2005, quoted in Ferreira 2015, 34)

ADB's Weakly Performing Countries (WPC) Index:

> Many of the region's poor people live in DMCs [developing member countries] that have weak governance, ineffective public administration and the rule of law, and civil unrest. These countries have been referred to variously as WPCs, fragile states, low-income countries under stress (LICUS), and difficult partnership countries. Service delivery systems in such countries seldom function well, and the government's ability to guarantee the basic security of its people is often limited. WPCs are more likely to experience largescale and civil conflict than other low-income countries.
>
> (ADB 2007, quoted in Ferreira 2015, 34)

OECD's Development Assistance Committee (OECD-DAC):

> [A fragile state or regions has] weak capacity to carry out [essential] governance functions, and lacks the ability to develop mutually constructive relations with society. Fragile states are also more vulnerable to internal or external shocks such as economic crises or natural disasters. More resilient states exhibit the capacity and legitimacy of governing a population and its territory. They can manage and adapt to changing social needs and expectations, shifts

> in elite and other political agreements, and growing institutional complexity. Fragility and resilience should be seen as shifting points along a spectrum.
>
> (OECD 2012, quoted in Ferreira 2015, 34)

For these scholars (whose datasets cover the period between 1999 and 2011), such definitions explain the significantly negative impact on economic development—provided the standard institutional, demographic and economic regressors are accounted for. Economic fragility explains, on the one hand, the causes and consequences of fragility for economic growth and aid governance, and their impact on state governance policies (see Chauvet and Collier 2008; Easterly, Levine and Roodman 2004; Baliamoune-Lutz and McGillivray 2011; Naudé, Santos-Paulino and McGillivray 2011). On the other hand, it also makes possible critical examination of the complex and differentiated economic, social, geographical and political characteristics of sub-Saharan African countries (Bertocchi and Guerzoni 2012, 3).

Barro's regressions—which include real per capita income/GDP, schooling, life expectancy, fertility rate, ethnic fractionalization, quality of institutions and civil liberties (all proxied by data from 1960 to 1985)—were developed to draw attention to the possibilities associated with alternative measures of fragility, with recognition of country-specific differences identified by the CPIA ratings developed by the World Bank (including investment, schooling, government expenditure, trade openness and inflation), and those identified (on an annual basis) by the International Development Association (IDA) and the OECD-DAC.

For its part, the Fund for Peace's (FfP) Fragile States Index contains 12 indicators, which we contend constitute the FfP's working definition of fragility. These indicators are: (1) security apparatus, (2) factionalized elites, (3) group grievance, (4) economic decline, (5) uneven economic decline, (6) human flight and brain drain, (7) state legitimacy, (8) public service, (9) human rights and rule of law, (10) demographic pressures, (11) refugees and internally displaced persons (IDPs) and (12) external intervention. We observed, based on our reviews of the literature on the episodic incidences of fragility in sub-Saharan Africa, that while these indicators affect each other, there are variations in the patterns of these impacts—an issue to which the FfP's Fragile States Index seems not have little attention. That said, our observation is that a fragility induced by the lack of adequate state security apparatus (indicator 1) affects all the indicators, but its impact is felt most in situations where the question of state legitimacy is unresolved, and—in situations where there is an increased number of refugees who have fled to neighboring countries—would also put pressure on indicators 1, 3, 8, 9 and 10 of the receiving country. Likewise, in a situation where the elites of a country are factionalized (indicator 2), indicators 8 (the public service) and 9 (human rights and the rule of law) will be affected disproportionately. We also believe that: indicator 3 has an increased impact on indicator 5; indicator 6 (especially brain drain to prosperous western countries[1]) on indicator 10 (but with reduced pressure on—and, in fact, ameliorating—indicators 8 and 10); indicators 1, 2 and 11 have a significant impact on the nature of indicator 12; and the outcome of indicator 12 may either resolve or exacerbate the problems associated with all the other indicators, most especially indicators 2, 3, 10 and 11.

Obviously, the definitions offered above are presented by institutions headquartered in the Global North (save for the ADB, based in Manila, in the Philippines), and their perspectives could be far-removed from the everyday realities and lived experiences of the peoples in conditions of fragility in sub-Saharan Africa. It is, therefore, vital that we draw also on the perspectives of the two institutions created by these peoples to address the problem of fragility in their communities. These institutions are the African Development Bank (AfDB) and the G7+ of Fragile States (otherwise known as the G7+).

For its part, the AfDB's defines fragility as:

> [the] imbalance between the strains and challenges (internal and external) faced by a state and society and their ability to manage them. At the extreme, fragility is expressed as conflict or collapse of state functions.... Fragility is thus the opposite side of the coin to state resilience, which is the ability of the state to manage such strains through effective institutions, processes, and capacities that build legitimacy and societal cohesion.
>
> (AfDB 2014, quoted in Ferreira 2015, 34)

For their part, the G7+ adopted a definition during the Juba (South Sudan) Ministerial Retreat in October 2011 (later affirmed at the Dubai Technical Meeting in May 2013) that ascribes to 'fragility' the characteristics of 'time-limit' and 'national identity,' reflecting the belief that they (the fragile states) must go through the shocks of fragility on their way to achieving sustainable peace, security and economic development. The definition states:

> A state of fragility can be understood as a period of time during nationhood when sustainable socio-economic development requires greater emphasis on complementary peacebuilding and state-building activities such as building inclusive political settlements, security, justice, jobs, good management of resources, and accountable and fair service delivery.
>
> (G7+ 2013, 1)

The G7+ also noted that it chose this definition of fragility because it:

> [1] captures the key concerns of the G7+ and the diversity of our experiences of fragility; and [2] is purposely broad so that it covers the key areas where our countries need to be strengthened, but not does prescribe what weaknesses in these areas look like.
>
> (G7+ 2013, 1)

These definitions notwithstanding, there is one major shortcoming we observed during our extensive reviews of the datasets that accompany these institutional definitions—namely, the lack of a stand-alone indicator on women and fragility, and children and fragility. It has been established by feminist political scientists, economists and sociologists that there is a correlation between gender structural inequality and the making of state fragility. For example, Mary Caprioli (a professor of gender, conflict and security studies at the University of Minnesota and a World Bank consultant) asks two fundamental questions: is gender a factor in the causes, course and consequences of intra-state conflicts? And, can we use gender structural inequality to predict conflicts and other forms of fragility? To answer these questions, she used empirically informed datasets to show that the grievance theory of Ted Gurr and Paul Collier (among others) cannot fully account for why the call to arms draws combatants in the civil conflicts of Africa, and to test whether "states characterized by higher levels of [gender-based] discrimination, inequality, and violence are more likely to experience intrastate conflict" (Caprioli 2005, 161). She ultimately confirms that there is a link between gender structural inequality and civil conflict, concluding that, between the years 1960 and 2001, countries with such inequalities experienced various forms of conflicts. Against this backdrop, she warns against circumscribing gender inequality as a social justice issue, and against overlooking sexual and gender-based violence in the analyses of conflicts. To do so, she argues, reinforces the effects of such violence on societies and, hence, increases the probability that conflicts will occur.

In Part II of this book, we provide statistically informed and empirically rich analyses to explain fragility with its dimensions of poverty, conflicts, child labor, food insecurity, pandemics and gender inequality within sub-Saharan Africa. Based on our empirical exploration, we hypothesize that if policy-makers and governments (including their institutions, the African Development Bank and the G7+) within the sub-regional bloc pay critical attention to addressing these dimensions, such countries will use their resilience in proactive ways to gradually move towards sustainable economic, political and social development. We proceed with our discussion by showing the advantages of including gender and childhood as stand-alone variables in the interpretations of the results on the convergences and divergences between the development/economic—and security—fragility nexuses on statehood.

Towards a theory of state resilience

For our study, there is no better way to begin our examination of the concept of resilience than to start with what psychologists have said about the term. In the field of psychology, which cannot be separated from social science and humanist studies on state fragility, resilience is defined as "the process of adapting well in the face of adversity, trauma, tragedy, threats or even significant sources of stress" (American Psychological Association 2014, quoted in Southwick et al. 2014, 2). Recognizing the other determinants of resilience—socio-cultural, psychological, political and economic—Steven Southwick et al. observe (with references to the study of Robert H. Pietrzak and Steven Southwick on the resilience of U.S. veterans who fought in Iraq and Afghanistan) that resilience is a "continuum that may be present to differing degrees across multiple domains of life" (Southwick et al. 2014, 2–3). For their part, David Fletcher and Mustafa Sarkar contend that the ability to survive traumatic situations makes people stronger. Even in extremely negative situations, such as those involving poverty, resilience means that mental and physical processes and capacity enable people to adapt successfully to challenging and even life-threatening situations (Fletcher and Sarkar 2013, 13). This capacity to cope tells of a continuum in people's abilities to "bend but not break, bounce back, and perhaps even grow in the face of adverse life experiences" (Southwick et al. 2014, 2).

This concept of a continuum suggests a narrative of resilience in the political institutions and peoples of sub-Saharan Africa throughout the long history of fragility in the region. The history of fragility, we suggest, should not be limited to the postcolonial era. It dates as far back as the fifteenth and sixteenth centuries—the period when the precolonial institutions and peoples of sub-Saharan Africa came into contact with European merchants, explorers and missionaries. From that time to the present, the idea of fragility and the responses it attracted were determined by the interests of market forces, and perspectives of market regulators, from outside the region. For instance, we discovered in the literature that between the 1500s and 1700s, fragility in sub-Saharan Africa was defined in terms of shocks to the political economy of the Transatlantic Slave Trade. During this time, piracy against slave ships, a reduction in the number of the inter-micro-kingdom conflicts that produced slaves, and the general resistance of the people in some of these micro-kingdoms against European slave traders, were the leading indicators of fragility that shaped European discourses on state-failure in sub-Saharan Africa. The slave trade officially ended in 1817 (although other forms of salary is still evident in many societies of SSA), and the resilience of African communities continued. Throughout the nineteenth and twentieth centuries, and ending only in the 1960s, discourses on state fragility reflected the imperial world order. All forms of resistance to European imperial expansion were seen as indicators of fragility. During this era, colonial policies against anti-colonial struggles were uncompromisingly militant. Rebellions against European colonial rule were numerous, and were brutally suppressed; examples can be taken from Sierra Leone (the Hut Tax War of 1898, the Haidara Kontorfilli rebellion of 1931), Malawi (the Nyasaland uprising of 1915), South West Africa (now Namibia; the Herero uprising of 1904), South Africa (the Sebatakgomo uprising of 1958 in Sekhukhuneland), Kenya (the Mau Mau uprising of 1952–1960), Rhodesia (now Zimbabwe; the war for independence, 1965–1979), and Mozambique, Angola, Cape Verde and Guinea-Bissau (the sporadic anti-colonial guerrilla wars between 1961 and 1974). In all these uprisings, unco-opted African traditional institutions (including secret societies, which were central to the idea of 'nationhood' and 'statehood': Osaghae 2006; Little 1966; Cleary 1990) were violently suppressed (Mamdani 1996, 2012; Rasmussen 1974).

In the postcolonial era (i.e., after the 1960s when most SSA countries secured political independence), while the struggle against European neo-colonial influences has not disappeared, it is the internal make-up of the successor-states, amid rising consciousness of the global implications of underdevelopment, that have led to a gradual acceptance that the resilience of the African states requires economic, social and political support. Of course, one cannot say that all forms of external support are in favor of development. Further, the ways in which some of the governments of these transitioning states confronted the problem of fragility exacerbated the problem and made the modes of societal resilience more complicated; and navigational strategies more perilous. That notwithstanding, in their overall response to external attempts to use the superior neoliberal peace project (with its intent of promoting Western political dominance of the fragile spaces of Africa: Richmond 2009; Young 1995) to re-direct the localized forms of resilience, the African states demonstrated their mindfulness of their social and political realities. It is difficult for African states to project an outlook of resilience that is overtly anti-Western if they are to escape the fragility-trap entirely. There is, therefore, a need for a compromise between the external and the internal realities, which the international community has taken into consideration as it attempts to help African states and protect its own self-serving interests at the same time.

It is this compromise that shapes the directions of the fragility-as-resilience turn. In theory, at least, this resilience turn has removed 'fragile states' from the 'failed' state (an irrevocable status) discourse and put them in the category of 'countries at risk' (Lemay-Hébert 2018; G7+ 2013). But, as Lemay-Hébert went on to argue, this emergent category of countries at risk comes with its own complications. First, it creates necessitating conditions, and legal justification for the elevation of the liberal peace alternative to resolve the institutional breakdown that accompanies societal collapse and violent conflict. Second, with the core elements of the liberal peace agenda framed to promote the liberal internationalist agenda of the western democracies, the possibilities for securitization of these neoliberal peace interventions increase. However, proponents of the Copenhagen school of securitization theory (McDonald 2008; Stritzel 2007; Buzan and Wæver 1997) have suggested several 'facilitating conditions' that should exist before a complex humanitarian emergency becomes a political/security concern. First, there should be a substantial political issue around the problems—of, say, pandemics and civil conflicts—that cannot be dealt with by the countries in which they have erupted. Second, the crises should have profound global implications as a result of their potential to cross national borders. Third, the crises should have the potential to feed into other geopolitically sensitive problems, and their impact must be of sufficient magnitude to warrant being treated by the international community as having the potential to disrupt global peace and security. That notwithstanding, the inferential securitization narratives around state fragility (without regard for the resilience of the peoples in conditions of fragility) would not achieve the intended goals—of securitization—were the 'inferential subjects,' the constituents of those seeking to securitize the fragile states, not receptive to the narratives of their political leaders (Huysmans 2011). Accordingly, where these inferential subjects are receptive to speech acts of insecurity, a crowd psychology of fear is created (Balzacq 2005). In such a situation, the people of the sending state (the philanthropists; the saviors) need to be reassured. While the desire should always be to resolve the crisis, there are other self-seeking factors that may lead to a situation wherein the savior becomes the devil. Then again, African leaders have, in some cases, called for the securitization of their own states when faced with complex political and medical emergencies. For example, following the outbreak of the Ebola pandemic in West Africa in 2014, the leaders of affected countries (Sierra Leone, Liberia and Guinea) framed their messages to the UN using 'dependency discourses' that were, according to John Idriss Lahai, designed to motivate the West to accept, as sacrosanct, its moral responsibility to produce a comprehensive response to the pandemic, and to help those countries mitigate the impact Ebola-related restrictions on trade and transportation were having on their respective economies (Lahai 2017).

Despite this negative impact, this turn from failed states to countries at risk is about recognizing the resilience of fragile states. Resilience matters because it is so perceptibly and fundamentally what survival is all about. There are various notions of resilience, and many platforms on which it is demonstrated. Thus, the resilience of a state may be the will and ability to endure in the face of threats to its sovereignty—territoriality, as the scholars of realism theory contend; or it may derive from the activism of civil society in compelling the state to do more to provide the basic needs of her peoples, and to promote and protect their fundamental human rights, as development experts and human rights advocates recommend. State resilience may ultimately rest in the processes of rebuilding the institutions of governance after every episode of fragility so as to prevent such episodes from happening again, as peacebuilding scholars and practitioners would have it; or it may reside in the willingness of the leaders of government to subject themselves to the political appraisals of their electorates—and, for those voted out of office, the willingness to accept the democratic verdict of their electorates, as the advocates of democracy advise. Then again, state resilience may circulate through political and cultural accommodation of the political and cultural 'others' for the sake of peace, as Kantian theorists (who propound the deontological perpetual/moral peace theory of Immanuel Kant) argue. State resilience may come from the acceptance of the fragile states in the international system. Here, the dominant states can transform the international system into a dais of equity to enable the fragile states to be recognized as equal (though emerging) sovereign states, as advocates of the democratic theory predict. Or state resilience may offer the state the means by which its people can eliminate all politically motivated and culturally regulated patriarchal institutions and narratives that prevent the attainment of gender equality in politics, economics and society, as liberal feminists have suggested.

Note

1 According to the joint World Bank and African Development Bank Migration and Remittances Household Surveys conducted for the Africa Migration Project, reported

that, sub-Saharan countries grew from its 2015 figures of $33 billion to $37.8 billion in 2017; with a two-year prediction that by 2019, it will increase to $39.6 billion. www.worldbank.org/en/topic/migrationremittancesdiasporaissues/brief/migration-remittances-data (accessed: June 14, 2018).

References

Anter, Andreas. 2014. *Max Weber's Theory of the Modern State: Origins, Structure and Significance*. Basingstoke, Hampshire: Palgrave Macmillan.

Baliamoune-Lutz, Mina, and Mark McGillivray. 2011. "State Fragility: Concept and Measurement." *Fragile States: Causes, Costs, and Responses*, 33–42.

Balzacq, Thierry. 2005. "The Three Faces of Securitization: Political Agency, Audience and Context." *European Journal of International Relations* 11 (2): 171–201.

Bates, Robert H. 2008. "The Logic of State Failure: Learning from Late-Century Africa." *Conflict Management and Peace Science* 25 (4): 297–314.

Bertocchi, Graziella, and Andrea Guerzoni. 2012. "Growth, History, or Institutions: What Explains State Fragility in Sub-Saharan Africa?" *Journal of Peace Research* 49 (6): 769–783.

Buzan, Barry, and Ole Waever. 1997. "Slippery? Contradictory? Sociologically Untenable? The Copenhagen School Replies." *Review of International Studies* 23 (2): 241–250.

Caprioli, Mary. 2005. "Primed for Violence: The Role of Gender Inequality in Predicting Internal Conflict." *International Studies Quarterly* 49 (2): 161–178.

Carment, David, and Yiagadeesen Samy. 2012. "Assessing State Fragility: A Country Indicators for Foreign Policy Report." Carleton University [with Canadian International Development Agency]. www.operationspaix.net/DATA/DOCUMENT/7374~v~Assessing_State_Fragility__A_Country_Indicators_for_Foreign_Policy_Report.pdf.

Chauvet, Lisa, and Paul Collier. 2008. "What Are the Preconditions for Turnarounds in Failing States?" *Conflict Management and Peace Science* 25 (4): 332–348.

Clapham, Christopher. 2000. "Failed States and Non-States in the Modern International Order." In *Failed States III: Globalization and The Failed State*, 1–15. Florence, Italy: Strategic Outreach Program of the U.S. Army War College and the Office of International Programs, Purdue University. www.comm.ucsb.edu/faculty/mstohl/failed_states/2000/failedstates.php.

Cleary, A. S. 1990. "The Myth of Mau Mau in Its International Context." *African Affairs* 89 (355): 227–245.

Dahl, Robert A. 1957. "The Concept of Power." *Systems Research and Behavioral Science* 2 (3): 201–215.

Dowdall, Harold Chaloner. 1923. "Word State." *Law Quarterly Review* 39: 98–112.

Dunleavy, Patrick, and Brendan O'Leary. 1987. *Theories of the State: The Politics of Liberal Democracy*. Basingstoke, Hampshire: Macmillan Education Ltd.

Easterly, William, Ross Levine, and David Roodman. 2004. "Aid, Policies, and Growth: Comment." *American Economic Review* 94 (3): 774–780.

Ferreira, Ines Afonso Roque. 2015. "Defining and Measuring State Fragility: A New Proposal." In, 39. Berkeley, CA. http://cega.berkeley.edu/assets/miscellaneous_files/109_-_ABCA_2015_Ines_Ferreira_Defining_and_measuring_state_fragility__A_new_proposal_May15.pdf.

Fletcher, David, and Mustafa Sarkar. 2013. "Psychological Resilience." *European Psychologist* 18: 12–23. https://doi.org/10.1027/1016-9040/a000124.

G7+. 2013. "Note on the Fragility Spectrum." G7+. www.g7plus.org/sites/default/files/resources/g7%2B%2BEnglish%2BFS%2BNote%2BDesign.pdf.

Giddens, Anthony. 1985. *The Nation-State and Violence*. Vol. 2. Berkeley, CA: University of California Press.

Grant, Thomas D. 1999. "Defining Statehood: The Montevideo Convention and Its Discontents." *Columbia Journal of Transnational Law* 37 (2): 403–457.

Hampel, Karl. 2015. "The Dark (Er) Side of 'State Failure': State Formation and Socio-Political Variation." *Third World Quarterly* 36 (9): 1629–1648.

Heath, Elizabeth. 2010. "Berlin Conference of 1884–1885." In *Encyclopedia of Africa*, edited by Kwame Anthony Appiah and Gates, 2: 177–175. Oxford, UK: Oxford University Press. www.oxfordreference.com/view/10.1093/acref/9780195337709.001.0001/acref-9780195337709-e-0467.

Helman, Gerald B., and Steven R. Ratner. 1992. "Saving Failed States." *Foreign Policy*, 89 (3): 3–20.

Huysmans, Jef. 2011. "What's in an Act? On Security Speech Acts and Little Security Nothings." *Security Dialogue* 42 (4–5): 371–383.

Klute, Georg, and Trutz von Trotha. 2004. "Roads to Peace: From Small War to Parasovereign Peace in the North of Mali." In *Healing the Wounds: Essays on the Reconstruction of Societies after War*, edited by Marie-Claire Foblets and Trutz von Trotha, 109–143. Portland, OR: Hart Publishing.

Krasner, Stephen D. 1999. *Sovereignty, International Relations Theory, and International Law*. Princeton, NJ: Princeton University Press.

Lahai, John Idriss. 2017. *The Ebola Pandemic in Sierra Leone: Representations, Actors, Interventions and the Path to Recovery*. Basingstoke, Hampshire: Palgrave Macmillan.

Lahai, John Idriss, and Nenneh Lahai. 2018. "The History and Representations of the Challenges of Governance in the Fragile States of Sub-Saharan Africa." In *Governance and Political Adaptation in Fragile States*, edited by John Idriss Lahai, Karin von Strokirch, Howard Brasted, and Helen Ware, 1: 35–50. Basingstoke, Hampshire: Palgrave Macmillan.

Lemay-Hébert, Nicolas. 2018. "From Saving Failed States to Managing Risks: Reinterpreting Fragility through Resilience." In *Governance and Political Adaptation in Fragile States*, edited by John Idriss Lahai, Karin von Strokirch, Howard Brasted, and Helen Ware. New York, NY: Palgrave Macmillan.

Levitov, Alex. 2016. *Normative Legitimacy and the State*. Oxford, UK: Oxford University Press. www.oxfordhandbooks.com/view/10.1093/oxfordhb/9780199935307.001.0001/oxfordhb-9780199935307-e-131.

Little, Kenneth. 1966. "The Political Function of the Poro. (Part II.)." *Africa: Journal of the International African Institute* 36 (1): 62–72.

MacGibbon, Iain C. 1957. "Customary International Law and Acquiescence." *British Year Book of International Law* 33: 115.

Mamdani, Mahmood. 1996. *Citizen and Subject: Contemporary Africa and the Legacy of Late Colonialism*. Princeton, NJ: Princeton University Press.

Mamdani, Mahmood. 2012. *Define and Rule: Native as Political Identity*. Cambridge, MA: Harvard University Press.

McDonald, Matt. 2008. "Securitization and the Construction of Security." *European Journal of International Relations* 14 (4): 563–587.

Naudé, Wim, Amelia U. Santos-Paulino, and Mark McGillivray, eds. 2011. *Fragile States: Causes, Costs, and Responses*. Oxford, UK: Oxford University Press.

Osaghae, Eghosa E. 2006. "Colonialism and Civil Society in Africa: The Perspective of Ekeh's Two Publics." *Voluntas: International Journal of Voluntary and Nonprofit Organizations* 17 (3): 233–245.

Otto, Dianne. 1996. "Subalternity and International Law: The Problems of Global Community and the Incommensurability of Difference." *Social & Legal Studies* 5 (3): 337–364.

Rabel, Ernst. 1941. "The Revision of the Treaties of Montevideo on the Law of Conflicts." *Michigan Law Review* 39 (4): 517–525.

Rasmussen, Thomas. 1974. "The Popular Basis of Anti-Colonial Protest." In *Politics in Zambia*, edited by William Tordoff, 40–61. Manchester, UK: Manchester University Press.

Redner, Harry. 1990. "Beyond Marx-Weber: A Diversified and International Approach to the State." *Political Studies* 38 (4): 638–653.

Richmond, Oliver P. 2009. "Becoming Liberal, Unbecoming Liberalism: Liberal-Local Hybridity via the Everyday as a Response to the Paradoxes of Liberal Peacebuilding." *Journal of Intervention and Statebuilding* 3 (3): 324–344.

Richmond, Oliver P. 2010. "Introduction." In *Palgrave Advances in Peacebuilding: Critical Developments and Approaches*, edited by Oliver P. Richmond, 1–13. New York, NY: Palgrave Macmillan.

Shaw, Malcolm N. 2017. *International Law*. 8th edition. New York, NY: Cambridge University Press.

Southwick, Steven M., George A. Bonanno, Ann S. Masten, Catherine Panter-Brick, and Rachel Yehuda. 2014. "Resilience Definitions, Theory, and Challenges: Interdisciplinary Perspectives." *European Journal of Psychotraumatology* 5 (1): 25338.

Stritzel, Holger. 2007. "Towards a Theory of Securitization: Copenhagen and Beyond." *European Journal of International Relations* 13 (3): 357–383.

Wilde, Ralph. 2002. "The Skewed Responsibility Narrative of the Failed States Concept." *ILSA Journal of International and Comparative Law* 9 (2): 425–429.

Young, Tom. 1995. " 'A Project to Be Realised': Global Liberalism and Contemporary Africa." *Millennium* 24 (3): 527–546.

3 Frames of impact

The contexts and correlates of armed conflicts on state fragility

Introduction

Armed conflicts have been theorized as one of the main factors for state fragility in sub-Saharan Africa (SSA) due, in part, to what scholars and practitioners make of the instrumental correlates of war (used interchangeably with war): battle-related deaths (Themnér and Wallensteen 2011; Wallensteen and Sollenberg 1999; Lacina and Gleditsch 2005), the gendered dimensions of the interactions between the warring factions (Caprioli 2005; El-Bushra 2000; El Jack et al. 2003), including the behaviors of their combatants towards women (and the vulnerable men) (Lahai 2015; Alison 2004; Fox 2004; Giles and Hyndman 2004), the economic (Ballentine 2003; Collier and Hoeffler 2004) and political (Zolberg 1968; Smith 2000; Le Billon 2001) impact of rebel groups, and the religion-induced issues that drive some groups to rebel. As such, the extensive multidisciplinary scholarly research on the correlations of conflicts and state fragility reflects not just the perspectives of the peoples living in conditions of fragility, but also the views of institutions (governmental and non-governmental) and intellectuals working in or with interests in the justice, development and security sectors in the so-named fragile states of SSA.

This extensive literature, and the broader concerns it produces, has generated definitions and typologies of conflicts using various, and sometimes contentious, methods and theoretical standpoints. To date, while there is general agreement over the meaning of 'armed conflicts' there has not been a consensus on how conflicts impact the states of SSA. There is an ongoing debate as to whether conflict should always be considered destructive; and, if so, who—within the zones of war—does it affect the most: the state institutions (Besley and Persson 2008), or the men (Sivakumaran 2007; Carpenter 2006), women (Kelly 2000) and children (Yule et al. 2004), or the international community of 'civilized' nations and institutions (Buzan 2007; Herbst 1990). As pointed out in Chapter 1, the debate also includes discourses that see conflicts as not necessarily bad. Some liberation conflicts produce dividends that contribute to the nationalistic re-awakening of the peoples in some (if not all) of the postcolonial states of SSA (Parry 1998) and, in tandem, have resulted in the making of new states (such as South Sudan (see LeRiche and Arnold 2013)) and an end to apartheid (Melber 2002) in the

SSA sub-region. Conflicts have created the 'disciplinary' economic and political conditions that necessitated the waves of liberal democracy and their gradual consolidation in previously undemocratic, but presently transitioning, countries in SSA and beyond (Hardt and Negri 2004; Fatton 1990; Abrahamsen 2000). Finally, conflicts have, in some respects, contributed to the opening up of markets and people's adaptation to globalization; to progressive social ideals and economic ideas that may change the peripherality of the sub-continent in the international political economy (IPE) (Ajayi 2003).

With the political economy of war seen as an outcome of humankind's insatiable desire for the means to achieve (though never be satisfied with) his or her wants, the first frame for the scholarly understanding of war was economics: what, financially, caused conflict to proliferate in spaces of material (and moral) scarcity. Through empirically informed desegregated datasets, scholars interested in the vertical economic character of war have gone to great lengths to trivialize all that cannot be quantified in terms of financial gain and loss whenever armed conflicts erupt or terminate (see Collier and Hoeffler 2004, 2005; Collier and Sambanis 2005). For them, the essence of theorizing conflicts is empirically and quantitatively explaining the economic shocks or volatility of (pseudo-)capitalist states. They see no relevance in the political and cultural dimensions of conflicts if these non-economic dimensions do not explain the need for a liberal economic order (driven by a liberal internationalist political power (Hardt and Negri 2000)) in a chaotic world with multiple centers of economic power that transcend the state (Goldgeier and McFaul 1992; Ikenberry 2010; Amin 1998, 2006). Rather, the focus, it was suggested, should be on vertical inequalities that are born out of greed (and its associated outcome of grievances) within fragile states (Collier and Sambanis 2005), and the remittances of the 'diasporas' of these conflict-prone countries (Collier and Hoeffler 2004, 568).

Without rejecting the entirety of the 'ultra-economic' framing of conflicts and the impact of inequalities on fragility, some have tried to centralize (and in so doing, problematize) the horizontal nature of inequalities—bringing to bear the hallmarks of 'relative' deprivation on the bases of identity: social (ethnic and language), political and economic (Stewart 2016; Østby 2008; Cederman, Weidmann and Gleditsch 2011; Nafziger and Auvinen 2002; Gubler and Selway 2012; Østby et al. 2009). There are also those who, inasmuch as they have not rejected vertical and horizontal explanations of the eruption and termination of conflicts, have approached the issue from the existential sequencing and interplay of the crises of poverty, cultural beliefs and political/financial powers (de facto or *de jure*) of political organizations (Arnson and Zartman 2005). Moreover, there are those who say we should focus on the question of 'what' makes wars persist, and not just on the question 'why' they erupt. The 'what,' they suggest, should enable us to shift our scholarly attention to the question 'what do state institutions do?' and 'what do people (within fragile states) make of the performance of their governments?' In essence, they are asking us to frame the impact of conflicts on fragility based on the beliefs and aspirations peoples have for the institutions working in the critical areas of human rights, economic development and security (military) of the state (see Easterly 2001; World Bank 2011).

In recent years, some schools of thought have attempted to locate the causes of conflicts, and what makes them intractable, on the borderless platforms of gender inequality. The increasing volume of feminist-centric research—while anchored on epistemologies that can be seen as feminisms-without-borders[1] and, therefore, not in favor of patriarchally conditioned strategies to undo the postcolonial foundations of war globally—have, in practice, generated an interest in the correlation between conflict and gender-based discrimination against women (Lahai 2015; Giles and Hyndman 2004; El-Bushra 2000). Scholarly works projecting a 'feminist' framing of the causes and course of conflicts have looked into the underlying agendas of actors (both state and non-state) in conflict zones and how their militarized manner of interaction affects their patterns of systematic and non-systemic attacks on civilians, and the gender-specific impacts on women (see Meintjes, Turshen and Pillay 2001)—who are considered, in most SSA communities as the people on whose wombs the continuity of the state rests (Dyer 2007). In short, they are interested in the issues inherently connected to patriarchy and the masculine character of militarism—induced by *culture* (which turns men into warriors, and women, into docile beings who must accept their status as those in need of protection), motivated by *politics* (the instrumental space in which illegitimate use of force is given legitimacy), and validated by *society* (the 'space' where the platforms of sexual and gender-based violence (SGBV)—which have conditioned the bodies of women as a platform for sex-based differences, gender-based discrimination and the 'uncivility' of civil wars in SSA.

Notwithstanding the existence of these, and many other, theories, and the methods and datasets that guide them, about the multi-dimensional framing of the correlation between conflicts and fragility, the lack of consensus on 'what causes conflicts' has had far-reaching consequences. Attempts to synchronize the context-specific agendas of professionals in the field (individuals, agencies and governments) into these multi-layered theoretical positions (be they dominant or peripheral) and their definitions of the various forms of conflicts, have had an impact on the measurement indicators of conflicts.

We recognize, however, that despite the existence of these, and many other, datasets and databases, the literature on the intersection between conflict and state fragility in SSA is not conclusive. Against this backdrop, our intention in the first part of this chapter is to present (a) the tools and adaptive indices that have been used to measure the causes and causal effect of conflicts, (b) summaries of the definitions and typologies of conflicts, and (c) the key theoretical perspectives (and their methodological frameworks) on the causes of conflict in SSA. In the second part of the chapter, we scrutinize the ways in which the proponents of those perspectives have imagined, understood and theorized the context-specific variations of the impact of conflict on state fragility. In addition, our aim is to contribute to the existing studies on conflict by focusing on the attempts to centralize the 'lived experiences' of states—that is, as actors representing the collective emotions (and 'knowledge') of the people within them. The goal is to reveal the convergences and divergences in the theoretical (and practical) underpinnings of conflict as a key indicator of state fragility and a tool for measuring the resilience of states in SSA.

Measuring the causes and causal effect of conflict: tools and adaptive indices

There has been a rise in attempts to quantify or measure the causal effect of conflicts, and their impact on the discourse of state fragility. Studies have adopted indices, such as the *State Fragility Index* of the Fund for Peace (SFI-FfP) or the *Conflict Database and Datasets* of the Uppsala Conflict Data Program/Peace Research Institute, Oslo (UCDP-PRIO).

The SFI-FfP is based on a conflict assessment framework—known as 'CAST'—that was developed in the 1990s to capture the levels of 'vulnerability' of states on the verge of 'collapsing' or failing (Fund for Peace 2017). This framework has four main indicators: (1) cohesion; (2) economic; (3) political; and (4) social. There are sub-indicators under each of these. Under the cohesion indicator, there are (a) security apparatus, (b) factionalized elites, and (c) group grievance. Under the economic indicator, there are (i) economic decline, (ii) uneven economic development, and (iii) human flight and brain drain. Under the political indicator, there are also three areas of focus: (a) state legitimacy, (b) public services, and (c) human rights and the rule of law. And, finally, under the social indicator there are: (i) demographic pressures, (ii) refugees and internally displaced persons (IDPs), and (iii) external intervention (in situations of 'vulnerability').

The UCDP-PRIO, on the other hand, contains various databases and datasets. They include, among others, the Data on Armed Conflict, the Urban Social Disorder v2, the GEO-SVAC Dataset, the Data on Religious Cleavages and Civil War, the Conflict Site Dataset, the Onset and Duration of Intrastate Conflict, the Armed Conflict Location and Event Data (ACLED), the Battle Deaths Data and the UCDP/PRIO Armed Conflict Dataset. These databases and datasets, which were developed (or at least some of them) in (or after) 1946, are primarily intended for scholarly use in statistical and macro-level research. According to the developers, the Department of Peace and Conflict Research at Uppsala University, this information "complements the annual compendium of ongoing armed conflicts published in the *Journal of Peace Research*, as well as the UCDP online database."[2] Collectively, they are being used to aid in forecasting conflict eruption, studying the duration of violence and, through what the developers refer to as "conflict polygons," estimating the number of battle-related deaths.[3]

The UCDP-PRIO are the most widely used statistical databases and datasets in attempts to understand the broader impact of conflicts on the indicators of fragility presented by SFI-FfP. However, to give recognition to the 'new' conflict—namely, terrorism, which until recently was not a typology of conflict in SSA—in the causal influence of war on fragility, new terrorism-related and associated datasets have been developed. Two prominent examples are (1) the open-access Global Terrorism Database of the National Consortium for the Study of Terrorism and Response to Terrorism (or START), hosted by the Centre of Excellence of the U.S. Department of Homeland Security and the University of Maryland,[4] and (2) the RAND Database of Worldwide Terrorism Incidents (RDWTI).[5]

Critical overview of the definitions of conflicts: histories, theories, and classifications

Many efforts have been made to understand the meanings of conflicts. Some have concluded that conflict is a part of the human condition, an integral aspect of the interactions between people in their natural state of being. In this Hobbesian view, it was the attempt to regulate the inherent impulse to violence (which made his life "solitary, poor, nasty, brutish, and short") of man (used here as a technical political term for the 'political person(s) or 'people') that led him to enter into civil society (the state) through a social contract with a government that was required to possess, and be able to demonstrate, absolute powers to govern impartially and prevent people from rebelling against it (Sorell 1996). After all, what

> power could have been strong enough either to gather scattered humanity into one place, or to lead it out of its brutish existence in the wilderness up to our present condition of civilization as men as citizens, or, after the establishment of social communities, to give shape to laws, tribunals, and civic rights?
> (Silver 1996, p. 331)

None, but the "Leviathan"—or the "matter, the form and power of a commonwealth ecclesiastical and civil" (Hobbes 2010[1651]).

For other political theorists, it is the cruelty of the civil society created for and governed by the so-called Leviathan that spurred 'man' (who was by nature 'good') to rebel (according to John Locke) (Dunn 1995); and, by rebelling, hope to regain his freedom in the face of the refusal of the state to fulfil his 'general will' (according to Jean Rousseau) (Shklar 1985). In trying to ground the root causes of the depravity of the political man in his 'unnatural state' of being and knowing—a state that frames man's contractual right to fight for his human rights as criminal, and the rules that occasion such criminality as the norm—the focus is on that which criminalizes the moral reasoning behind, and action toward, the right of man to rebel (according to Locke and Rousseau) (Riley 1982)—although, an empiricist reading of David Hume's rule-consequentialist reconstruction of Locke's and Rousseau's social contract theories, as sources of social and political obligations, lends legitimacy to the state's power to control some of the excesses of man (see Chwaszcza 2013).

However, for proponents of structural political realism, such as Kenneth Neal Waltz (Waltz 2001) and John J. Mearsheimer (Mearsheimer 2001), conflicts are a necessary condition for states because, as for humans, the space for state interaction is, by nature, primed to survive through the 'Darwinian' concepts of 'natural selection' and 'survival of the fittest.'

For others, conflicts first began as human constructs and were later given actual meanings by society to legitimate gender-based differences, embedded in narratives of power that call for the exclusion of women from political and security spheres. Those who adopt this standpoint are called western liberal feminists. They saw the histories of wars—World Wars I and II, the Cold War and its proxy wars that raged in postcolonial Africa and beyond—as the fulfillment of Niccolò Machiavelli's recommendation to the 'militant men and states' to resist the inclusion of women in the governance of states. As John Idriss Lahai notes (with reference to other eminent feminist scholars—Mary O'Brien, Emanuele Saccarelli, Christine Sylvester and Maria J. Saxonhouse—critical of the role of men in politics) this anti-woman standpoint in Machiavelli's philosophical works.

> In his treatise, *The Discourse*, Machiavelli lists women among the enemies of the state and argues that [they] are biologically not designed for the 'bad acts which boys must be taught' [quoting Mary O'Brien (1989)]. In other words, a sure means through which a state is destroyed is by allowing women to play active roles in the management of the state, including the regulation of war and peace [citing Emanuele Saccarelli (2009)]. To prevent this situation, Machiavelli argues there should be a distinction between public and private spheres. The home, which he understands as the sphere of private morality, should be the place for women. And the sphere of public morality, the public, and the political landscape, where matters of state politics and security are dealt with, should be a place reserved for men [citing Christine Sylvester (1994)]. This is the domain which women should be discouraged from entering.
>
> (Lahai 2016a, 18)

For this reason, Lahai goes on to state,

> Machiavelli, suggest[ed] that men, especially those aspiring for or [are] in positions of political authority (i.e., in government or the military), should not be judged by their conduct at home, because whatever they do there is an expressive pursuit of their sexual desires [here Lahai endorses the position of Maria Saxonhouse (2004)]. In the same way, whatever role women play behind the scenes that may result in their husbands making wise political decisions and [militarily] strategically important moves their efforts should not be recognised.
>
> (Lahai 2016a, 18)

To others, conflicts are outcomes of class differences created by the state (the machinery for the societal oppression of the working class) and sustained by competition for limited resources. This social (dis)order is maintained by oppressive domination of the proletariat and the power of the bourgeoisie, rather than on the general consent of the oppressed. According to this view's leading proponent, Karl Marx, conflicts thrive in human societies because of the structure of society "in relation to its major classes, and the struggle between them" (Rummel 1977, 35). This 'struggle,' Marx argues, is, in practice, the apparatus for 'structural' change—with this structural change (an outcome of class struggle), in turn, being the only constant in humankind's lived experiences (Marx 1973, 59). What makes the experiences of people always volatile, we are told, is what society attaches to 'private property' (a representation of class interest) or the will to acquire it (through the manipulation of political organization and power). This idea of class differences—defined by materialism—is about power, which, in the Marxist sense, is defined as the capability to "exclude others from the property and to use it for personal purposes" (Rummel 1977, 75). Power, therefore, creates irreconcilable divisions between the powerful (the bourgeoisie, who controls the main drivers of production: capital), the semi-powerful (the landowners, whose income or power is rent), and the powerless (or the proletariat, whose power is labor). And since the proletariat has been conditioned by the artificial scarcity created by the state (under the control of the bourgeoisie), the powerless are required to sell their labor for menial wages. While the transition from one class to another is possible, the merger between capital and land has created class interests that makes it difficult for an individual proletarian to succeed. But, were the proletariat to come together and understand their deprived conditions, a class consciousness would arise and eventually enable them to cooperate in their struggle to overthrow the state—and with it, their oppression by the bourgeoisie. This triumph, R. J. Rummel informs us, would

> eliminate the basis of class division in property through public ownership of the means of production. With the basis of classes thus wiped away, a classless society will ensure [in theory], and since 'political power' to protect the bourgeoisie against the workers is unnecessary, political authority and the state will wither away.
>
> (Rummel 1977, 313)

Thus, according to Rummel, if the attainment of justice can only be achieved in a classless society, then 'aggression'—or what he referred as a "disposition, power, or manifestation characterized by assault, attack, invasion" (Rummel 1977, 25)—aimed at overthrowing the state (to make it possible for the creation of a classless society) should be seen as good, instrumental, defensive and altruistic (Rummel 1977, 184–185)—with altruism being the "intellectual, and authoritative form of power" that makes it possible for 'love, persuasion, or authority to thrive after the toppling of the state" (Rummel 1977, 196).

Arguably, and in view of what we have said so far, conflict is what people say it is. It is both physical and emotional; it is both intra-personal and interpersonal;

although it time-limited, it can also transcend time; and, hence, it is what regulates the timeless histories of political beings/people in their evolutionary societal adaptations in war and peace. Conflict can be induced by economic or ethnicity-based inequality, and has far-reaching consequences for habitable spaces. It can be made and unmade; learnt and unlearnt; studied and managed. And although it is situationally circumstantial in nature, its violent (and non-violent) forms thrive in conditions of state fragility—which is the unintended outcome of social, political and economic power.

That notwithstanding, there have been, in recent decades, attempts to define the most disastrous forms of conflicts—armed conflicts—based on a set of criteria. These include the actors involved, their modes of interaction, the magnitude of the harm that follows their interactions, and the impact of their actions on the pillars of development: state institutions, capital flow and markets. Thus, according to the widely used characterization of conflict, that of the UCDP-PRIO, armed conflict—with a focus on the category of non-international conflicts—is:

> [A] contested incompatibility that concerns governments and/or territory over which the use of armed force between the military forces of two parties, of which at least one is the government of a state, has resulted in at least 25 battle-related deaths each year.
>
> (Gleditsch et al. 2002, quoted in Bartusevičius 2016, 106)

The aggregate variables on the number of battle-related deaths, Lars-Erik Cederman et al. argue, can be observed over time and through the following interrelated parameters: (1) intensity level of the conflict, (2) location of the conflict, (3) conflict type (for example, rebel vs. government, rebel vs. rebel, government vs. government), (4) composition of the parties to a conflict, and (5) the dyads of parties' incompatibility (Cederman, Buhaug and Rød 2009).

In addition to the parameters identified by Cederman et al., the UCDP-PRIO's Armed Conflict Dataset identifies five separate elements that better explain, if not operationalize, its definition of the aggregate category of intra-state conflicts (quoted above). These elements, which we quote *in extensio* from the Uppsala Conflict Data Program (UCDP 2013, 1–3), are as follows:

1 *Use of armed force*: use of arms in order to promote the parties' general position in the conflict, resulting in deaths.
   1.1 *Arms*: any material means, e.g., manufactured weapons but also sticks, stones, fire, water, etc.[6]
2 *25 deaths*: A minimum of 25 battle-related deaths per year and per dyad (see Item 3.3 in this definition) in an incompatibility [UCDP-PRIO's Armed Conflict Dataset argues that

> incompatibility involving two opposition groups, each involved in clashes with the government resulting in 20 deaths, would not be

recorded as a conflict (neither dyad reached the minimum casualty threshold), whereas an incompatibility involving a single opposition group that caused 25 battle-deaths would be included in the dataset.

(footnote, p. 2)]

3 *Party*: A government of a state or any opposition organization or alliance of organizations.

UCDP distinguishes between primary and secondary parties. Primary parties are those that form an incompatibility by stating incompatible positions (see Item 5 in this definition). At least one of the primary parties is the government of a state. Secondary parties are states that enter a conflict with troops to actively support one of the primary parties. The secondary party must share the position of the primary party it is supporting in the incompatibility.

3.1 *Government*: The party controlling the capital of a state

3.2 *Opposition organization*: Any non-governmental group of people having announced a name for their group and using armed force to influence the outcome of the stated incompatibility (see Item 5 in this definition).
The UCDP only deals with formally organized opposition. The focus is on armed conflict involving consciously conducted and planned political campaigns rather than spontaneous violence.

3.3 *Dyad*: A dyad consists of two conflicting primary parties. At least one of the primary parties must be the government of a state. In interstate conflicts, both primary parties are state governments [here the dataset stated an exception of three: "the primary parties interstate conflict consist of only one actor on each side (and thus only consist one dyad" (footnote, p. 2)]. In intrastate and extra-systemic conflicts, the non-governmental primary party includes one or more opposition organization(s). A conflict can include more than one dyad (if, for example, a government is opposed by three rebel groups over the same incompatibility, the conflict is made up of three dyads. Note that secondary parties (i.e., intervening states supplying troops to one of the primary parties) do not lead to the formation of additional dyads).

4 *State*: A state is an internationally recognized sovereign government controlling a specific territory or an internationally unrecognized government controlling a specified territory whose sovereignty is not disputed by another internationally recognized sovereign government previously controlling the same territory.

5 *Incompatibility concerning government or territory*: The incompatibility, as stated by the parties, must concern government and/or territory.

5.1 *Incompatibility*: The stated general incompatible positions.

5.2 Incompatibility concerning government: Incompatibility concerning type of political system, the replacement of the central government, or the change of its composition.

> 5.3 Incompatibility concerning territory: Incompatibility concerning the status of a territory, e.g., the change of the state in control of a certain territory (interstate conflict), secession or autonomy (internal conflict). (UCDP 2013, 1–3)

Another definition of armed intra-state conflict has been presented by the Working Group on Militarism and Underdevelopment, otherwise known as 'Project Ploughshares.' This defines an armed conflict as

> a political conflict in which armed combat involves the armed forces of at least one state and one or more armed factions seeking to gain control of all or part of the state; and in which at least 1,000 people have been killed by the fighting during the course of the conflict.[7]

Project Ploughshares' definition of conflict differs from UCDP-PRIO's in several areas: the number of battle-related deaths, the cause(s) of such deaths and the types of conflict in which these deaths occur. Relating to the first, Project Ploughshares' definition sets a threshold of 1,000 deaths, while the UCDP-PRIO suggests 25 deaths (per annum). On methods, the UCDP-PRIO, with a concern for the difference between 'direct' and non-conflict related deaths, explains that its data only captures

> those deaths caused by the warring parties that can be directly related to combat over the contested incompatibility. These include traditional battle-field fighting, guerrilla activities (e.g., hit-and-run attacks/ambushes) and all kinds of bombardments of military bases warfare (bombs, explosions, and assassinations) [which] does not resemble what happens on a battlefield, but such deaths are considered to be battle-related. The target for the attacks is either the military forces or representatives for the parties, though there is often substantial collateral damage in the form of civilians being killed in the crossfire, indiscriminate bombings, etc. all fatalities—military as well as civilian—incurred in such situations are counted as battle-related deaths.
>
> (UCDP 2013, 5)

In relation to the third difference—the types of conflict in which these deaths occur—the UCDP-PRIO Armed Conflict Dataset's Correlates of War identifies the following types of conflict: (1) inter-state (or a conflict between two or more governments); (2) extra-state (also known as extra-systemic conflict), a conflict "between a state and a non-state group [like a terrorist group/network] outside its own territory"; such conflicts can be classified as territorial if a government (either the home government of the group or another) sides with the non-governmental group;[8] (3) intrastate (or a conflict between a government and a non-governmental party, with no interference from other countries); and (4) internationalized internal conflict (or conflict between a government and a non-governmental party where the government side, the opposing side, or both sides, receive troop support from other governments that actively participate in the conflict).[9] For its part, Project Ploughshares identifies three overlapping types of conflicts: (a) state-controlled wars, (b) state formation conflicts, and (c) failed state wars. On what constitutes state-controlled wars, Project Ploughshares notes that these wars are centered on struggles for control of the central governing apparatus of the state. It argues:

> State control struggles have typically been driven by ideologically defined revolutionary movements, decolonization campaigns or simply as a mechanism for the transfer of power from one set of elites to another. In some instances, communal [...] interests are significant to the fight to transfer power, and in other instances, religion becomes a defining feature of the conflict.[10]

With regard to 'state formation conflicts,' Project Ploughshare defines these as armed confrontations that are concerned with the

> form or shape of the state itself and generally involve particular regions or a country fighting for a greater measure of autonomy or for outright secession or for the right to decide in a fair and binding referendum whether or not to secede. Communal or ethnic interests are usually central to struggles for regional autonomy or secession, and in some instances, religion also becomes a defining feature of the conflict.[11]

Finally, and perhaps most importantly (because it is the focus of this book), there are 'failed states wars.' Before examining the Project Ploughshares definition, it is important to reiterate, from our review of the literature on the characteristics of failed state conflicts in SSA, that these are conflicts that erupt due to several interrelated causes. They can erupt from the spasmodic forms of societal violence within the state; they erupt when an exclusive group of people attempts to take control of the governing apparatus of the states—particularly, in postcolonial SSA, between the 1970s and 1990s. By way of clarification, when we say an 'exclusive group of people' we are referring to what Ali A. Mazrui termed the *lumpen militariat*, "a class of semi-organized, rugged, and semi-literate soldiery which has begun to claim a share of power and influence in what would otherwise have become a heavily privileged meritocracy of the educated" (Mazrui 1973, 1). Apart from the activities of the 'militariat' in the making of failed state conflicts, there are cases in which conflicts have erupted as a result of a state-sponsored crackdown on dissident groups, and the desire of the oppressed to free themselves from the autocratic governments that succeeded European colonial rule.

That said, we return to the Project Ploughshares' definition, according to which failed state conflicts are wars in which the aim is

> [n]either about state control nor state formation, but about more local issues and disputes involving violence in the absence of effective government control. The primary failure is *incapacity* to provide minimum *human security* for individual citizens.[12]

Two key words in the quoted definition—'incapacity' and 'human security'—have shaped western imaginations of Africa (as a 'burden') in the development discourse, and within associated scholarly and global policy-making interests. With a focus on the role of state 'incapacity' in the making of human insecurity, which leads ultimately to failed states conflicts, we scrutinize, in the next section, the contexts and correlates of conflicts on state failure.

What causes conflicts?

A review of existing theories and methods

Table 3.1, below, is a summary of (1) the theoretical standpoints and, (2) the methodologies that have been deployed to explain the causes of conflict. Our focus is on their key indicators, which the proponents of these perspectives argue create the conditions for state failure conflicts to erupt. It should be noted here that we recognized the existence of countervailing variables that support the contrary position (namely, that state incapacity does not usually lead to conflict) and thus call into question the accuracy of these key indicators. Moreover, due to our emphasis on the tensions around the elements of 'state performance' (that is, place and power, as a measure, in part, of state incapacity), we have not attempted to score these perspectives on disciplinary merit and scholarly citations. We remind readers to focus on context when doing their own evaluations. As for us, we are of the view that 'what' (ever) makes conflicts possible carries equal weight—even if the consequences (for states and for people) differ. Below we discuss (and compare) these theoretical perspectives on the causes of conflict,

A Vertical inequality theory

We begin with the *vertical inequality* theory. Initiated by Paul Collier (director of the Development Research Group of the World Bank, and a professor in Oxford University's Economics Department) in the 1990s, this empirically informed and statistically imbued theory is, undoubtedly, a common if controversial perspective. It has been used to examine the conflicts in several SSA countries: Sierra Leone (1991–2002), Liberia (1898–1997, 1998–2003), Chad (1980–1988, 1998–2002, 2005–2010), Democratic Republic of Congo (formerly Zaire; 1997–to date) and Nigeria (1966–1970, 2009–to date), among others. At the core of this theory is the 'motive' (to begin the conflict)–'opportunity' (that continuation of the conflict presents) dichotomy, on the one hand; and, on the other, the recognition of the intersections of 'greed' and 'grievance' in the triggering of conflicts. While greed, in economic terms, is the forceful, and perhaps the excessive, desire to accumulate wealth by the few (even where such accumulation leads to poverty for the many), grievance, as our review of the works of Collier and others reveals, is about injustices in the distribution of the dividends of the country's exportable primary and secondary commodities and resources. These injustices, it has been argued, have the capacity to generate a 'real' sense of hurt in the narratives of the people (marginalized despite being the majority), which, in turn, can transform spasmodic incidences of conflict into full-blown conflicts that satisfy the UCDP-PRIO's criteria for 'armed conflict' and the Project Ploughshares' characterization of 'failed state conflicts.' In such a situation, proponents of vertical inequality tell us, the mere incidents of conflict do not meet the threshold of failed state conflicts. For failed states conflicts to occur, the proxies of grievance should persist until (and after) the state moves from being a country-at-risk to a collapsed war-torn state. These proxies of genuine grievance include: (1) lack of economic and financial equality—measured by the flow of wealth that does not trickle down to the poor and marginalized peoples and communities; and (2) the political uses of the resource-curse, which according to Paul Collier and Anke Hoeffler (2004), can easily warrant the disaggregation of a country's primary commodity exports into different sectors of the rogue economy (which must have rendered the formal economic sector dysfunctional and non-responsive to the needs of the marginalized) through a neo-patrimonial network that is more powerful than the state—with the rogues of this network firmly in control of the institutions of the state, especially those responsible for justice, security and development.

The vertical inequality theory has a set of indicators that can be used to measure (using a Gini coefficient) the impact of vertical inequality on the eruption and termination of conflicts. These indicators include: asset (including land ownership), income and employment inequality, financial and economic flows from the state to the rogue elements of the informal economy (Collier and Hoeffler 2004), natural resource distribution limited to the affluent and politically powerful (Collier and Hoeffler 2005), and diaspora remittances and financial contributions from hostile governments (Collier and Hoeffler 2004). In their work *Greed, and Grievance in Civil War* (2004), Collier and Hoeffler use a logit regression to predict the risk of conflicts that set in motion the path to full-blown conflict. Although this method is open to anodyne interpretations, these scholars, after painstakingly observing the control measures for possible errors and comprehensively accounted for them, argue that there is a robust correlation between vertical economic inequality and conflicts (of the UCDP-PRIO characterization). This, they suggest, is especially true in situations where there are available proxies or opportunities, such as exploitable natural resources such as diamonds to finance the military adventures of rebel groups. Put another way, according to proponents of vertical inequality, the defining factor for real grievance is economic deprivation, which is generated by 'greed'—or the motivation of the marginals to engage in armed conflicts to better their lives or destroy everything in the state (including themselves) in the process (Cederman, Gleditsch and Buhaug 2013; Dixon 2014; Collier and Sambanis 2005).

B Horizontal inequality theory

Moving beyond the limitations of the macro/micro-economic proxies to the demographic and relational, we turn next to the horizontal inequality (HI) theory.

HI theory, according to some schools of thought, finds its origins in the works of Frances Stewart of Oxford University. Its central premise is that if deprivation, be it relative or direct, is caused by the societal make-up of a state, such as ethnicity, religion, and gender, then the roots causes of conflict are 'grievance' rather than 'greed'—as the vertical inequality theorists suggest. In essence, the HI theory seeks to shift the focus from economic abstraction to the everyday lived experiences of people, across the gender, age, religion, and ethnicity divide within countries. It hypothesizes the political outcomes of 'everyday' social relations by contending that, despite the existence of intra-group inequality, when inequality is perpetrated by, say, an ethnic other in control of governance, this will not only lead to the politicization of ethnicity but also to increased calls for war mobilization by the disadvantaged ethnic group(s). For this 'call to war' to occur, Stewart (2016) says, there are certain benchmarks that must be present. These include (1) exclusionary government: a government that promotes, by the sternest means possible, political inclusion based solely on people's identities—biologically proven ethnic belonging and language of the leadership of the governing party;[13] (2) the government's response to the initial protests of the disadvantaged group(s) should favor the wishes of the group in control of the state; (3) the marginalization of the disadvantaged group(s) should be consistent—that is, it should cut across income, asset, employment, education, health, and access to justice, and both be and be seen to be discriminating against or excluding the disadvantaged groups; put another way, the disadvantaged group should not be in control of any governmental sector; and (4) the ethnic markers of the disadvantaged group(s), namely, language and cultural belief systems (including beliefs of gender and household/community relations), should also be marginalized or not recognized by the state.

In terms of methods, HI theory employs the following: (a) the classification of relevant (i.e., dominant) identity groups (excluding those with multiple identities and ethnicities) based on the percentage of their numbers in key positions of government (the legislature, the executive, the judiciary, the police, and the military) and the private sector; (b) group boundaries that influence the in-group kinship connections of people and their space, the land, on the datasets; (c) in-depth review of the history and political economy of a country; (d) surveys of people's own subjective perceptions; and (e) population-weighted group coefficient of variance (to measure the overall dissatisfaction of the collective, excluding the day-to-day individual experiences of people.

C Need, creed, and greed theory

Another theoretical perspective has been developed by William Zartman (see Zartman 2000; Arnson and Zartman 2005). This theory is called the 'Need, Creed, and Greed (NCG)' theory. In sum, NCG can be understood as follows.

> Need is the shorthand for poverty or inequality in a society. Creed denotes religious or ethnic identity. The inequalities in the studied societies

> [contained in Zartman's works on this subject, published in 2000; and in Cynthia J. Arnson and William Zartman's edited volume published in 2005] broke along these fault lines. Greed meant that conflicts resulted in the amassing of wealth by the leadership of the physical organizations.
>
> (Hill 2009, 154)

NCG theory uses a multidisciplinary mixed-method approach to explain the correlations between poverty, religion, ethnicity, income inequality and civil wars. This method, Zartman suggests, may include ontological surveys, discourse theory, statistical regression, game theory and econometric approaches. The scholars who contributed to Arnson and Zartman's edited volume, *Rethinking The Economics of Wars: The Intersection of Need, Creed, and Greed*, employed such methods to discover the following correlates of NCG and the eruption of conflicts. NCG creates (1) the conditions for uneven distribution of natural resources; (2) heightened levels of economic deprivation, creating the conditions for the economic motives for war; and (3) with economic interests already polarized, the structures for the "advent of peace, democracy, and accountability for human rights abuses," are compromised (Malone and Sherman 2005, 239). The net effect is the emergence of identity (creed)-induced discrimination, which, in turn, reinforces greed (i.e., the concentration of wealth in the hands of rogue politicians). Political violence and full-blown civil conflict erupt from the competition between the leadership of political organizations to sustain their ill-gotten wealth and power.

D Institutional trust theory

The vertical, horizontal and NCG causes of conflicts, the World Bank argues, would not arise in societies and countries where there is general trust in public, governmental, political, justice and security institutions. Against this backdrop, the World Bank has suggested another theory, that of 'institutional trust,' in its World Development Report of 2011. Premised on 'vulnerability and risk management,' this institutional trust perspective seeks to identify the stresses induced by World Bank's Country Assistance Strategies (CASs). It can be used to investigate, or rather assesses, the deficits in the capacities of key national institutions that are responsible for security, justice and development in weak (i.e., donor-dependent) countries. Finally, this perspective's theoretical standpoint endeavors to find the best pathways to end or mitigate the cycle of conflicts.

To understand the institutional aspects of the antecedents of conflicts, and find ways of resolving them, the World Bank has employed qualitative analysis, longitudinal studies, statistics and econometric approaches. Through these methods, they discovered that the lack of public trust in government institutions could lead to conflicts in the following ways. First, the lack of trust prevents the development of violence-prevention-focused governmental policies. Second, the lack of trust perpetuates suspicions between the government institutions responsible for security, development and justice, thus rendering them powerless to prevent gross violations of human rights prior to conflict. Cases such as those of countries with entrenched dictatorships in SSA in the 1970s and 1990s reveal, to find political legitimacy in the eyes of the leaders, these government institutions will collaborate to prevent or suppress political dissent. It is this oppression, history teaches us, that leads to the outbreak of conflicts. Third, entrenched dictatorships rely more on the military and the police to protect individual politicians, and neglect what actually prevents the eruption of conflict: that is, risk-mitigation and early-warning systems that are human-security-focused.

E Gender-based structural inequality theory

These theoretical standpoints discussed thus far share two main characteristics: (1) they all employ the definitions (and threshold) of intra-state conflicts presented by the UCDP-PRIO Armed Conflicts Dataset and (2) they are gender-neutral, blind or insensitive to the place of 'gender-based structural inequalities' in their explanations of the causes of conflict—including the 'gender-based' differences on the impact of inequality and conflict on men and women. To address this insensitivity, Mary Caprioli developed, between 1998 and 2000, a feminist-centric theory called a 'gender-based structural inequality' theory (Caprioli 2000, 2005). Through a gender-based lens, scholars of the theory have concluded that there is a direct connection between discrimination against women (including pre-war sexual and gender-based violence) and the onset of conflicts at the international, national and sub-national levels (see Caprioli and Boyer 2001; Caprioli and Trumbore 2003a, 2003b; Hudson et al. 2009).

With regard to research methods, Caprioli (in the papers 'Gendered Conflicts,' published by the *Journal of Peace Research* in 2000) and 'Primed for Violence: The Role of Gender Inequality in Predicting Internal Conflict,' in the *International Studies Quarterly* in 2005), employs (and in doing so, gives them a feminist outlook) multivariate and logistic regressions. She uses the multivariate regression to observe the linkages between the outset of wars and (1) the percentage of women in parliament; (2) female suffrage; (3) women in the labor force; and, (4) fertility. Her observations confirm her hypothesis that states characterized by higher levels of gender inequality are more likely to experience intra-state conflicts. To minimize the negative impact (standard error of the sampling variance) of marginal errors, she uses logistic regressions in developing her control variables, namely, political alliances, political continuity, wealth, democracy, transnational political influences, party/government type, GDP per capita (constant dollars, 1995 U.S.$), and GDP per capita growth rate prior to the outbreak of conflict in her select countries. To generate and store the list of countries (from a poll of countries in UCDP-PRIO's Correlates of War continuity dataset) to test her hypotheses and to generate raw utility scores (including risk scores on the occurrence of conflict) and equilibrium predictions (of the dyad year unit of analysis of gender-based variables), Caprioli uses EUGene software. She also employs cross-national surveys and a longitudinal study to cover the period between 1960 and 2001.

Through a longitudinal study, Caprioli finds that gender inequality in the economy, in the home (where children are born and fertility ratios created), and in politics, the following conditions that make conflicts possible are created: (1) political preferences for military spending ('warfarism,' e.g., the buying of arms and the training of military forces) over welfare (social services, such as family planning, public schools and healthcare); (ii) the politicization of sexual and gender-based violence (SGBV) at the domestic and national levels—in ways that feed into the war narratives of combatants who are either out to 'get' (rape) women or to protect them from SGBV; (iii) preferences for male children (by government, when assessing what should be counted as favorable in their national fertility ratio), children who will eventually aspire to join the fighting ranks of either rebel or government armies; armies that ultimately abduct women on the basis of gender-based constructs that dictate that those female abductees should continue with their nurtured (gender-based division of household chores) and natural (reproductive) roles in fighting communities.

Thus far, we have explained the definitions and causes of conflicts. In the next and final sub-section, we identify the impact of conflict on state fragility.

Frames and contexts of impact

Identifying the impact of conflict on state fragility

As demonstrated by the various studies reviewed above, despite the fact that, in practice, the magnitude and consequences of conflicts for human life and property is one of the root causes of fragility, the concept of conflict is a relative term. Against this backdrop, its impact on state fragility should also be assessed contextually. In the main, and by way of examples, the drivers of conflicts can be territorial. Examples include the conflicts between Ethiopia and Eritrea over the territory of Badme (1993–2018), and between Sudan and South Sudan over the territories of Abyei, Heglig, Jodha, Kaka and Kafia Kingi (after 2011).

Conflicts can be ideological, with power as the ultimate goal. An example is the Angolan civil war between two liberation (from Portuguese colonial rule) movements, the *Movimento Popular de Libertação de Angola* (MPLA; the People's Movement for the Liberation of Angola) and the *União Nacional para a Independência Total de Angola* (UNITA; the National Union for the Total Independence of Angola).

Conflicts can also be resource-driven, such as the 'second' Congo (Democratic Republic of Congo) war, which began in August 1998 and is ongoing at the time of writing.[14] Since 1999, UN peacekeepers have been in the Congo trying to settle the conflicts between the rebel (and splinter) forces. Despite the presence of peacekeepers (and documents to prove that the war officially came to an end in 2012), the natural resources of the country have led to the rise of a new rebel faction, the M23.

Conflicts in SSA can be religious–ideological. For example, after the 2001 terrorist attacks against the United States, a new type of conflict, terrorism, has

Table 3.1 Theoretical standpoints and methodologies that have been deployed to explain the causes of conflict

References	*Typology of conflict*	*Contextual effect on state fragility*
1 Collier and Hoeffler 2004 2 Directorate-General for External Policies of the EU 3 Collier, Hoeffler and Söderbom	Vertical inequality-induced conflict	• Rogue (informal) economy creates a dysfunctional formal economic sector, and an increase in the severity of pre-conflict political repression. • Gains from primary agricultural and mineral exports not reflected in GDP growth due to large rents. • Prevalence of organizations of aggrieved people. • Diaspora remittances lead to currency appreciation (with negative impact on export flow), inflation, aggravates regional inequalities (between receiving and non-receiving areas), dependence between the sender and receiver (and the sender sometimes dictates the actions of the receivers). • Extortion/corruption of the returns from primary commodity export (such as natural resources) creates, and reinforces, high rents.
1 Stewart 2002; 2009; 2016	Horizontal inequality-induced conflict	• Ethnic and ethno-linguistic fractionalization leads to polarization of sub-nationalism. • Regional inequalities in, say, health and education services in areas where such services are needed most. • Statelessness for some marginalized groups as a result of restrictive citizenship. • Cultural genocide (i.e., the extermination of cultures and identities) due, in part, unequal cultural recognition, and resistance to accept the identities of the 'ethnic' and religious' other. • Political exclusion breeds political autocracy and, ultimately, governance policies non-responsive to the plight of the marginalized and the poor. • Ethnicity-based political and economic marginalization robs the country the needed financial contributions and human resource power for economic development.

1 Arnson and Zartman 2005 2 Zartman 2000	Need, creed and greed-induced conflict	• Widespread societal grievance. • Structures for the promotion of democracy, peace and democracy replaced by structures that perpetuate poverty, ethno-religious divisions, and wealth concentration in the hands of the few. • Natural resources distribution limited only to those with connections to the political establishment. • Rent-seeking patronage-clientele networks determine outcomes of governmental policies and interventions. • Elite fractionalization and competition between political organizations leads reinforce the volatility of the political space, and an increase in political violence and intimidation. • Ideology-based international support for competing political organizations[1]—hence the loss of local political legitimacy of these organizations, and the political irrelevance of the people within the country.
1 World Bank 2011	Institutional trust-induced conflicts	• Lack of national legitimacy of government institutions responsible for justice, development and security. • Non-existence of risk management and early warning systems. • Non-accountability and transparency of governmental fiscal policies and spending. • Proliferation of 'organized crimes' and uncontrolled criminal activities, including drugs and human trafficking.
1 Caprioli 2000, 2005 2 Caprioli and Boyer 2001 3 Caprioli and Trumbore 2003a, 2003b, 2003 4 Hudson et al. 2009 5 Lahai 2016, 2014	Gender-based structural inequality induced conflicts	• Low or non-impactful welfare services. • Increased levels of sexual and gender-based violence (SGBV) at all levels of the society. • Gender-based discrimination in employment, education, health and politics. • Increased GDP per capita spending on armament. • Over-population (as preferences for male children serves both military and economic purpose). • Cultural resistance to the best governance practices—entrenches resistance to gender-responsive governance.

Note

1 For example, in pre-conflict Angola, the USSR and Cuba supported the Neo-Marxist group, MPLA; the US and South African government supported UNITA (Bender 1978; Minter 1994; Guimarães 2001).

emerged in Nigeria (the Boko Haram insurgents; see Agbiboa 2013) and Somalia (Al-Shabaab; see Solomon 2014)). These terrorist factions have strong links to terrorist groups outside sub-Saharan Africa: in the Maghreb, the Middle East, and south-east and south-central Asia (see Agbiboa 2014a, 2014b, 2015). Conflicts can also be an outcome of the horizontal inequality and neglect of regions on the basis of race, such as the ongoing 'genocidal' conflict in Darfur, which began in 2003 (Lahai 2016b, 56).

Unfortunately, when assessing the implications of conflicts for state fragility in SSA, conclusions are often about trivializing (if not silencing) the resilience of the state. The dominant narrative of these discourses, in analyzing the problem of state incapacity, is the urgency of embracing a neoliberal path to peace, governance and democracy. It has been argued, however, that this path empowers, in the political sense, the very actors (warlords) whose military actions contribute to state fragility during conflicts, while also reinforcing the economic and political structures for fragility to persist in the aftermath of the conflict (see Pitcher et al. 2009; Englebert and Ron 2004; Willett 2005; Hansen 2006; Reno 1999; Lahai and Lyons 2016). As a corrective measure, we propose a contextual assessment of the impact of conflict on state fragility in SSA. As we have already noted, what we tabulate here are outcomes of our review of the relevant literature on the theories of conflict. With this in mind, we recognize that the complexities (relating to the symptoms, correlates and causes) of war may have cross-theoretical conclusions. Moreover, we do not attempt to scale impact based on which theory offers either the best (or worst) explanation.

Notes

1 Feminisms-without-borders, as we understand it (and as it relates to the study of feminist movements in SSA) denotes, what is intuitively 'pro-womanism' or what concerns the identity and plight of the 'Black African woman' in the fragile gendered-spaces of the sub-continent, on the one hand; and, on the other, what is, theoretically speaking, pro-western feminism or the projection of the 'high theories' of the western feminists (for more on this, and the clashes between African and western feminists, see, for example, Lyons 2004, 3–8).

2 Department of Peace and Conflict Research, Data on Armed Conflict, www.prio.org/Data/Armed-Conflict/ (accessed: June 27, 2018).

3 Ibid.

4 This database contains more than 170,000 systematic national (on U.S. soil) and international (elsewhere, outside the U.S.) terrorists attacks between 1970 and 2016 (with annual updates). SEE, www.start.umd.edu/gtd/ (accessed: June 18, 2018).

5 The RDWTI is a compilation of data from 1968 through 2009. See the following links (accessed: June 27, 2018): www.rand.org/nsrd/projects/terrorism-incidents.html; www.rand.org/topics/terrorism.html.

6 But, for all the obvious reasons, some feminist scholars have suggested that 'the penis' (the male organ) should be included as a weapon of war (see, Mullins 2009; Carter 2010). Thus, as the lived experiences of women in the civil wars of SSA reveals, rape crimes were systemically used to dislocate families and communities, and sometimes to effect population transfer in genocidal wars as was the case of

Rwanda (see, Mullins 2009) and Darfur (see, Miller 2009); or to transfer sexually transmitted diseases to the women who would eventually infect their men (within their ethnic group of same) (see, Ruby Reid-Cunningham 2008). In some instances, rape of the women and girls was aimed at demoralizing the male members of the warring faction to whom these women victims belong (Clifford and Slavery 2008; Trenholm, Olsson, and Ahlberg 2011; Coulter 2009).

7 Project Ploughshares. n.d. Defining Armed Conflicts. http://ploughshares.ca/armed-conflict/defining-armed-conflict/.

8 See, Department of Peace and Conflict Research. n.d. Definitions. www.pcr.uu.se/research/ucdp/definitions/#Extra-systemic_conflict.

9 Ibid., www.pcr.uu.se/research/ucdp/definitions/.

10 Project Ploughshares. n.d. Types of Armed Conflict. http://ploughshares.ca/armed-conflict/types-of-armed-conflict/.

11 Ibid.

12 Ibid.; emphasis added.

13 An example of this was pre-1994 Rwanda, where the government of Juvénal Habyarimana had a state policy that called for the empowerment of only the Hutu ethnic group, and the marginalization of the Tutsi ethnic group (including any Hutu who was found to be sympathetic to the plight of the Tutsis) (Scott 2006). In response, the Tutsis formed a rebel group, the *Front Patriotique Rwandais* (FPR; or the Rwanda Patriotic Army, under their leaders, Fred Gisa Rwigyema (who was the leader of the FPR until his death October 1990 (Waugh 2004, 42–47)) and Paul Kagame and declared war on the Hutu-government in 1990 (Mamdani 2001).

14 However, there are other international factors responsible for the outbreak of this conflict. According to the BBC, in 1998, Rwanda accused the government of President Laurent Kabila of either supporting or not acting against the Hutu rebels who had fled into the Democratic Republic of Congo (DRC) after they were defeated by the Rwanda forces loyal to President Kagame. In response to Kabila's inaction, Rwanda declared war on the Hutu rebels inside Congo. With the Rwandan forces inside his country, Kabila sent his soldiers to support to the Hutu rebels. This conflict raged between 1988 and 2003. But the conflict between the Tutsis (loyal to President Kagame of Rwanda) and the Hutu rebels (who want the Tutsi exterminated continues in eastern DRC. See, www.bbc.com/news/world-africa-11108589.

References

Abrahamsen, Rita. 2000. *Disciplining Democracy: Development Discourse and Good Governance in Africa*. London, UK: Zed Books.

Agbiboa, Daniel. 2015. "Shifting the Battleground: The Transformation of Al-Shabab and the Growing Influence of Al-Qaeda in East Africa and the Horn." *Politikon* 42 (2): 177–194.

Agbiboa, Daniel E. 2014a. "Terrorism without Borders: Somalia's Al-Shabaab and the Global Jihad Network." *Journal of Terrorism Research* 5 (1): 27–34.

Agbiboa, Daniel E. 2014b. "Ties That Bind: The Evolution and Links of Al-Shabab." *The Round Table* 103 (6): 581–597.

Agbiboa, Daniel Egiegba. 2013. "Why Boko Haram Exists: The Relative Deprivation Perspective." *African Conflict & Peacebuilding Review* 3 (1): 144–157.

Ajayi, S. Ibi. 2003. "Globalisation and Africa." *Journal of African Economies* 12 (suppl 1): 120–150.

Alison, Miranda. 2004. "Women as Agents of Political Violence: Gendering Security." *Security Dialogue* 35 (4): 447–463.

Amin, Samir. 1998. "Spectres of Capitalism." *Monthly Review* 50 (1): 36.

Amin, Samir. 2006. "Beyond Liberal Globalization: A Better or Worse World?" *Monthly Review* 58 (7): 30.

Arnson, Cynthia J. and I. William Zartman, eds. 2005. *Rethinking the Economics of War: The Intersection of Need, Creed, and Greed*. Washington, DC: Woodrow Wilson Center Press.

Ballentine, Karen. 2003. *The Political Economy of Armed Conflict: Beyond Greed and Grievance*. Boulder, CO: Lynne Rienner Publishers.

Bartusevičius, Henrikas. 2016. "Introducing the Categorically Disaggregated Conflict (CDC) Dataset." *Conflict Management and Peace Science* 33 (1): 89–110.

Bender, Gerald J. 1978. "Angola, the Cubans, and American Anxieties." *Foreign Policy* 31: 3–30.

Besley, Timothy, and Torsten Persson. 2008. "Wars and State Capacity." *Journal of the European Economic Association* 6 (2–3): 522–530.

Buzan, Barry. 2007. *People, States & Fear: An Agenda for International Security Studies in the Post-Cold War Era*. Wivenhoe Park, UK: ECPR Press.

Caprioli, Mary. 2000. "Gendered Conflict." *Journal of Peace Research* 37 (1): 51–68.

Caprioli, Mary. 2005. "Primed for Violence: The Role of Gender Inequality in Predicting Internal Conflict." *International Studies Quarterly* 49 (2): 161–178.

Caprioli, Mary, and Mark A. Boyer. 2001. "Gender, Violence, and International Crisis." *Journal of Conflict Resolution* 45 (4): 503–518.

Caprioli, Mary, and Peter F. Trumbore. 2003a. "Ethnic Discrimination and Interstate Violence: Testing the International Impact of Domestic Behavior." *Journal of Peace Research* 40 (1): 5–23.

Caprioli, Mary, and Peter F. Trumbore. 2003b. "Identifying Rogue States and Testing Their Interstate Conflict Behavior." *European Journal of International Relations* 9 (3): 377–406.

Carpenter, R. Charli. 2006. "Recognizing Gender-Based Violence against Civilian Men and Boys in Conflict Situations." *Security Dialogue* 37 (1): 83–103.

Carter, Kathleen R. 2010. "Should International Relations Consider Rape a Weapon of War?" *Politics & Gender* 6 (3): 343–371.

Cederman, Lars-Erik, Halvard Buhaug, and Jan Ketil Rød. 2009. "Ethno-Nationalist Dyads and Civil War: A GIS-Based Analysis." *Journal of Conflict Resolution* 53 (4): 496–525.

Cederman, Lars-Erik, Kristian Skrede Gleditsch, and Halvard Buhaug. 2013. *Grievances and Inequality in Civil Wars*. New York, NY: Cambridge University Press.

Cederman, Lars-Erik, Nils B. Weidmann, and Kristian Skrede Gleditsch. 2011. "Horizontal Inequalities and Ethnonationalist Civil War: A Global Comparison." *American Political Science Review* 105 (3): 478–495.

Chwaszcza, Christine. 2013. "Hume and the Social Contract. A Systematic Evaluation." *Rationality, Markets and Morals* 4 (73): 108–130.

Clifford, Cassandra, and Stop Modern Slavery. 2008. "Rape as a Weapon of War and Its Long-Term Effects on Victims and Society." In *7th Global Conference Violence and the Contexts of Hostility*. Budapest, Hungary. www.peacewomen.org/sites/default/files/vaw_rapeasaweaponofwar_stopmodernslavery_may2008_0.pdf.

Collier, Paul, and Anke Hoeffler. 2004. "Greed and Grievance in Civil War." *Oxford Economic Papers* 56 (4): 563–595.

Collier, Paul, and Anke Hoeffler. 2005. "Resource Rents, Governance, and Conflict." *Journal of Conflict Resolution* 49 (4): 625–633.

Collier, Paul, and Nicholas Sambanis. 2005. *Understanding Civil War: Africa*. Vol. 1. Washington, DC: World Bank Publications.

Coulter, Chris. 2009. *Bush Wives and Girl Soldiers: Women's Lives through War and Peace in Sierra Leone*. Ithaca, NY: Cornell University Press.

Dixon, Jeffrey S. 2014. *What Causes Civil Conflicts? Back to "Grievance vs. Greed."* Oxford, UK: Blackwell Publishing Ltd.

Dunn, John. 1995. *The Political Thought of John Locke: An Historical Account of the Argument of the 'Two Treatises of Government'*. 6th paperback reprint edition. Cambridge: Cambridge University Press.

Dyer, Silke J. 2007. "The Value of Children in African Countries – Insights from Studies on Infertility." *Journal of Psychosomatic Obstetrics & Gynecology* 28 (2): 69–77.

Easterly, William. 2001. "Can Institutions Resolve Ethnic Conflict?" *Economic Development and Cultural Change* 49 (4): 687–706.

El Jack, Amani, Emma Bell, and Lata Narayanaswamy. 2003. *Gender and Armed Conflict: Overview Report*. Brighton, UK: BRIDGE, Institute of Development Studies, University of Sussex Brighton.

El-Bushra, Judy. 2000. "Transforming Conflict: Some Thoughts on a Gendered Understanding of Conflict Processes." In *States of Conflict: Gender, Violence and Resistance*, edited by Susie Jacobs, Ruth Jacobson, and Jennifer Marchbank, 66–86. London, UK: Zed Books.

Englebert, Pierre, and James Ron. 2004. "Primary Commodities and War: Congo-Brazzaville's Ambivalent Resource Curse." *Comparative Politics* 37 (1): 61–81.

Fatton, Robert. 1990. "Liberal Democracy in Africa." *Political Science Quarterly* 105 (3): 455–473.

Fox, Mary-Jane. 2004. "Girl Soldiers: Human Security and Gendered Insecurity." *Security Dialogue* 35 (4): 465–479.

Fund for Peace, The. 2017. "Fragile States Index: Indicators." Fragile States Index: Presented by The Fund for Peace. http://fundforpeace.org/fsi/indicators/.

Giles, Wenona, and Jennifer Hyndman, eds. 2004. *Sites of Violence: Gender and Conflict Zones*. Berkeley, CA: University of California Press.

Goldgeier, James M. and Michael McFaul. 1992. "A Tale of Two Worlds: Core and Periphery in the Post-Cold War Era." *International Organization* 46 (2): 467–491.

Gubler, Joshua R. and Joel Sawat Selway. 2012. "Horizontal Inequality, Crosscutting Cleavages, and Civil War." *Journal of Conflict Resolution* 56 (2): 206–232.

Guimarães, Fernando Andresen. 2001. *The Origins of the Angolan Civil War: Foreign Intervention and Domestic Political Conflict, 1961–76*. Basingstoke, Hampshire: Palgrave Macmillan.

Hansen, Stig J. 2006. "Warlords and Peace Strategies: The Case of Somalia." *Journal of Conflict Studies* 23 (2): 57–78.

Hardt, Michael, and Antonio Negri. 2000. *Empire*. Cambridge, MA: Harvard University Press.

Hardt, Michael, and Antonio Negri. 2004. *Multitude: War and Democracy in the Age of Empire*. New York, NY: Penguin Books.

Herbst, Jeffrey. 1990. "War and the State in Africa." *International Security* 14 (4): 117–139.

Hill, Walter W. 2009. "Reviewed Work(s): Rethinking the Economics of War: The Intersection of Need, Creed, and Greed by Cynthia J. Arnson and I. William Zartman." *International Journal on World Peace* 26 (1): 153–156.

Hobbes, Thomas. 2010. *Leviathan, or, The Matter, Forme, & Power of a Common-Wealth Ecclesiasticall and Civill [First Published in 1651; Reprint 2010]*. (Rethinking the Western Tradition). New Heaven, CT: Yale University Press.

Hudson, Valerie M., Mary Caprioli, Bonnie Ballif-Spanvill, Rose McDermott, and Chad F. Emmett. 2009. "The Heart of the Matter: The Security of Women and the Security of States." *International Security* 33 (3): 7–45.

Ikenberry, G. John. 2010. "The Liberal International Order and Its Discontents." *Millennium* 38 (3): 509–521.

Kelly, Liz. 2000. "Wars against Women: Sexual Violence, Sexual Politics and the Militarised State." In *States of Conflict: Gender, Violence and Resistance*, edited by Susie Jacobs, Ruth Jacobson, and Jennifer Marchbank, 45–65. London, UK: Zed Books.

Lacina, Bethany, and Nils Petter Gleditsch. 2005. "Monitoring Trends in Global Combat: A New Dataset of Battle Deaths." *European Journal of Population/Revue Européenne de Démographie* 21 (2–3): 145–166.

Lahai, John Idriss. 2015. "Gendering Conflict and Peace-Building in Sierra Leone." In *Female Combatants in Conflict and Peace*, edited by Seema Shekhawat, 132–148. Palgrave Macmillan UK. https://doi.org/10.1057/9781137516565_9.

Lahai, John Idriss. 2016a. *Gender in Practice: Culture, Politics and Society in Sierra Leone*. 14 vols. http://dx.doi.org/10.3726/b11126. Oxford, UK: Peter Lang Ltd.

Lahai, John Idriss. 2016b. "The International Responsibility to Protect and the Conflict in Darfur." In *African Frontiers: Insurgency, Governance and Peacebuilding in Post-colonial States*, edited by John Idriss Lahai and Tanya Lyons, 55–68. Abingdon, UK: Routledge.

Lahai, John Idriss, and Tanya Lyons. 2016. "The West African Warscapes: Rebe Factions, Insurgent Opportunism and State Governance." In *African Frontiers: Insurgency, Governance and Peacebuilding in Postcolonial States*, edited by John Idriss Lahai and Tanya Lyons, 17–30. Abingdon, UK: Routledge.

Le Billon, Philippe. 2001. "The Political Ecology of War: Natural Resources and Armed Conflicts." *Political Geography* 20 (5): 561–584.

LeRiche, Matthew, and Matthew Arnold. 2013. *South Sudan: From Revolution to Independence*. Oxford, UK: Oxford University Press.

Lyons, Tanya. 2004. *Guns and Guerilla Girls: Women in the Zimbabwean National Liberation Struggle*. Asmara, Eritrea: Africa World Press.

Malone, David M. and Jake Sherman. 2005. "Economic Factors in Civil Wars: Policy Considerations." In *Rethinking the Economics of War: The Intersection of Need, Creed, and Greed*, edited by Cynthia J. Arnson and I. William Zartman, 234–256. Washington, DC: Woodrow Wilson Center Press.

Mamdani, Mahmood. 2001. *When Victims Become Killers: Colonialism, Nativism, and the Genocide in Rwanda*. New Jersey, NJ: Princeton University Press.

Marx, Karl. 1973. *Karl Marx on Society and Social Change: With Selections by Friedrich Engels*. Edited by Neil J. Smelser. Chicago, IL: University of Chicago Press.

Mazrui, Ali A. 1973. "The Lumpen Proletariat and the Lumpen Militariat: African Soldiers as a New Political Class." *Political Studies* 21 (1): 1–12.

Mearsheimer, John. 2001. *The Tragedy of Great Power Politics*. New York, NY: Norton.

Meintjes, Sheila, Meredeth Turshen, and Anu Pillay. 2001. *The Aftermath: Women in Post-Conflict Transformation*. London, UK: Zed Books.

Melber, Henning. 2002. "From Liberation Movements to Governments: On Political Culture in Southern Africa." *African Sociological Review/Revue Africaine de Sociologie* 6 (1): 161–172.

Miller, Sarah Clark. 2009. "Moral Injury and Relational Harm: Analyzing Rape in Darfur." *Journal of Social Philosophy* 40 (4): 504–523.

Minter, William. 1994. *Apartheid's Contras: An Inquiry into the Roots of War in Angola and Mozambique*. Johannesburg, SA: Witwatersrand University Press.

Mullins, Christopher W. 2009. " 'He Would Kill Me with His Penis': Genocidal Rape in Rwanda as a State Crime." *Critical Criminology* 17 (1): 15–33.

Nafziger, E. Wayne, and Juha Auvinen. 2002. "Economic Development, Inequality, War, and State Violence." *World Development* 30 (2): 153–163.

O'Brien, Mary. 1989. "The Root of the Mandrake: Machiavelli and Manliness." In *Reproducing the World: Essays in Feminist Theory*, edited by Mary O'Brien, 103–127. Boulder, CO: Westview Press.

Østby, Gudrun. 2008. "Polarization, Horizontal Inequalities and Violent Civil Conflict." *Journal of Peace Research* 45 (2): 143–162.

Østby, Gudrun, Ragnhild Nordås and Jan Ketil Rød. 2009. "Regional Inequalities and Civil Conflict in Sub-Saharan Africa." *International Studies Quarterly* 53 (2): 301–324.

Parry, Benita. 1998. "Liberation Movements: Memories of the Future." *Interventions: International Journal of Postcolonial Studies* 1 (1): 45–51.

Pitcher, Anne, Mary H. Moran and Michael Johnston. 2009. "Rethinking Patrimonialism and Neopatrimonialism in Africa." *African Studies Review* 52 (1): 125–156.

Reno, William. 1999. *Warlord Politics and African States*. Boulder, CO: Lynne Rienner Publishers.

Riley, Patrick. 1982. *Will and Political Legitimacy: A Critical Exposition of Social Contract Theory in Hobbes, Locke, Rousseau, Kant, and Hegel*. Cambridge, MA: Harvard University Press.

Ruby Reid-Cunningham, Allison. 2008. "Rape as a Weapon of Genocide." *Genocide Studies and Prevention* 3 (3): 279–296.

Rummel, R. J. 1977. *Understanding Conflict and War: Vol. 3: Conflict in Perspective Beverly Hills*. Vol. 3 vols. Beverly Hills, California: Sage Publications Ltd.

Saccarelli, Emanuele. 2009. "The Machiavellian Rousseau: Gender and Family Relations in the Discourse on the Origin of Inequality." *Political Theory* 37 (4): 482–510.

Saxonhouse, Arlene W. 2004. "Niccolo Machiavelli: Women as Men, and Men as Women, and the Ambiguity of Sex." In *Feminist Interpretations of Niccolò Machiavelli*, edited by Maria J. Falco, 93–116. Pennsylvania, PA: Pennsylvania State University Press.

Scott, Straus. 2006. *The Order of Genocide: Race, Power, and War in Rwanda*. Ithaca, NY: Cornell University Press.

Shklar, Judith N. 1985. *Men and Citizens: A Study of Rousseau's Social Theory*. Paperback edition. Cambridge, UK: Cambridge University Press.

Silver, Victoria. 1996. "Hobbes on Rhetoric." In *The Cambridge Companion to Hobbes*, edited by Tom Sorell, 329–345. Cambridge, UK: Cambridge University Press.

Sivakumaran, Sandesh. 2007. "Sexual Violence against Men in Armed Conflict." *European Journal of International Law* 18 (2): 253–276.

Smith, Zeric Kay. 2000. "The Impact of Political Liberalisation and Democratisation on Ethnic Conflict in Africa: An Empirical Test of Common Assumptions." *The Journal of Modern African Studies* 38 (1): 21–39.

Solomon, Hussein. 2014. "Somalia's Al Shabaab: Clans vs Islamist Nationalism." *South African Journal of International Affairs* 21 (3): 351–366.

Sorell, Tom, ed. 1996. *Hobbes's Political Philosophy*. Cambridge, UK: Cambridge University Press.

Stewart, Frances, ed. 2016. *Horizontal Inequalities and Conflict: Understanding Group Violence in Multiethnic Societies*. Basingstoke, Hampshire: Palgrave Macmillan.

Sylvester, Christine. 1994. *Feminist Theory and International Relations in a Postmodern Era*. Vol. 32. Cambridge, UK: Cambridge University Press.

Themnér, Lotta, and Peter Wallensteen. 2011. "Armed Conflict, 1946–2010." *Journal of Peace Research* 48 (4): 525–536.

Trenholm, Jill E., Pia Olsson, and Beth Maina Ahlberg. 2011. "Battles on Women's Bodies: War, Rape and Traumatisation in Eastern Democratic Republic of Congo." *Global Public Health* 6 (2): 139–152.

Uppsala Conflict Data Program (UCDP). 2013. "UCDP/PRIO Armed Conflict Dataset Codebook (Version4–2013)." Uppsala, Oslo: Centre for the Study of Civil Wars, International Peace Research Institute, Oslo (PRIO). www.pcr.uu.se/digitalAssets/167/a_167198-f_codebook_ucdp_prio-armed-conflict-dataset-v4_2013.pdf.

Wallensteen, Peter, and Margareta Sollenberg. 1999. "Armed Conflict, 1989–98." *Journal of Peace Research* 36 (5): 593–606.

Waltz, Kenneth Neal. 2001. *Man, the State, and War: A Theoretical Analysis*. New York, NY: Columbia University Press.

Waugh, Colin M. 2004. *Paul Kagame and Rwanda: Power, Genocide and the Rwandan Patriotic Front*. Jefferson, NC: McFarland & Company, Inc., Publishers.

Willett, Susan. 2005. "New Barbarians at the Gate: Losing the Liberal Peace in Africa." *Review of African Political Economy* 32 (106): 569–594.

World Bank. 2011. "Operationalizing the 2011 World Development Report: Conflict, Security, and Development." (Development Committee's Joint Ministerial Committee of the Borad of Governors of the Bank and the Fund on the Transfer of Real Resources to Developing Countries; DC2011-0003 (April 4). Washington, DC: World Bank. http://siteresources.worldbank.org/DEVCOMMINT/Documentation/22884392/DC2011-0003%28E%29WDR2011.pdf.

Yule, William, Rune Stuvland, Florence K. Baingana, and Patrick Smith. 2004. "Children in Armed Conflict." In *Trauma Interventions in War and Peace*, edited by B. L. Green, M. L. Friedman, J. de Jong, S.D. Solomon, T.M. Keane, J. A. Fairbank, B. Donelan, and E Frey-Wouters, 217–242. Boston, MA: Springer.

Zartman, I. William. 2000. "Mediating Conflicts of Need, Greed, and Creed." *Orbis* 44 (2): 255–266.

Zolberg, Aristide R. 1968. "The Structure of Political Conflict in the New States of Tropical Africa." *American Political Science Review* 62 (1): 70–87.

4 Behavioral language frames, conflict de-escalation, and battle-related deaths

A panel estimation survey of peace accords across zones of conflict

In the context of state-centric processes of conflict escalation and de-escalation, proponents of the Copenhagen School of securitization theory (Balzacq 2011, 2005; Floyd 2011) contend, to quote Mark B. Salter (2008, 321), that before an existential threat becomes a real security problem that could justify the invocation of "emergency" or "executive powers," state actors must, first, identify the existential threat and, second, use speech acts (that speak of a clear and present danger) to an audience (mostly the electorate) to excise that threat from the sphere of normal politics. In this chapter, we ask—and answer—two main questions: (1) would the mainstreaming of conflict de-escalation words (CDWs) in the outcome documents—Peace Accords (PAs)—of state-led political settlements of conflicts lead to a reduction in battle-related deaths in the year or two following the conclusions of peace negotiations? and (2) would the demystification and the social and cultural conditioning of threats—through conflict de-escalating words result in a reduction of battle-related deaths?

In answer to the first question we show, using the pooled ordinary least squares (OLS) and a random effects model, why and how these frames of conflict de-escalation have contributed to reductions in battle-related deaths. Our findings demonstrate that the effect of reconciliatory words on battle-related deaths exhibits an inverted-U relationship. This finding called for a rigorous, statistically verified threshold analysis to discover the number of words that can trigger this relationship. We focused on 49 Peace Accords across countries in sub-Saharan Africa from 1990 to 2003, not only to count the number of times conflict de-escalation words were used, but also to deconstruct their meanings and connections to state-led efforts to resolve conflicts and reduce battle-related deaths. Our threshold analyses peg the number of conflict de-escalating words at 35. What this means is that increasing the number of reconciliatory words in a peace accord beyond 35 can reduce the number of battle-related deaths. Some of the vital conflict de-escalating words and phrases we searched for are: human rights, ceasefire, release of political prisoners, reconciliation, free movement of people, peace, demilitarization, rehabilitation, disarmament, demobilization, humanitarian assistance, economic reform, reintegration, resettlement and repatriation, civil society, liberal democracy, good governance, power-sharing, social inclusion, women and gender, and words relating to peace monitoring bodies. What we found implies that the fewer the reconciliatory words in a peace accord, the higher the number of subsequent battle-related deaths; conversely, the number of deaths begins to decline with the increase in reconciliatory words. In this context, the choice to wage the war of CDWs—to get parties to a conflict to think less about warfare and more about ways of getting out of the adversarial trap—is a primordial motivator for the mainstreaming of 'soundbite' semantics. Linguistically speaking, they are two different frames, but, in the discourse of securitization, they are not opposed to each other. Whereas peace, as an '*affect*,' depicts an end (the absence of existential threats), words—or, rather, political speech acts—contribute more than any other natural human phenomenon to the securitization of incidents that do not merit securitized executive action (Williams 2003).

In response to the second question, we contend—in line with the conventional discourse of securitization theory—that, "securitizing moves" are speech acts with performative sociopolitical consequences for the objects (i.e., the people; the inferential audience) (Watson 2011; Bagge et al. 2000)—with the objects being those who should approve the extraordinary measures intended by the securitizing actor to address the subject matter (i.e., the existential threat) (Léonard and Kaunert 2011; Williams 2003; Balzacq 2010). We infer that the more CDWs to be found in PAs, the higher the probability that actors—including those who initially do not want to be part of, or are excluded from, the peace process—will seize the opportunity to embrace peace, gain political legitimacy. This finding trivializes frames favoring, say, the idea that war is profitable (for vertical inequality-induced conflicts) or is the means to end indifference to one's identity markers (for horizontal inequality-induced conflicts), or is the means of replacing untrustworthy state institutions (for institutional mistrust-induced conflicts). The outcome of PAs, if the 'peace spoilers' and peacemakers are dialogically controlled, is a reduction in post-accord battle-related deaths. Conflict de-escalation, unlike escalation, is a situation whereby states (and inter/nationally recognized governments) experiencing intrastate armed conflicts can employ less costly resources (such as alternative dispute resolution, or ADR) to shift warring factions from focusing on their incompatible goals to focusing on what would lead them towards peaceful co-existence.

Put another way, with cognizance of the context-based conclusions of securitization theory, peace is an 'end' that is unwanted by security actors; and words are a 'means' to an end that is preferred—stalemate, state of emergency, war and political uncertainty. The illocutionary logic of words—as a means to a violent end in the paradigmatic field of securitization theory—has the hallmarks of inferent actors who want to create 'special politics' for their inferential audiences (Vuori 2008). It bears the ontological cosmology of an inferent actor whose attempts at securitization are attempts to place their individuality above the collective (Keskinen 2017), their linear and rigid rejection of time over the non-linear and flexible receptiveness of the apolitical society to time (Holbraad and Pedersen 2013)—with time being (at least in the imaginations of a desecuritized society) a non-relativist, independent, indefinite progress of existence that proceeds independent of the perceiver (Whitrow and Soulsby 2003). As such, when actors fixated with frames of war begin to use frames of peace ('peace words'), they are demonstrating the de-securitization of self, and, with it, a resilience in the face of the temptation to securitize existential threats. This kind of resilience, hinging on the use of positive, transformative words, suggests the state actors' recognition of their compatibility, the possibility of their co-existence, with their enemies. Apart from the role this recognition plays in the normalization of tensions, the symmetricalization of status and power on the negotiating table also reduces the chances of war. In the end, parties will naturally accept the peace option.

Why is 'language' important? A review of the literature

Language as communicative interaction (the theory of frame analysis). The study of the role of language in the making and unmaking of human relations and societies took a theoretical turn with the publication of Erving Goffman's book, *Frame Analysis: An Essay on the Organization of Experience* in 1974. Goffman's pioneering study has generated broad scholarly interest in the humanities and social sciences, including sociology (especially in the study of social movements), media and communication studies, experimental political science, and critical security studies. In defining frame analysis, Goffman writes,

> Goodman reminds readers that the definitions of a situation are built up in accordance with principals of organization which govern events—at least social ones—and our subjective involvement in them; frame is the word I use to refer to such of these [essential] elements as I am able to identify. My phrase "frame analysis" is a slogan to refer to the examination in these terms of the organization of experience.
>
> (Goffman 1974, 10–11)

By "framing," Goffman wants people to recognize that their social worldviews are born out of subjective attempts to use their identities to locate and understand their communities (understood here as non-static sociocultural, political and economic spaces). By defining their objective and subjective situations—through what Jacobsen and Kristiansen, in their study of the social thought of Goffman, call "matrices of perceptions" (Jacobsen and Kristiansen 2015, 122)—people are merely trying to systematize their worldviews to give legitimacy to the institutions regulating their subjective experiences.

Expanding on Goffman's work, some have defined 'frame analysis' as "the process by which a communication source, such as a news organization, defines and constructs a political issue or public controversy" (Nelson, Clawson and Oxley 1997, 221). Here, new frames of social and political problems are arranged to subtly steer audiences to think about "an unfolding strip of events and weave a connection among them" (Gamson and Modigliani 1987, 143). Research suggests that the ideational concept of frames (used, henceforth, interchangeably with 'words'), which sees language as a communicative interaction between actor and audience, is a theorization that seeks to show actors' "capacity" and inclination to use concrete, actual activities—activities that are meaningful in their own right—to create "deception, experiment, and rituals" (Goffman 1974, 560). These activities, which Goffman calls "shadows of events," should be taken seriously; it is the ordinariness of words that makes frames potent ideological drivers that shape political events. In practice, ordinary words are reinforced by shared societal assumptions, whose subtle meanings shape the political interpretations of political events (Johnston and Oliver 2000, 41).

Our readings of the varied scholarly interpretations of Goffman's seminal work led us to the realization that the political uses of frames to interpret, say, security events (existential or actual) are outcomes of actors' attempts to build systems—methodical pathways—for self-preservation, while also demonstrating a commitment to the substantive, procedural and normative values that promote or resist political change. In Goffman's view—which is supported by Foucauldian and Deleuzean discourse on language and power relations (see Deleuze and Foucault 1977; Foucault 2005; McNay 2013)—there is more to the political use of frames than their subjective incidental positionalities. In this respect, words in the language called, say, English—and the language of English words—offer a relational (but still under-researched) conception of the transformations of 'speech acts' into marketable political moves, whose social resonance is spatial and impact on the audience unpredictable. Ironically, words emerged from human constructs; and their unpredictability, political theorists argue, should be case-managed by specialist state institutions—institutions that would naturally exploit these constructs for their self-interested gain.

Those writing from the viewpoint of ethnography would argue that these tendencies are malleable because the actors (the people) and space (societies) change over time. Those writing from the linguistic and cognitive psychology traditions would say, inasmuch as constructs are not fixed schemes, that they function as 'intelligible, cognitive structures' of stored memories of the everyday. If, as Bartlett (1932, 197–214) hypothesized in his theory of remembering, memory is reconstructive, and if people store and retrieve information according to expectations formed by cultural schemas, then we can agree with Oliver and Johnston's argument that the theoretical and practical relevance of Goffman's concept of the frame lies in its being an "instrument by which we can infer 'what is going on' with the caveat that they [what actors say and how people understand what they say] are under constant revision based on new occurrences and unexpected actions by other" (Johnston and Oliver 2000, 40). It is the attempt to understand what "is going on" that has captivated sociologists. They are interested in the relationships between stored memories (which can act as communicative code-switchers (Downes 1998, 85)) and the constant evolution of socialized platforms where political actors, who are in the process of becoming social, can (non)permissibly move in and out based on their current circumstances (Goodenough 1981; Romaine 2000; Montgomery 2008).

Thus, with reference to Goffman's frame analysis and the sociological discourses of every day, it is assumed that the framing of language (especially that focusing on the political language of war and peace) is a driver of cognitive structures that appeal to the ordinary people, whose 'ordinariness' can be transformed into a politically significant instrument for the authentication and validation of securitization and de-securitization (see, for example, Gledhill 2008; Goldstein 2016; Hansen 2011). Our empirical assumption, then, is that the elements of language frames can be elicited through various methodological observations, including ethnographic interviews, providing an anthropocentric perspective on the interaction between people and institutions, the impact of their identities on their linguistic positionalities, and cognate modes of reception and rejection of securitized and de-securitized political moves. Such perspectives can also be obtained through longitudinal surveys of statistically tested and verifiable working schema or algorithms.

Language is a social fact (the theories of linguistics structuralism). After Goffman published his work in 1974, several schools of structural linguistics emerged and attempted to understand the usefulness of language in social systems analysis. The central premises of structural linguistics are two-fold. On the one hand, the Saussurean School (founded by the Swiss linguist Ferdinand de Saussure (1857–1913)) emphasizes the primary object of language, and the impact of social constructs (or what Saussure called "systems" of "social facts" (Sampson 1980, 34)) on the state of language over time. These social facts, the argument goes, are regulated by the content-elements of the 'meanings' of words in all human-given languages (written and spoken). Conversely, the Prague school (founded by the Czech linguist Vilém Mathesius (1882–1945)) stresses the functional aspects of the expression-elements of the 'sound' of words within a language. Irrespective of their methodological differences, both schools agree that language is a socially constituted system of signs—and symbols, and the consequences of symbolism—that are quite arbitrary, and that people's constructs of what words mean to them can only be "defined in terms of their relationship within the system" of signs, arbitrariness, linearity, and change (Holdcroft 1991, 186). The Saussurean and Prague schools of structural linguistics made significant in-roads into the development of formal models of language, however inadequate they may seem. That notwithstanding, they lost popularity in the political and behavioral sciences due, in part, to the rise of (1) *Glossematics* structural linguistics (founded in 1931 by the Linguistic Circle of Copenhagen, among whom were Louis Hjelmslev and Viggo Brøndal), and (2) Noam Chomsky's revolutionary theory of language: 'rational grammar.'

Language is an expression of substance (according to the 'glossematics' structural linguistics theory). Glossematics structural linguistics stresses, perhaps, the most interesting radical alternative to contemporary linguistics. Using an elaborate system of algebraic symbolism to explain a "highly complex, sparsely illustrated terminology for describing hypothetical relationships of various kinds," Louis Hjelmslev (the co-founder of this theory) argues that

> language manifests two distinctions, *form* v. *substance* and *content* v. *expression* (the latter pair of terms refers to the opposition between meaning and speech-sound-or-writing-or-Morse); and these distinctions intersect one another to produce four 'strata,' namely *content-substance, content-form, expression-form*, and *expression-substance*, of which the middle two belong to language proper, and the first and last are the external realities which it is the task of a language to link with one another. A language consists purely of relationships: 'external' relationships between elements in different strata and 'internal' relationships between the elements in one stratum, but, except for the sounds and meanings in the two outer strata, the 'elements' between which these relationships obtain are themselves relationships—there is nothing else. A truly general, pure theory of language will discuss only the various possible categories of relationship which may obtain in language, ignoring the properties of extralinguistic 'substance.'
>
> (Quoted in Sampson 1980, 167)

Language is a quantifiable generative construct (according to Noam Chomsky's 'behavioral linguistics rationalism' or 'rational grammar'). This theory is a critic of structuralism's fundamental problems with behaviorism. In Chomsky's theory of language, "there are linguistic syntactic universals in the domain of syntax" (Sampson 1980, 131). With reference to Chomsky's first book, *Syntactic Structures* (1957), Geoffrey Sampson further argues Chomsky might have shown a special interest in how language should be treated, from a syntactic standpoint, "as a particular subset of the class of all possible sequences of the items in its dictionary" (ibid., 133). Chomsky's interest here is in 'discovering' the types of dialectically 'affective,' declaratively well-constructed and grammatically sequential language that comes naturally to an human being.

Chomsky's concept denotes two logical possibilities: first, the applicability of words is endless; or, second, that every word is intentionally well-defined, whether it has been or is waiting to be discovered and classified into distinct classes to perform interrelated sequential functions. In his attempt to generate a formal means to classify functions of words, Chomsky developed a mathematical model called generative grammar, which continues to attract interest in applied linguistics and behavioral and social sciences (such as political science). In an attempt to sequence the morphological unit (or morpheme) of a language that cannot be further divided (e.g., *peace, full* to create the word *peaceful*), Chomsky developed a mathematical technique, the transformational grammar. As outlined in his *Syntactic Structures* (1957), this equation—which can be used to understand, say, the ways in which sociopolitical speech acts (re)create security—contains three elements: the 'phrase-structure' element' (which can be treated as an independent variable), and the transformational and morphophonemic elements (the dependent variables). Each of these elements is guided by a specific set of language rules whose functional inputs are supposed to generate a specified set of probable outputs.

Language is a dramaturgical 'act' with a transformative effect on the performative functions of identities in the making of the securitization moves (according to the theory of dramaturgical analysis). For the proponents of this theory, it is the 'act' of speech that matters. To understand the role of language performance in the making and unmaking of peace, some writers have employed 'dramaturgical analysis' (Fisher 2015; Salter 2008; Gimenez-Salinas 2004; Huysmans 2011). According to Mark B. Salter (2008), this refers to the dramatized uses of the vocabulary of the theater to understand the social settings, roles, and performances of identity in the escalation and de-escalation of conflicts (Salter 2008, 328). Salter also observes that,

> [T]his dramaturgical theory argues that the setting of a securitizing move is determined by the actors and their roles, the rules of the discourse permissible within that space, and the expectations of the audience. When we push this theatrical metaphor, we can classify the different types of securitizing moves that all share similar conventions, narratives, characters, and tropes. The use of specialized language, procedural forms, and common conventions all suggest a common setting [he explains in the footnote that: "These dynamics have been explored in international relations, particularly in the domain of foreign policy analysis, strategic studies (strategic culture), public administration, and organizational anthropology"]. For example, terms, precedents, or issues whose specialized meanings both speaker and audience share.
>
> (Ibid.)

The dramaturgical standpoint makes a case for scholarly engagement with the concept of 'act' in the study of securitization and de-securitization. While other scholarly works have focused on the dialogic aspects of securitizing, they have noted the need for closer scrutiny of the concept of 'act,' which, Jef Huysmans (2011) says, "has been relatively ignored," despite its usefulness in the study of the " 'politicality' of the speech-act approach." With respect to the changing dynamics of security in recent times, Huysmans explores the impact that the displacement of 'acts' by securitizing practices (and devices that appear as banal) can have on the discipline of securitization.

In this context, and with particular reference to the United Kingdom's war on terror, Kathryn Marie Fisher (2015) argues that the essence of taking into consideration the ways identities are dramatized is to relationally construct and produce discourses that influence the conditions of "meaning-making" of what a threat is, and of "action-legitimation" of state and non-state actors' responses. Fisher also observes (for the years between 2000 and 2006) the correlates between dramatized identities and the frequency of terrorist attacks, concluding that the way identity framings are used to measure the frequency of attacks augments their intensity and dramatizes their consequences beyond what can be perceived as normal. Beyond what can be classified as normalized language frames of "threat" is the observation that identity does to drama what the 'resonance' of the securitizing speech acts of political actors does to the crowd psychology of a political audience. This relationship explains the inseparability of the audience and the performer in the (re-)configuration of the processes of how speech acts are made and received (Salter 2008, 330). Salter also suggests (quoting Goffman 1959, 66) that, whether the intention of the speaker is entirely intelligibly calculative or incomprehensibly emotive, the rule of the setting remains the same. Because of this, the dramatized language (be it the language of political resilience or incapacity) should adhere to the same logic (of arousing the interests of the audience), even if the outcomes are different. This logic, Salter tells us, is understandably located in the "grand narratives by which some truths are legitimated, and others de-legitimated"; and the characters of the speaker and their audiences, having been authenticated by identity-induced meta-narratives (hence, the relevance of Fisher's observation above), become the means through which they can find their voice to speak about their lived experiences and their relationships (Salter 2008, 329).

The linearity of the semantical and syntactical elements of language causes wars and peace (according to Johan Galtung's reading of Walter J. Ong's 'Literacy and Oracy,' and D. M. Topping's 'Tyranny of Literacy'). Developed in 1987 by the doyen of peace studies, Johan Galtung, this theory says there is a direct connection between language (semantics and syntax) and society's appreciation of the frames of war and peace. This perspective is not a questionable claim of quantifiable correlates between language and war (or peace). Instead, it is an observation of the connection between the "linear, irreversible language presentation" of the war frames about victory (which encourages conflict) rather than defeat (which discourages conflict, since the outcomes are negative); and the "linear, irreversible expansion into space" (and across time) of deceptive semantics of, say, life—when, in actual fact, the coded message is death.

The intent of creating symbolic pointers to the society, it can be argued, is about persuading the audience to feel they are part of it. Thus, inasmuch as the logic of words resonates with dramaturgical power (see Salter 2008) and identity (see Fisher 2015), it should not be divorced from the questions of semantics and syntax. Hence, the relevance of Galtung's question: "is there a connection between language and war?" Galtung looked first at the logical semantics, with a view to identifying what makes sense, and also the lexical aspects of semantics, to understand the presuppositions and implications of their coded textual, etymological meanings. He was interested in what these meanings contain so as to ascertain whether the coded frames/words are "tilted in favor of peace, or in favor of war" (Galtung 1987, 2).

Galtung's observations on semantics and war (although lack any discussion of the methodological framework he used) are as follows. When militarized words are used by state/non-state actors, the intent is either to create stalemate (the condition of no-war-no-peace) in situations of conflict, or to escalate conflict. In this regard, he argues the language of war can be defined as a "linguistic crime" committed by those who control the discourse of violence, and by those who have used semantics to persuade people to conceive peace as the absence of violence, rather than "violence as the absence of peace" (Galtung 1987, 2). As such, when the word 'defense' is used, political actors are indirectly making a case for 'offensive' weapons in defensive war; they logically create the condition for the legitimate use of offensive weapons. When the word 'modernization' is emphasized by state actors, they are using it as a euphemism in political speech acts that, on the one hand, call on their citizenry to approve their securitizing moves and investment in new weapons; and, on the other hand, to encourage the citizenry to become aggressively fascinated with the offensive and defensive use of these new weapons against others (people and countries) whose civilizations are opposed to, or are incompatible with, theirs; hence, the emergence of a 'clash of civilization.' Furthermore, when the phrase 'balance of power' is used, Galtung is of the view that it signifies the need to move from the equilibrium between military powers (with the mutually assured destructive nuclear capability) to power asymmetry or unipolarity in the geopolitical ordering of the international system (with far-reaching implications for states on the margins of this system's periphery). Conversely, the use of 'peacemaking,' when mentioned by supporters of securitization and political realism, might raise misgivings among those conversant with the history of how the Reagan Administration (which formulated the term 'peacemaking' in American security discourse) used the term it as its "people-killing" securitization move (in the guise of humanitarian interventions) in other parts of the world, including sub-Saharan Africa. While by no means arguing against Galtung's view on the political uses of such words, we contest that with the rise of the doctrine of a responsibility to protect—which obligates states and the international community to protect populations from all forms of war (Bellamy and Reike 2010)—it is highly unlikely that conflict de-escalating words like 'peacemaking' would contribute to the escalation of conflict. Against this backdrop, our panel estimation dataset on the correlates of conflict de-escalation words and peace—and, hence, the reduction of battle-related deaths—should be seen as a response to Galtung's conclusions on political uses of peacemaking.

On the syntactical aspects of language, Galtung took a birds-eye view of what drives states (a) to theatrically tell their stories of military victories and the defeat of enemies (but not their defeat by enemies); (b) to celebrate their forward march into the territory of the enemy (but not retreat from these territories); and (c) to preference narratives that feed into their securitizing moves and augment their power (and not their powerlessness). Galtung conceptualizes the syntactical influences—literacy and oracy—that create a gestalt around the violent past of societies, and how these influences shape societal memory of that past. This memory, according to Galtung, is a symbol-cum-information that is stored, in literate societies, in books and kept in archives for "easy retrieval as long as the person [that is, any person, whether victim, perpetrator or bystander] has some idea, roughly, where on the rather long string of words … something would approximately be located" (Galtung 1987, 3). This, he tells us, forces upon people and governments in non-western societies specific subdivisions of speech approximately mirroring 'phonemes' in oral communication (that is, the minimum elements capable of carrying some kind of meaning, in the sense of making a difference). Central to these phonemes are the gestaltized elements—of time, knowledge, space, human nature, people-to-people relationships—message coding (by the speaker or writer) and decoding (by the listener or reader). Amid all this, Galtung reminds his readers that what holds for spoken or written words holds also for the belief systems that produce them. It is in recognition of this that he argues that "even more important is how language steer[s] our epistemology, organize[s] the whole dimension of knowledge—again, not in any unambiguous way, but in the sense of making us incline in one direction rather than the other" (Galtung 1987, 5).

In this regard, Galtung suggests the need to find a "positive and an assertive language" that "do[es] not see peace as a deviation, to be singled out terminologically, or even as a negation of the normal" (Galtung 1987, 2). One way of finding this "positive" language is through the recognition that (1) what state/non-state actors think is not independent of subjective, dramaturgical political speech acts of political survival; hence, the people for whom and by whom the quest for survival is legitimated must accept their responsibility to re-direct the political narrative from war to peace; and, (2) the events that occur as a result of these acts are guided by cultural symbolism of the identity of the individual (the actor) and the collective (the inferential audience).

Introducing the concept of conflict de-escalation words

What is the concept of conflict de-escalating words (CDWs), and why did we develop it? Before explaining what CDWs are, readers are reminded that our emphasis on CDWs is self-evident in our attempt to revise and expand on exploratory analysis (Weaver 1995; Balzacq 2005, 2011; Stritzel 2007; Taurek 2006; Floyd 2011, 2016) of the Copenhagen School's securitization theory—with our focus on the "process opposite to securitization [theory] which involves the return of an issue from urgent, securitized situation to the area of normal negotiations in political sphere" (Putnik and Milošević 2018, 18). Moreover, CDWs should be seen as an elaborative attempt to fuse Goffman's (1974) frame analysis, Fillmore's (1976) frame semantics, and Galtung's (1987) 'semantics, syntax and war' in the discourses of peace and conflict studies in sub-Saharan Africa. Through this revised and elaborated engagement with these theories, we not only address the definitional issues but also make up for the discursive issues—relating to the correlates between CDWs and battle-related deaths—not explained in the panel data estimation technique we employed. Capturing the discursive aspects of CDWs is a way of reminding readers that CDWs are frames about actors' compatibility that not only got them to the negotiating table but made agents for the mainstreaming of peace words that favor the de-escalation of conflict in the warscapes of sub-Saharan Africa.

CDWs are politicized speech acts that recognize the positive contribution of alternative dispute resolution mechanism. They are words that are deliberately mainstreamed in highly sensitive political statements (be they in written or oral form) that remove security issues from the domain of extra-ordinary, militarized executive decisions and situate them as normalized existential threats to be put forward to the people (including the governmental and non-government warring factions), who then have the opportunity to factor in their everyday lived experiences when scrutinizing these security issues. Figure 4.1 below presents a conceptual framework of CDWs and how they can be used to transform the linear frames of conflict into the non-linear frames of peace. In this framework, we see that the politicized narratives on death toll, unmet needs, cost of war, factions' rent-seeking, societal inequality, international communities' sanctions and embargos, the proliferation of arms, and sexual violence during the fighting are captured as 'conflict frames' that shape actors' (here, the mediators are identified as actors because they are the people seeking to de-securitize the war frames) views on the kind of peace frames to include in the peace accord. But the effectiveness of these peace frames depends on the social frames or 'socialized attributes' of the relationships between the actors and their audience (here, the warring factions are the audience because they are the one who would give legitimacy to the de-securitizing moves of the actors, the mediators); and, taken

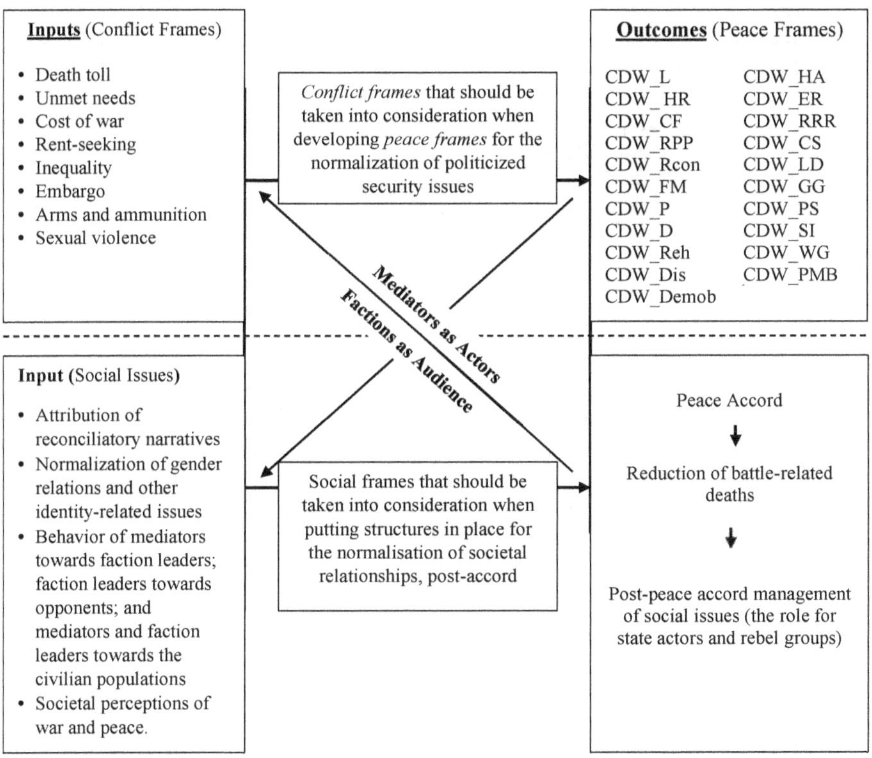

Figure 4.1 Conflict frames—inputs, outputs and expected outcomes.

together, what the actors and the audience think about the civilian population—attending especially to their socialized perceptions of war and peace.

We suggest that CDWs are about actors' understanding of their readiness (see Pruitt's (2007) *Readiness Theory*) to talk peace based on their judgment of the ripeness (see Zartman's (1989) *Ripeness Theory*) of the conflict. Readiness and ripeness theories suggest that conflicts are exposed to the 'principles' of diminishing marginal productivity of the desires to keep fighting. That is to say, the desire to continue (propelled by the profitability of conflict) or discontinue fighting hinges on inputs. Changes in societal and in-group perceptions of the conflict (addressing the question, "why do we fight when we cannot win?"), increased pressure from allies of the warring parties (not forgetting that these allies would also be under pressure from their constituents) and general optimism regarding the success of political negotiations (especially if a neighboring country has successfully ended their conflicts) will lead to a reduction of combatant effectiveness. Military gains will be reduced due to the asymmetrical rise of conflict de-escalation words within (and then, between) warring factions.

Table 4.1 Abbreviations for CDW—Conflict de-escalation word

Abbreviations	
CDW—Conflict de-escalation word	
↓	
CDW_L	Love
CDW_ HR	Human Rights
CDW_CF	Ceasefire
CDW_RPP	Release of Political Prisoners
CDW_Rcon	Reconciliation
CDW_FM	Free Movement of civilian population and humanitarian workers, mediators and peacekeepers
CDW_P	Peace
CDW_D	Demilitarization
CDW_Reh	Rehabilitation
CDW_Dis	Disarmament
CDW_Demob	Demobilization
CDW_HA	Humanitarian Assistance
CDW_ER	Economic Reform
CDW_RRR	Reintegration, Resettlement and Repatriation
CDW_CS	Civil Society (as peacebuilders)
CDW_LD	Liberal Democracy (including the transformation of rebel groups into political parties and free and fair elections
CDW_GG	Good Governance
CDW_PS	Power Sharing
CDW_SI	Social Inclusion (and social integration)
CDW_WG	Women and Gender (emphasis on the needs and concerns of women; and gender-sensitive language of peace
CDW_PMB	Peace Monitoring Bodies with an operational mandate based on the consensus of conflicting parties

Consequently, CDWs should be seen as a frame of 'interpretation' of state's resilient move to factor emotions into the resolution of conflicts. Language is emotion; and the systematic act of putting feeling into words, images and symbols is a self-regulatory way of dealing with emotions. It is arguable that, by transforming feelings into oral frames, the inhibitor is a step closer to being reconciled. Various ADR schools of thought, as well as scholarly works written from the standpoint of cognitive linguistics (see Lakoff 2016; Lindquist and Gendron 2013), critical ontological security studies and international relations (Mercer 2006; Crawford 2000), and feminist international relations theorists have also used these conclusions to explain the gendered nature of the psycho-dynamics of emotion in world politics. With reference to the nature–nurture dichotomy (in feminist essentialism, which states that men are warlike and women 'peace-loving') and the masculinization of the structures of war (feminist constructivism), feminists believe that by putting their feelings, needs and concerns into language frames, they can transcend structural inequalities and wars (Sylvester 1994; Bleiker and Hutchison 2008; Cockburn 2010).

In relation to the second part of the question outlined at the beginning of this chapter—why did we develop the concept of CDW—readers are reminded that the receptor and transmitter (the African person) of the language of war and peace is a being who understands war and peace as things that are cultural, illogical and non-linear. As a result of this unscientific perspective on war and peace, political speech acts are socialized dramaturgical acts that do not require the suggestive linearity of securitization theory. Let us take, for instance, the processes involved in the normalization of politicized security issues. In western democracies, every existential or actual security crisis is thoroughly researched, and the processes of addressing the existential threat of, say, terrorism, are guided by logical thought, laws and depoliticized regulatory institutions, staffed by professionals applying linear thinking. While individuality is factored into the way in which issues of peace and security are imagined and understood, subjective conclusions are objectified through the scholarly corroboration of viewpoints. Outcomes are validated not just by the means employed to achieve them, but also by reference to classified and unclassified documents and reports accessible to both the actors and (after declassification) the inferent audience.

This is not the case for much of sub-Saharan Africa. We recognize that historical European–African colonial contacts, and ongoing westernization and globalization, have resulted in significant social, cultural, economic and political changes in sub-Saharan Africa; and that the rise of institutions owned, funded and regulated by states and the international community makes the application of this distinction across the war/peacescapes of sub-Saharan Africa challenging. Nonetheless, we believe, based on our individual observations and our lived experience in our respective communities in the sub-region (Sierra Leone and Ghana), that a distinctive characterization of the typical sub-Saharan African community (outside the cities) is visible and offers a useful tool to understand how the language of war and peace is imagined, understood, stored and transmitted across time and space.

Table 4.2 Methods of imaginations, comprehension, storage and transmission of conflict escalation and de-escalation words in situations of conflicts in sub-Saharan Africa

Methods	*What they mean in practice and how they impact conflict de-escalation words*
Oracy	Here the emphasis is placed on the eloquence of speech, imagination and memory. Eloquence about issues affecting war and peace is measured by the amount of personal knowledge the speaker has, not how well-constructed his/her grammar is. In fact, the abilities of writing, reading, and spelling using the semantics and syntax of European languages are hardly rewarded in the narratives of war and peace.
Thoughts and expressions	Here the emphasis is on the psychodynamics of first oral cultural thinking that to 'look up something' that has already been conceptualized can only lead to emptiness. Thoughts and expressions tend to be of the following sorts: (a) *Additive rather than subordinate. This is because discourses have meanings that cannot be determined by grammar;* (b) *Aggregative rather than analytic.* This is because oral expression carries epithets and other formulary baggage that high literacy rejects as cumbersome and redundant because of its aggregative weight; (c) *Redundant or 'copious.'* What this means is that, since redundancy characterizes oral thought and speech, it is, in a profound sense, more natural to thought and speech than the systemic linearity found in, say, the 'literate' western societies. Sparsely linear or analytic thought and speech is an artificial creation, structured by the technology of writing; (d) *Conservative or traditionalist.* Since in primarily oral cultures conceptualized knowledge that is not repeated aloud soon vanishes, oral societies must invest great energy, in saying over and over again what has been learned arduously over the ages; (e) *Close to the human lifeworld.* In the absence of elaborate analytic categories that depend on writing to structure knowledge at a distance from lived experience, oral cultures must conceptualize and verbalize all their knowledge with more or less close reference to the human lifeworld, assimilating the alien, objective world to the mort immediate, familiar interaction of human beings; (f) *Agonistically toned.* By keeping knowledge embedded in the human lifeworld, orality situates knowledge within a context of struggle; (g) *Empathetic and participatory rather than objectively distanced.* For an oral culture, learning or knowing means achieving close, empathetic, communal identification with the known, the bearer of the story; (h) *Non-homeostatic.* Oral societies live in the past as much as they live in present. Interestingly, to keep the balance between the asymmetries or non-homeostasis that emerges out of people's attempts to use the past (which is sometimes esoterically fused to cosmological beliefs of gods, saints, and demons) to understand their present circumstances, people have used proverbs (thought-based expressions) to filter memories. The relevant expressions are presented as they are, and non-relevant ones are given inter-generational tones of being 'children's talk.' (i) *Situational rather than abstract.* Oral cultural narratives (including those that are documented in writing) tend to use impressions of situational frames that draw both actors and audience (and the living and the dead) together. Where references of constructs of war and peace are made, it is done with the myth-making reverence for the world of the dead—as if to say, they have not died in vain.

Oralature (as opposed to 'literature')	What this means is that stories are heard in an informal setting (say, under the tree or around the campfire) and are mostly told by people to their living audiences. Personal experience that shapes Oralature narratives refers to experiences during social growth and development. This personal experience is unique to the individual and can be referred to as knowledge gained from things they have actually done. To properly use personal experience, one must engage in personal reflection. This requires thinking about who one is, what one does and one is living; the nature of the culture one is experiencing; and the specific environment one experiences. Personal experience is intertwined with micro-factors molding the gender, age, place of origin, and fearlessness.
Customs	Rules on human conduct in war and peace, and on social organization (including those concerned with inter-gender/inter-generational relations) are known and understood by all, and they are arbitrated by designated people who hold their authority based on the dictates of their time-honored belief systems. Laws are not written; they are cataloged in the minds of people, who transmit them from one generation to another through informal means.
Memory storage	Despite the fact that peace accords are written in printable documents and can be retrieved, the truths and lies about the past are stored in the memory of a designated group of people—mostly the elderly—who became the natural repository of information; stored information in books, museums, files, libraries, and archives is suspect; with memory in the minds of the elderly, they (the elderly) must be able to recall the events reported in books. If they cannot, then what is contained in that book is maligned and annulled
Source of wisdom and rationality	*Instinct, empathy, knowledge, spirituality (in what can be attributed to the community's pre-colonial religious belief systems).*
Community (more important than the individual)	Individuality is not accepted; the individual is part of the community; there is an emphasis on the familial. In fact, the familiar adage in sub-Saharan African communities are: "it takes a man and a woman to bring a child into the world, but it takes a community to raise that child." As such, the *id* is communalized. In making sense of it, several issues are taken into consideration: religion, family and friends, place and location, profession, social class, political beliefs, history of one's family, community and country, and gender.
Success–failure image	Opinions about failure and success is determined by one's acceptance of customs and traditions regulating each individual place in the public (community) and private (home; family) spaces; the idea of place is hierarchical, with age, gender, and the status of one's family (landed gentry, royal, peasant etc.) determining success or failure.

continued

Table 4.2 continued

Methods	*What they mean in practice and how they impact conflict de-escalation words*
Social continuity	Social continuity is static; it is the repetition of patterns in thinking and behavior and the social trends which have occurred are not subjected to the past. Time is timeless, and its indefinite continuum is evident in esoteric cultural norms, heritage, traditional customs and values in a given society. Continuity serves to unify a given community and link sense of past and present. The primary drivers of change are beliefs, identity and the family. *Beliefs* form a system of values that systematically outline the complicated ways people should perceive their social, cultural, political, peaceful or violent, physical and psychological worlds. This also takes into consideration people's perceptions of the relationship between the cosmological world of the dead (ancestors) and the physical world of the living (mostly limited by tribal and village boundaries). *Identity* is defined here as the understanding that people, irrespective of their circumstances, have subjective representations of themselves, and the 'otherness' of others. In almost all cases, what they think and feel about self and others are conditioned by the collective: the family, the community and the state. *Family*—the idea of family, especially in sub-Saharan African societies, where the 'family unit' remains a strong determinant of social continuity with political functions, is mostly patriarchal and was constituted to give men public (political) power and women symbolic domestic (private) powers. Even so, in all war-affected sub-Saharan African countries, the ability of the woman to give birth to a male child or children—who would later populate the world of war, and the spaces where peace deals are negotiated—is one aspect of the role of women in the projection of the family unit as a political space where frames of war and peace are domesticated, and narratives on the causes and consequences of conflicts and peace are reinforced.
Causes of conflict and peace	On Conflict: in some cases, popular opinion points to the mythopoetic, fatalist thinking of curses from angry gods and ancestral spirits (Summerfield 2002; Pfeiffer 2005; Behrend 1999). On Peace: the narratives point to conciliatory cosmic forces who are appeased through prayer and the pouring of libation (see Park 2010; Dugdale and Gerstbauer 2017; Howard 2012; Kelsall 2005).

Sources: The analysis presented in this table is based on our Afro-centric readings, modifications and context-based application of Walter J. Ong's (1979, 2015, 1982) 'literacy' and 'oracy'; and other referenced works. However, our interpretations of the mythopoetic differences in the way the frames of war and peace are imagined, understood, memorialized and transmitted in sub-Saharan African societies, also draw from our lived experiences as citizens of sub-Saharan African countries.

The question to ask, then, is: 'on what platform (or platforms) do CDWs give political meaning and social resonance in the political settlement of disputes in sub-Saharan Africa?' In answering this question, we refer to the hagiography of the political emotions (the desire for self-determination) that created the decolonized spaces where the idea of state-led regional integration and collective security was born in sub-Saharan Africa. To this ends, we trace the statist history of the institutionalization of CDWs to the Organization of African Unity (the OAU, which was replaced on July 9, 2002 by the African Union, or AU) and its alternative dispute resolution strategy, the Mechanism for Conflict Prevention, Management and Resolution (hereafter, the Mechanism). In the 1970s, the primary aim of sub-Saharan African leaders, under the nominal leadership of pan-African political radicals like presidents Nkrumah (of Ghana), Tubman (of Liberia) and Touré (of Guinea), was the creation of a "political union for Africa in which economic, cultural and military activities would be coordinated centrally in order to advance much-needed development and make the African voice in world politics both more effective and respected" (Franke 2009, 52). The focus of these radical leaders was 'military security' against an existential threat to their 'sovereign nations' from 'neo-imperial' western nations. This was opposed by the moderates of the OAU, who called themselves, the Brazzaville group (later known as the 'Liberian group'). For them, African countries should be advocating for a union that was not "political integration of sovereign states, but the unity of aspirations and of action" (Chime 1977, 64).

In the end, it was the aspirations of the moderates that led to the emergence of peaceful resolution of conflicts in the discourses of state sovereignty, peace and security in sub-Saharan Africa. In March 1991, during the African Leadership Conference on "Security, Stability, Development, and Cooperation" in Kampala, Uganda, the OAU Secretariat proposed the mainstreaming of 'peace frames' in the Union's joint efforts to prevent conflicts and put to an end to battle-related deaths. In June 1991, during the Abuja Summit of the Heads of State and Government, a decision was taken to authorize the OAU Secretary-General, Salim Ahmed Salim, to develop a comprehensive conflict prevention framework. In 1992, Secretary-General Salim issued a report titled *Resolving Conflicts in Africa: Proposals for Action.* Although much focus has been on the Agenda for Peace of then-UN Secretary-General Boutros Boutros-Ghali, also released in 1992, Ahmed Salim's report was the first to create a path for sub-Saharan African countries to gravitate from an emphasis on war frames to an emphasis on peace frames. The report was endorsed by all countries in the sub-region[1] and in June 1993, the Assembly of Heads of State and Government, meeting in Cairo, Egypt, for its 29th assembly meeting, adopted a resolution authorizing the creation of the Mechanism. In November 1993, at a joint meeting of the defense and foreign affairs ministers of the OAU member-states in Addis Ababa, Ethiopia, a set of guidelines for the implementation of the Mechanism were drawn up. Seven months later—in June 1994—the Mechanism came into force, signaling the institutionalization of a mandate revolving around the use of conflict de-escalating words. As such, this mechanism, later incorporated into the OAU's successor (the AU), marked the beginning of sub-Saharan African countries' second-generation peace and security agenda. Second, it strengthened and harmonized their peacemaking policies; and, third, it reversed states' emphasis on the policy of non-involvement in their internal affairs by other member states of the sub-regional bloc.

As a show of commitment to the removal of this non-interference clause, the sub-regional security and economic integration groupings of sub-Saharan African countries followed the example of the continental body by creating their own zonal mechanisms between 1995 and 2000. One example is the Intergovernmental Authority on Development (IGAD) Mechanism for the Prevention, Management, and Resolution of Inter-state and Intra-state Conflicts in the IGAD subregion. The IGAD mechanism (which came into force following the Khartoum Summit of November 2000) is based on a five-point program, which included building IGAD member states' good governance institutional capacity, documenting peacemaking initiatives in their regional early-warning systems and establishing a peace fund to help their peacemaking activities in the region (Franke 2009, 72). The ECOWAS Mechanism for Conflict Prevention, Management and Resolution, Peacekeeping and Security was adopted by the ECOWAS Authority of Heads of State and Government in Lomé, Togo, on December 10, 1999, and the ECOWAS Conflict Prevention Framework (ECPF) in 2008. The

> goal of the conflict prevention framework is to ensure the creative transformation of conflict, diffusion of tensions and prevent conflict outbreak, escalation, spread or relapse. Put another way; it involves institutionalizing measures to ensure that conflicts do not arise in the first place or if they do, that they do not reoccur.
>
> (Odobo, Andekin and Udegbunam 2017, 148)

The Southern African Development Community (SADC) Politics, Defense and Security (OPDS) mechanism, established in 1996, has several objectives but, for the purpose of this chapter, we will only focus on "Conflict Management, Prevention, and Resolution."[2] It emphasizes alternative dispute resolution for both inter-member states and intra-state conflicts through the incorporation of the elements of frames that seek to persuade the parties to cease fighting and promote non-violent means to resolve their conflicts.

Accordingly, the embodiment of statism in the development of these subregional bodies, and their methodical approaches to conflict resolution, are not about the mere suppression of conflicts or the use of ADR to resolve them. Instead, they should be about giving a national outlook to localized forms of conflict. In fact, the legalizing protocols that created the ADR mechanisms of these sub-regional organizations transfer responsibility for the arduous work of negotiating peace from the national populations of member states to their super-national groupings. The institutionalization of ADR—and with it, CDWs—at state levels has been criticized for compromising people's participation, a cherished political value of liberalism and democracy (Makoa 2005). Nonetheless, it provides an internationalized legitimating political outlook to peacemaking, through which a collective identity provides the platform in which CDWs become a tool for understanding, storing, memorializing, retrieving, and disseminating war and peace, as well as dealing with the imagery of those who died during the conflict.

Data description and estimation technique

Data description

The data used is a panel of 13 countries for the period 1990 to 2013 sourced from the Uppsala Conflict Data Program (UCDP). The choice of this period is mainly informed by data availability specifically for countries that signed peace accords. Countries that signed only one peace accord within the period under consideration were excluded from the dataset so that we could have, at least, two data points for each country. We employed three measures of battle-related deaths—the best, low and high measures for battle-related deaths measured by the UCDP. The definitions, sources and variables are presented in Table 4.3 below.

The summary statistics for the variables are presented in Panel A of Table 4.4, while countries included in the study are presented in Panel B. It can be seen from the means that the variables are comparable; the standard deviations also indicate the variables are substantially varying. This implies that corresponding

Table 4.3 Definitions and sources of variables

Variable	*Definition/type*	*Source*
Battle-related deaths		
Best measure (bdBest)	Best estimate for battle-related deaths in the conflict/dyad in the given year	*UCDPэж*
Low measure (bdLow)	Low estimate for battle-related deaths in the conflict/dyad in the given year	*UCDP*
High measure (bdHigh)	High estimate for battle-related deaths in the conflict/dyad in the given year	*UCDP*
Conflict de-escalation words (9) *(reconciliation, peace, rehabilitation, disarmament, demobilization, economic reform, power sharing, and peace monitoring bodies).*	Count/discrete variable for number of conflict de-escalation words in all peace accords that have be signed from 1990 to 2003	See Appendix A4.2
Peace accord signed previous year	Dummy variable	See Appendix A4.3
Election year	Dummy variable	See Appendix A4.3
Dominant religion	Dummy variable	See Appendix A4.3
International interest in conflict	Dummy variable	UCDP
Dominant resource	Categorical variable	See Appendix A4.3
Sub-regional location of country	Categorical variable	See Appendix A4.3

эжUCDP: The Uppsala Conflict Data Program (see also Appendix A4.3)

estimations could yield feasible relationships. We can see from the means that reconciliatory words featured most across the sample than conflict de-escalation words. About 57% of countries in the sample are predominantly Christian, while about 17% of the conflicts had international aspects. From Figure 4.2 to Figure 4.4, the conclusion drawn is that Liberia had the most reconciliatory words featuring in peace accords signed, while Somalia counted the most battle-related deaths. The existence of outliers is also visible and accounts for the use of robust standard errors, also known heteroskedasticity-corrected standard errors.

Table 4.4 Summary statistics and presentation of countries

Panel A: Summary statistics					
Variable	*Mean*	*Std. Dev.*	*Min*	*Max*	*Obs*
Battle-related deaths					
Best measure	787.531	1,076.688	25	8,119	144
Low measure	731.000	1,024.057	18	7,344	144
High measure	1,330.676	1,803.412	25	9,823	144
Conflict de-escalation words					
Reconciliation	1.724	11.235	0	131	144
Reconciliation squared	128.331	1,425.383	0	17,161	144
Peace	3.486	14.058	0	136	144
Rehabilitation	0.403	2.721	0	30	144
Disarmament	0.729	4.099	0	44	144
Demobilization	0.778	3.724	0	34	144
Economic reform	0.604	2.902	0	22	144
Power sharing	0.556	3.715	0	43	144
Peace monitoring bodies	0.313	1.611	0	13	144
Peace accords (previous year) (Yes = 1; No = 0)	0.152	0.360	0	1	144
Election year (Yes = 1; No = 0)	0.069	0.254	0	1	144
Dominant religion (Christian = 1; Islam = 0)	0.566	0.497	0	1	144
Dominant natural resource					
Oil	0.393	0.490	0	1	144
Gold/copper/diamond/bauxite	0.303	0.461	0	1	144
Tantalum/uranium/tin ore	0.179	0.385	0	1	144
Timber/cocoa	0.124	0.331	0	1	144
International interest (Yes = 1; No = 0)	0.166	0.373	0	1	144
Sub-region					
West Africa	0.193	0.396	0	1	144
Eastern/Southern Africa	0.683	0.467	0	1	144
Central Africa	0.124	0.331	0	1	144
Panel B: Presentation of countries					
Angola; Burundi; Chad; Guinea-Bissau; Ivory Coast; Liberia; Mozambique; Niger; Rwanda; Sierra Leone; Somalia; Sudan; Uganda					

Std. Dev.: Standard Deviation. Min: Minimum. Max: Maximum. Obs.: Observations.

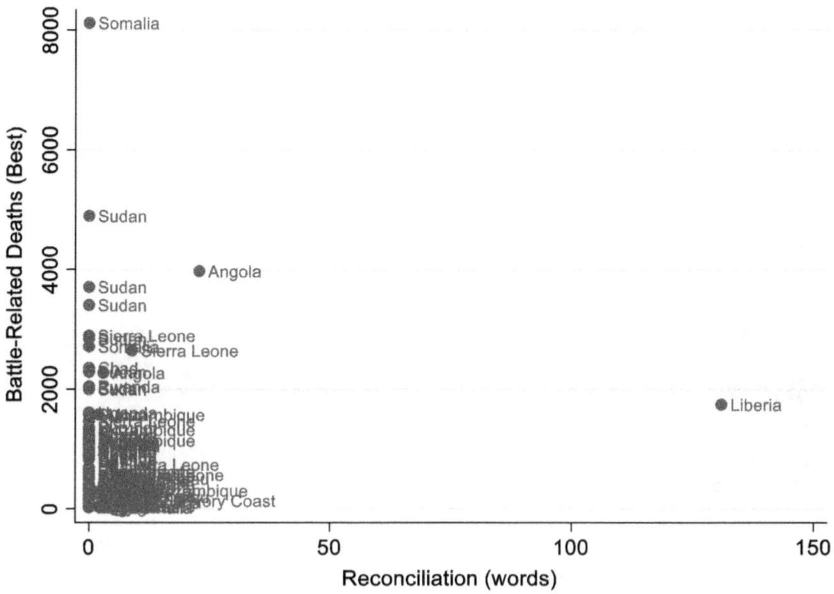

Figure 4.2 Scatter plot of battle-related deaths (best measure) and reconciliatory words.

Source: Authors' Construct (2018).

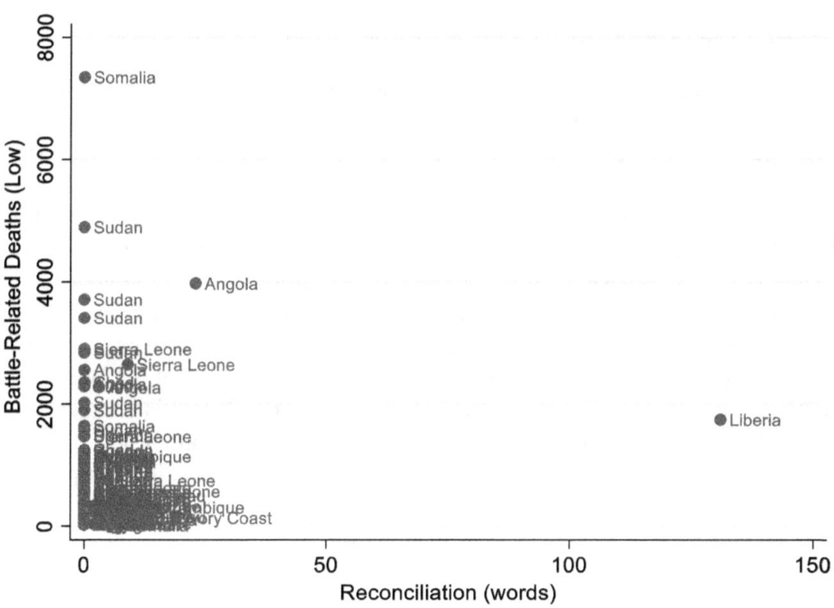

Figure 4.3 Scatter plot of battle-related deaths (low measure) and reconciliatory words.

Source: Authors' Construct (2018).

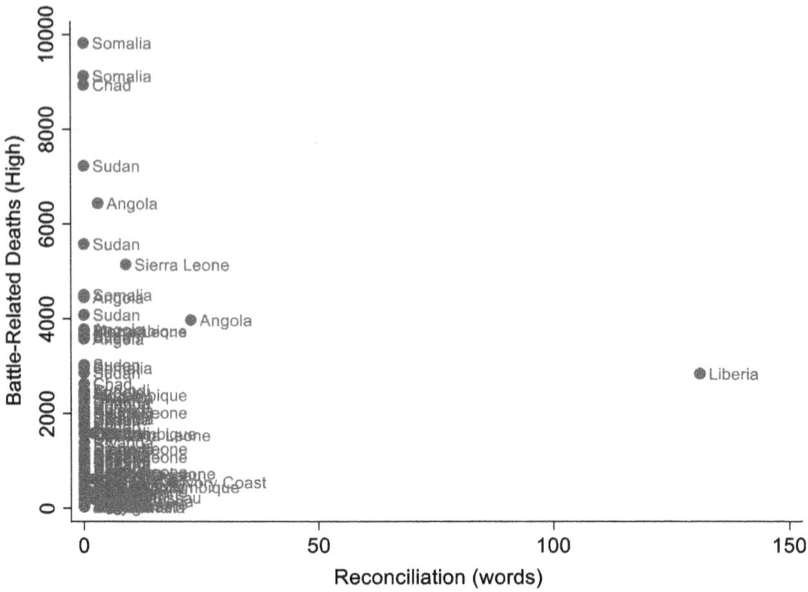

Figure 4.4 Scatter plot of battle-related deaths (high measure) and reconciliatory words.
Source: Authors' Construct (2018).

Estimation technique: pooled OLS and random effect models

The choice between the pooled OLS and the random effects model is determined by the Breusch-Pagan Lagrange multiplier test. This is a test of zero individual- or time-specific variance components in the random effects model (Baltagi, 2008; Cameron and Trivedi, 2010; Torres-Reyna, 2007). In other words, if the null hypothesis is not rejected, it means the data structure favors the pooled OLS (Park, 2010). We chose the random effects over the fixed effects model because we have an unbalanced panel, and, for such a data structure, the random effects model has been identified as the better estimator. Additionally, we have time-invariant independent variables and their inclusion supports use of the random effects model (Asteriou and Hall, 2011; Nguyen, 2010). Looking at the Breusch-Pagan test across the three models presented in Appendix 1 of this chapter, we can see that none fails to reject the null hypothesis at the 5% alpha level; thus, we have chosen the pooled OLS over the random effects model. The empirical model for the pooled OLS that captures the effect of conflict de-escalation on battle-related deaths is presented below in equation (4.1):

$$BRD_{it} = \alpha_0 + \sum_{i=1}^{9} \sigma_i CDW_{it} + \beta_1 PAprev_{it} + \beta_2 Elecyr_{it} + \beta_3 Domrel_{it} + \beta_4 Int_{it} + \beta_5 Domres_{it} + \beta_6 Subreg_{it} + \varepsilon_{it} \tag{4.1}$$

where *BRD* represents battle-related deaths and *CDW* captures all nine conflict de-escalation words counted (reconciliation and the square of it, peace, rehabilitation, disarmament, demobilization, economic reform, power sharing and peace monitoring bodies). *PAprev* is a dummy that takes a value of 1 if a peace accord was signed the previous year and 0 otherwise; *Elecyr* is a dummy variable for election year and is captured as 1 if election and 0 otherwise; *Domrel* is a dummy variable for dominant religion which is denoted 1 for Christian and 0 for Islam; *Int* is also a dummy variable and captured as 1 if the conflict has an international influence and 0 otherwise. *Domres* is a categorical for dominant resource (ranging from oil to timber/cocoa) while *Subreg* is a structural variable that accounts for the three sub-regions that the data covers (West Africa, East/Southern Africa and Central Africa). α, σ, and β are parameters to be determined while ε is an error term.

Analyses and discussion

Regarding battle-related deaths, we rely on the best measure of battle-related deaths and focus our analyses on the first column of Table 8.5. For model specification diagnostics using the link test, the *p*-value for *_hat* and *_hatsq*, which is significant and insignificant respectively, shows that the pooled OLS is correctly specified and does not suffer from omitted-variable bias. We also present robust standard errors indicative of heteroskedasticity-corrected variances. Having ensured the robustness of the models, we continue with an analysis of the findings.

The effect of reconciliatory words on battle-related deaths describes an inverted-U relationship and calls for a threshold analysis to identify the number of words that can trigger this relationship. This implies that, where there are fewer reconciliatory words included in a peace accord, the number of battle-related deaths increases per additional reconciliatory word but begins to decline with higher numbers of reconciliatory words. Threshold analyses peg this threshold at 35 words (see Appendix 4 to this chapter for calculations). This means that increasing the amount of reconciliatory words in a peace accord to more than 35 can reduce the number of battle-related deaths. Continuing, we can see that, increasing words that connote peace by an extra word has the potential to reduce battle-related deaths by 33. By inference, when words of peace take prominence in the signing of peace accords, the minor conflicting group(s) begins to develop a sense that such is the expectation and intention of the major party. This goes a long way to calming tensions, resulting in reduced deaths.

In addition, including words that depict power-sharing can reduce battle-related deaths by about 37. Similarly, increasing words that that advocate the adoption of peace-monitoring bodies (PMB) with an operational mandate based on the consensus of conflicting parties reduces battle-related deaths by a greater magnitude, with a stronger effect. The formal nature of consensus building, and group dynamics are important determinants of PMBs' contributions to peace.

As C.T. Lawrence Butler reminds us, "if war is the violent resolution of conflict, then peace is not the absence of conflict, but rather, the ability to resolve conflict without violence" (quoted in Butler and Rothstein 1987, v). To this end, one way to achieve a non-lethal approach to resolving conflicts is through the formalization, mainstreaming and diffusion of competing goals through the formation of peace-monitoring bodies with operational mandates based on consensus or, rather, the equalization of participation. Of course, conflict avoidance, denial of wrongdoing and repression of the truth are core characteristics of actor/audience participation in the activities of PMBs. But the neutrality of the mediators (the agenda planners, the facilitators, the time-keepers, and peacekeepers), the centralization of win–win peace narratives (that equally seek to benefit the vulnerable civilian populations) and belief in the formalities of the process will mitigate against these peace-spoilers. We also infer that, since PMB is about the formalization of decision-making through consensus, the dictatorship of the majority—which leads to competition and the circle of violence—gives way to cooperation and democratic decision-making. Thus, PMBs allow equal access to power, promote empowerment and create a sense of individual responsibility for the actions of the collective. Where there is an objection, the objector's premise is reflective of the terms of the peace accord. Thus, the objector's aim is to ensure that all parties adhere to rules of engagement and, hence, to promote the interests of the collective and prevent situations whereby what was publicly agreed and formalized is secretly disrupted and de-formalized. Put another way, the goal of a PMB is to eliminate the possibilities of win–lose competition and lose–lose attrition. Through the synthesis of all possible options based on actor/audience consent, a Kantian liberal peace—whose central guiding principle is 'political accommodation' (Doyle 2005)—takes root. It is against this backdrop that we agree with Lawrence Butler and Amy Rothstein's argument that

> consensus process ... creates a cooperative dynamic. Only one proposal is considered at a time. Everyone works together to make it the best possible decision for the group. Any concerns are raised and resolved, sometimes one by one, until all voices are heard. Since proposals are no longer the property of the presenter, a solution can be created more cooperatively.
>
> (Butler and Rothstein 1987, 5)

Besides the positive impact of PMB on the number of deaths, we also discovered that the signing of peace accords significantly drives down battle-related deaths in the years *after* those accords come into force. The analysis shows that in the years after peace accords are signed, battle-related deaths tend to be 228 fewer than when they were signed.

Interestingly, we discovered that the dominant religion of a country also plays a significant role in affecting battle-related deaths. In periods of conflict, the number of battle-related deaths in predominantly Muslim countries tend to be 581 more than those recorded in Christian-dominated countries. Moreover, the sub-regional component of the analysis indicates that battles fought in eastern and southern Africa recorded about 585 more deaths than those experienced in the western part of the African continent.

Notwithstanding the above discussion, some of the conflict de-escalation words have counter-intuitive results. Specifically, rehabilitation, disarmament and economic reforms were all seen to have a positive relationship with battle-related deaths. There are several possible explanations for this. In relation to the issue of rehabilitation, there is less focus on the mental rehabilitation of

Table 4.5 Pooled OLS regression for the effect of conflict de-escalation words on battle related deaths

Battle-related deaths	*Best measure*	*Low measure*	*High measure*
	Pooled OLS	*Pooled OLS*	*Pooled OLS*
Conflict de-escalation words			
Reconciliation	69.522*	70.219*	35.657
	(37.621)	(37.592)	(85.051)
Reconciliation squared	−0.993***	−0.971***	−1.247***
	(0.196)	(0.193)	(0.392)
Peace	−33.164**	−33.222**	−49.386
	(16.478)	(16.704)	(32.823)
Rehabilitation	242.803***	226.363***	463.603***
	(49.667)	(48.468)	(80.050)
Disarmament	140.728*	134.734	296.359*
	(81.441)	(81.317)	(157.298)
Demobilization	−64.625	−48.088	−135.625*
	(42.273)	(40.428)	(80.067)
Economic reform	139.341***	126.640**	194.074**
	(51.107)	(49.196)	(97.544)
Power sharing	−36.892***	−35.211***	−8.061
	(11.465)	(11.521)	(19.903)
Peace monitoring bodies	−228.176***	−210.729***	−382.232***
	(53.917)	(50.486)	(88.875)
Peace accords (previous year)	−369.305*	−349.370*	−445.285
	(214.199)	(200.185)	(376.194)
Election year (Yes = 1; No = 0)	295.102	291.570	246.383
	(346.872)	(346.987)	(556.253)
Dominant religion (Christian = 1; Islam = 0)	−581.151*	−625.004**	−882.423*
	(337.824)	(311.059)	(524.718)
International interest (Yes = 1; No = 0)	284.557	211.803	854.832**
	(180.902)	(185.163)	(387.418)
Dominant natural resource (Base = oil)			
Gold/copper/diamond/bauxite	−280.841	−238.319	−746.467
	(262.000)	(249.997)	(469.081)

continued

Table 4.5 continued

Battle-related deaths	*Best measure*	*Low measure*	*High measure*
	Pooled OLS	*Pooled OLS*	*Pooled OLS*
Tantalum/uranium/tin ore	2.092	–219.131	318.744
	(439.045)	(397.891)	(682.920)
Timber/cocoa	–322.314	–329.228	–524.500
	(281.654)	(265.242)	(471.397)
Sub-region (Base = West Africa)			
Eastern/Southern Africa	584.921**	588.228***	948.872***
	(226.930)	(215.175)	(351.671)
Central Africa	–471.666	–468.936	–268.683
	(289.084)	(286.123)	(634.138)
Constant	869.824***	867.795***	1,340.587***
	(260.440)	(256.790)	(403.223)
Observations	144	144	144
R-squared	0.245	0.262	0.224
Number of country	—	—	—
Breusch-Pagan LM (Prob > chibar2)	—	—	—
Link test (P>|t|)			
_hat	0.030	0.024	0.043
_hatsq	0.237	0.205	0.132

Notes
***$p<0.01$;
**$p<0.05$;
*$p<0.1$.
Robust standard errors in parentheses.

combatants and their victims before the closure of reintegration processes. Several studies have shown that failure to focus on the mental health of combatants, and the trauma of victims of war, has an impact on the level of community violence, leading to resentment and killings (Pedersen 2002; Miller 2009; Miller and Rasmussen 2010; Mollica et al. 2004; Betancourt et al. 2011). This is especially true where the disarmament process has not been transparent and rebel leaders and government politicians do not trust the process.

On the relationship between economic reforms and battle-related deaths, economic analysis of the foundations of armed conflict, while having a lengthy history (see, e.g., Lane 1958; Schelling 1960; Silver 1974) has made substantial advances through the works of Garfinkel and Skaperdas (1996), Hirshleifer (2001), Collier (2000), Collier and Hoeffler (2004), and Ballentine and Sherman (2003). These studies have concluded that, because resolution of conflicts is about fighting against the power arrangements of the economic spoilers of peace (who stand to benefit from the political economy of conflict), mediators are often positioned in the narratives of those opposed to the signing of peace accords as people or institutions that lack local legitimacy. The aim is to persuade the oppressed communities and their enemies to seek allies and form militant organizations for the purpose of using conflict to correct perceived micro-financial and economic injustices (see Gates 2002) that mediators may have either trivialized or excluded from the list of core issues during negotiations (Kaplow 2015).

Summary and recommendation

In this pioneering chapter we have shown that, whereas the escalation of conflicts has substantial social, cultural, economic and political consequences for 'resources' (lootable wealth and political agendas) at risk of being appropriated by the contending factions (see, e.g., Lacomba et al. 2014; Skaperdas 1991; Hirshleifer 1988; Ke, Konrad and Morath 2013), the de-escalation of conflict through the mainstreaming of multiple CDWs (above the 35 threshold) to reduce battle-related deaths is essentially a benign choice to stop fighting, on the one hand; and, on the other, to achieve win–win outcomes during and after the conclusion of negotiations. In this way, conflict de-escalation words offer state/non-state actors the opportunity to cooperate. This cooperation (an outcome of the typology of behavioral language frames employed by the mediators and included in the final peace accords) can also take the form of conditional or unconditional reciprocation—first, to the opponent's act of conciliatory language (an example of a change from belligerent posture to peaceful behavior); and, second, to the resilient actions of 'forgiving'; 'reconciling'; and 'moving on,' which spur the other party (or parties) to reciprocate. Of course, those drawing from game theory may argue otherwise. Their understanding is that "people should not be unconditionally cooperative because such [behavior], in game theory research, encourages exploitive strategies" of "egocentric beholders" of defensive and offensive postures of war (Hale 1998, 160).

We also find that including words that connote peace, and that call for power sharing, can significantly drive down the number of battle-related deaths. This is mainly because such words soften the stands of belligerent forces and prompt them to embrace peaceful coexistence. Contrary to the hawkish argument that positions the 'personhood' (identity) and 'knowing' (worldviews and epistemic narratives of 'self') of the political 'man' as naturally competitive and egoistically violent, we infer the opposite—namely, that the capacity to reconcile outweighs the desire for non-reconciliation. Thus, we suggest (by way of a recommendation) that where there is a focus shift from the irreconcilable "wants" (the root cause) of the warring factions to the reconcilable "needs" (the driver of altruistic 'peace-lovingness') of the civilian populations, the choice to adopt more CDWs ultimately creates opportunities to reduce battle-related deaths. It is against this backdrop that we contend that behavioral language frames (of peace and reconciliation) offer rebel factions, the state and the people a path to achieve their goals in a nonviolent or less violent way, Even where these goals do not lead to a Galtungian 'positive peace,' they will at least result in fewer battle-related deaths.

Table A4.1 Pooled OLS regression for the effect of conflict de-escalation words on battle related deaths

	Best measure		*Low measure*		*High measure*	
Battle-related deaths	*Pooled*	*Random effects*	*Pooled*	*Random effects*	*Pooled*	*Random effects*
Conflict de-escalation words						
Reconciliation	69.522*	69.522**	70.219*	70.219**	35.657	35.657
	(37.621)	(27.940)	(37.592)	(32.308)	(85.051)	(66.455)
Reconciliation squared	–0.993***	–0.993***	–0.971***	–0.971***	–1.247***	–1.247***
	(0.196)	(0.208)	(0.193)	(0.220)	(0.392)	(0.413)
Peace	–33.164**	–33.164**	–33.222**	–33.222**	–49.386	–49.386*
	(16.478)	(14.802)	(16.704)	(14.480)	(32.823)	(27.081)
Rehabilitation	242.803***	242.803***	226.363***	226.363***	463.603***	463.603***
	(49.667)	(39.456)	(48.468)	(38.134)	(80.050)	(72.876)
Disarmament	140.728*	140.728*	134.734	134.734*	296.359*	296.359*
	(81.441)	(82.918)	(81.317)	(80.215)	(157.298)	(151.270)
Demobilization	–64.625	–64.625	–48.088	–48.088	–135.625*	–135.625
	(42.273)	(47.966)	(40.428)	(49.761)	(80.067)	(95.959)
Economic reform	139.341***	139.341***	126.640**	126.640**	194.074**	194.074**
	(51.107)	(52.917)	(49.196)	(49.818)	(97.544)	(96.281)
Power sharing	–36.892***	–36.892***	–35.211***	–35.211***	–8.061	–8.061
	(11.465)	(9.194)	(11.521)	(11.288)	(19.903)	(15.668)
Peace monitoring bodies	–228.176***	–228.176***	–210.729***	–210.729***	–382.232***	–382.232***
	(53.917)	(45.403)	(50.486)	(42.090)	(88.875)	(89.565)
Peace accords (previous year)	–369.305*	–369.305	–349.370*	–349.370	–445.285	–445.285
	(214.199)	(263.224)	(200.185)	(244.374)	(376.194)	(499.203)
Election year (Yes = 1; No = 0)	295.102	295.102	291.570	291.570	246.383	246.383
	(346.872)	(285.245)	(346.987)	(282.553)	(556.253)	(426.250)
Dominant religion (Christian = 1; Islam = 0)	–581.151*	–581.151***	–625.004**	–625.004***	–882.423*	–882.423***
	(337.824)	(121.166)	(311.059)	(97.640)	(524.718)	(289.530)
International interest (Yes = 1; No = 0)	284.557	284.557	211.803	211.803	854.832**	854.832
	(180.902)	(235.657)	(185.163)	(208.106)	(387.418)	(568.712)

Dominant natural resource (Base = oil)						
Gold/copper/diamond/bauxite	–280.841	–280.841*	–238.319	–238.319	–746.467	–746.467**
	(262.000)	(159.121)	(249.997)	(151.175)	(469.081)	(302.937)
Tantalum/uranium/tin ore	2.092	2.092	–219.131	–219.131*	318.744	318.744
	(439.045)	(163.515)	(397.891)	(114.011)	(682.920)	(463.260)
Timber/cocoa	–322.314	–322.314**	–329.228	–329.228***	–524.500	–524.500**
	(281.654)	(137.182)	(265.242)	(125.568)	(471.397)	(255.503)
Sub-region (Base = West Africa)						
Eastern/Southern Africa	584.921**	584.921**	588.228***	588.228**	948.872***	948.872**
	(226.930)	(244.768)	(215.175)	(238.096)	(351.671)	(408.880)
Central Africa	–471.666	–471.666	–468.936	–468.936*	–268.683	–268.683
	(289.084)	(287.058)	(286.123)	(284.492)	(634.138)	(439.985)
Constant	869.824***	869.824***	867.795***	867.795***	1,340.587***	1,340.587***
	(260.440)	(302.196)	(256.790)	(295.426)	(403.223)	(474.334)
Observations	144	144	144	144	144	144
R-squared	0.245	0.245	0.262	0.262	0.224	0.224
Number of country	—	13	—	13	—	13
Breusch-Pagan LM (Prob > chibar2)	—	1.000	—	1.000	—	1.000
Link test ($P>\|t\|$)						
_hat	0.030	—	0.024	—	0.043	—
_hatsq	0.237	—	0.205	—	0.132	—

Notes
*** $p<0.01$;
** $p<0.05$;
* $p<0.1$.
Robust standard errors in parentheses.

Table A4.2 Variables, sources and comments on conflict de-escalating words

Variable	*Comment*	*Sources*
Conflict de-escalation words *Reconciliation, peace, rehabilitation, disarmament, demobilization, economic reform, power sharing, and peace monitoring bodies).*	We took all the conflict de-escalating words from the peace accords signed between the governments and rebel factions in 13 countries between the years 1990 and 2003. Below is the list of the peace accords for each country: Angola • *The Bicesse Accord (signed in 1991)* • *The Lusaka Protocol (signed in 1994)* • *Luanda Tripatite Protocol (signed in 1999)* • *The Memorandum of Understanding (Luena Agreement) (signed in 2002)* Burundi • *The Arusha Peace and Reconciliation Agreement for Burundi (signed in 2000)* Chad • *Peace Agreement between the Government of the Republic of Chad and the Movement for Democracy and Justice in Chad (MDJT) (signed in 2002)* • *Peace Agreement Between the Government of Chad and the Mouvement pour ka democratie* et al. *justice au Tchad (MDJT) (signed in 2003)* Ivory Coast • *Linas-Marcoussis Agreement (signed in 2003)* Liberia • *Joint Statement of the Warring Parties (INPFL, NPFL, AFL); otherwise known as Banjul IV Agreement (signed in 1990)* • *Lome Agreement (signed in 1991)* • *Yamoussoukro I peace accord (or the Outcome of Deliberations of the Meeting held in Yamoussoukro) (signed in 1991)*	For the whole of sub-Saharan Africa, the peace accords can be accessed from the website of the UN Peacemaker.Org, https://peacemaker.un.org/somalia-implementingdisarmament93 For the West African Region, the list of the peace accords, decisions and protocols is also available here: *Compendium of ECOWAS Peace and Security Decisions: Protocols, Declarations and Peace Agreements* (compiled by: Emmanuel Kwesi Aning, Emma Birikorang, and Thomas Jaye); published by the Kofi Annan International Peacekeeping Training Centre (KAIPTC) (in collaboration with the German Development Cooperation with support from the Training for Peace Programme). Link: https://drive.google.com/file/d/0B40UDxMwk8FASmRwZEVJM1F2RFU/view For the English translated copies of the peace accords of Francophone sub-Saharan Africa, see the *Uppsala Conflict Data program (UCDP)* website: http://ucdp.uu.se/downloads/

	• *Yamoussoukro II (or the Final Communique of The First Meeting of The Committee of Five on Liberia, Yamoussoukro) (signed in 1991)* • *Yamoussoukro III (signed in 1991)* • *Yamoussoukro IV (or the Final Communiqué of the Fourth Meeting of the Committee of Five of the Economic Community of West African States on the Liberian crisis) (signed in 1991)* • *Agreement on Ceasefire and Cessation of Hostilities Between the Government of the Republic of Liberia and Liberians United for Reconciliation and Democracy and the Movement for Democracy in Liberia (signed in 2003)* • *Comprehensive Peace Agreement Between the Government of Liberia and the Liberians United for Reconciliation and Democracy (LURD) and the Movement for Democracy in Liberia (MODEL) and Political Parties (signed in 2003)*	
Conflict de-escalation words *Reconciliation, peace,rehabilitation, disarmament,demobilization,economic reform,power sharing andpeace monitoring bodies).*	Mozambique • *Joint Communique (signed in 1990)* • *Declaration by the Government of the Republic of Mozambique and RENAMO on the guiding principles for humanitarian assistance (signed in 1992)* • *Joint Declaration (signed in 1992)* • *General Peace Agreement for Mozambique (signed in 1992)* Niger • *Ouagadougou Accord Joint Communiqué (Accord de paix entre le Gouvernement de la Republique du Niger et la Coordination de la Resistance Armee (CRA) (signed in 1994)* • *Agreement Establishing Permanent Peace Between the Government of The Republic Of Niger And The "Organisation De La Résistance Armée (O. R. A.)" (Organisation of the Armed Resistance Ora) (signed in 1995)*	For the whole of sub-Saharan Africa, the peace accords can be accessed from the website of the UN Peacemaker.Org,https://peacemaker.un.org/somalia-implementingdisarmament93 For the West African Region, the list of the peace accords, decisions and protocols is also available here:*Compendium of ECOWAS Peace and Security Decisions: Protocols, Declarations and Peace Agreements* (compiled by: Emmanuel Kwesi Aning, Emma Birikorang, and Thomas Jaye); published by the Kofi Annan International Peacekeeping Training Centre (KAIPTC) (in collaboration with the German Development Cooperation with support from the Training for Peace Programme). Link: https://drive.google.com/file/d/0B40UDxMwk8FASmRwZEVJM1F2RFU/view

continued

Table A4.2 continued

Variable	*Comment*	*Sources*
	Rwanda • *Arusha Accord (Peace Agreement between the Government of the Republic of Rwanda and the Rwandese Patriotic Front) (signed in 1993)* Sierra Leone • *The Abidjan Peace Agreement between the Government of the Republic of Sierra Leone and the Revolutionary United Front of Sierra Leone (signed in 1996)* • *Conakry Peace-Plan (the Economic Community of West African States six-month peace plan for Sierra Leone) (signed in 1997)* • *Lome Peace Accord (Peace Agreement Between the Government of Sierra Leone and the Revolutionary United Front of Sierra Leone (RUF) (signed in 1999)* Somalia • *The General Agreement (signed in 1993)* • *The Agreement on implementing the cease-fire and modalities of disarmament (signed in 1993)* • *Agreement on the Establishment of an* Ad hoc *Committee (signed in 1993)* • *Declaration by the Leaders of the Somali Political Organizations (signed in 1994)*	For the English translated copies of the peace accords of Francophone sub-Saharan Africa, see the *Uppsala Conflict Data program (UCDP)* website: http://ucdp.uu.se/downloads/
Conflict de-escalation words *Reconciliation, peace,rehabilitation, disarmament,demob ilization,economic reform,power sharing, andpeace monitoring bodies).*	Sudan (Darfur Conflict) • *Humanitarian Ceasefire Agreement on the Conflict in Darfur (signed in 2004)* • *Agreement with the Sudanese Parties on the Modalities for the Establishment of the Ceasefire Commission and the Deployment of observers in the Darfur (signed in 2004)* • *Protocol between the Government of Sudan, SLM/A and the JEM on the improvement of the Humanitarian Situation in Darfur (signed in 2004)*	

- *Protocol between the Government of the Sudan, SLM/A and JEM on the Enhancement of the Security Situation in Darfur in accordance with the N'Djamena Agreement (signed in 2004)*
- *Framework Agreement to Resolve the Conflict in Darfur between the Government of Sudan and the JEM (signed in 2010)*

Sudan (South Sudan's War for Independence)

- *Agreement between the Government of Sudan, the Sudan Liberation Movement (LSM), and the Justice and Equality Movement (JEM) (signed in 2004)*
- *Protocol between the Government of the Sudan and the Sudan People's Liberation Movement (SPLM) on Power Sharing (signed in 2004)*
- *Protocol between the Government of Sudan (GoS) and the People's Liberation Movement (SPLM) on the Resolution of Abyei Conflict (signed in 2004)*
- *Protocol between the Government of Sudan (GoS) and the Sudan People's Liberation Movement (SPLM) on the Resolution of Conflict in Southern Kordofan/Nuba Mountains and Blue Nile States (signed in 2004)*
- *Nairobi Declaration on the Final Phase of Peace in the Sudan (signed in 2004)*
- *Declaration on the Conclusion of IGAD Negotiations on Peace in the Sudan (signed in 2004)*
- *Permanent Ceasefire between the Government of the Republic of the Sudan (GoS) and the Sudan People's Liberation Movement/Army (SPLM/A) (signed in 2004)*
- *Juba Declaration on Dialogue and National Consensus (signed in 2009)*

Uganda

- *Ceasefire Agreement between the Government of the Republic of Uganda and the Uganda National Rescue Front I (signed in 2002)*
- *The Yumbe Peace Agreement (the Peace Agreement between the Government of the Republic of Uganda and the Uganda National Rescue Front II) (signed in 2002)*

Table A4.3 Names and sources of (and comments on) the dummy variables (cross-referenced in Table 4.3—Definitions and sources of variables)

Variable	*Definition/type*	*Source*	*Additional comment*
Peace accord signed previous year	Dummy variable	For the whole of sub-Saharan Africa, the peace accords can be accessed from the website of the UN Peacemaker.Org, https://peacemaker.un.org/somalia-implementingdisarmament93	
Election year	Dummy variable	African Elections Database: http://africanelections.tripod.com/	By election year, our focus is on multi-party elections. We did not take into consideration the contentious question of whether the electoral process was free and fair. Rather we limited it only to 'elections.' As to who conducted the elections, our analysis accommodates the multiparty elections conducted by either the governments or the international community (specifically, the UN and regional security bodies).
Dominant religion	Dummy variable	The Pew Research Center's Forum on Religion and Public Life www.pewforum.org/interactives/africa/	This interactive database—of the Pew Research Centre on religion—allows users to explore public opinion in 19 sub-Saharan African nations on topics ranging from religious beliefs and practices to views on religious extremism and morality. The findings come from more than 25,000 face-to-face interviews in more than 60 languages or dialects in 19 countries, representing 75% of the total population of sub-Saharan Africa.
International interest in conflict	Dummy variable	UCDP Battle-related deaths dataset Pettersson, Therése and Kristine Eck. 2018. Organized violence, 1989–2017. *Journal of Peace Research*, vol. 55, no. 4, 535–547	In UCDP's observation, 3 represents internal conflict (between the government and rebel groups) with no involvement of the troops of foreign governments. 4 represents internationalized conflicts with either party (government or rebels) supported by foreign interests. See page 4 www.ucdp.uu.se/downloads/brd/ucdp-brd-172.pdf

Dominant resource	Categorical variable	Geopolitical Features website https://geopoliticalfutures.com/sub-saharan-africa-natural-resource-deposits/	We observe here that, sub-Sahara Africa's natural resource deposits are a key feature that tie the region into mainstream geopolitics (including the trends in civil wars and battle-related deaths). According to the developers of the Geopolitical Features data, "countries in the region have historically depended highly on export of raw materials, which fuelled economic growth in industrialized economies. This strong dependence on the sale of natural resources has also made many Sub-Sahara African countries very susceptible to the exporters' crisis (for more on the victims and vulnerable countries affected by this exporters' curse, see https://geopoliticalfutures.com/the-export-crisis-the-10-worst-hit-countries-and-the-5-most-at-risk/)—both in terms of falling commodity prices and lower demand from major customers like China. Nigeria's oil and gas sector accounts for about 35 percent of GDP, while hydrocarbons account for about 45 percent of Angola's GDP. Oil and petrol account for 90–95 percent of exports in both countries. The price of other commodities, including gold, iron ore, platinum and copper, has remained low." They also observe that, the production of "these materials figure prominently in the GDPs of South Africa, the Democratic Republic of the Congo (DRC), Zimbabwe, Zambia and Mozambique."
Sub-regional location of country	Categorical variable	Gleditsch, Nils Petter; Peter Wallensteen; Mikael Eriksson: Margareta Sollenberg and Håvard Strand, 2002. "Armed Conflict 1946–2002, A New Dataset", *Journal of Peace Research*, vol. 39, no. 5, pp. 615–637.	This dataset's identification of civil wars with international dimensions also borrows from Gleditsch and Ward system membership table (see page 2) http://ucdp.uu.se/downloads/peace/ucdp-codebook-peace-agreements.pdf In relation to the identification of the region (and countries) of the location. The following regions are given in the original UCDP-PRIO Armed Conflict Dataset: Europe (1), Middle East (2), Asia (3), Africa (4), and the Americas (5). After cleaning the data (by eliminating the non-sub-Saharan African regions and countries) we use the interactive maps of Google to locate the sub-regions where each of the 13 country case studies is located within sub-Saharan Africa. We cross-checked our categorization with World Bank's database and list of sub-Saharan African countries (https://data.worldbank.org/region/sub-saharan-africa) before concluding our categorization.

Appendix 4: Calculation of the reconciliation words threshold

$$\frac{dBRD}{dRcon} = \sigma_i + 2\sigma_i Rcon = 0$$

$$69.522 + 2(-0.993)Rcon = 0$$

$$1.986Rcon = 69.522$$

$$Rcon = \frac{69.522}{1.986} = 35.006$$

where *BRD* = battle-related deaths; *Rcon* = Reconciliation words

Notes

1 With the exception of Somalia, which, at the time, had no functional government as a result of the fighting between the forces of Fareer Aideed and Ali Mahdi.
2 For more on this, see www.sadc.int/sadc-secretariat/directorates/office-executive-secretary/organ-politics-defense-and-security/ (accessed July 28, 2018).

References

Asteriou, Dimitrios, and S. G. Hall. 2011. *Applied Econometrics: A Modern Approach Using Eviews and Microfit*. Basingstoke, UK: Palgrave Macmillan.

Bagge Laustsen, Carsten, and Ole Waever. 2000. "In Defence of Religion: Sacred Referent Objects for Securitization." *Millennium* 29 (3): 705–739.

Ballentine, Karen, and Jake Sherman, eds. 2003. *The Political Economy of Armed Conflict: Beyond Greed and Grievance*. Boulder, CO: Lynne Rienner Publishers.

Baltagi, Badi. 2008. *Econometric Analysis of Panel Data*. Chichester, UK: John Wiley & Sons.

Balzacq, Thierry. 2005. "The Three Faces of Securitization: Political Agency, Audience and Context." *European Journal of International Relations* 11 (2): 171–201.

Balzacq, Thierry. 2010. "Enquiries into Methods: A New Framework for Securitization Analysis." In *Securitization Theory: How Security Problems Emerge and Dissolve*, edited by Thierry Balzacq, 45–68. Abingdon, UK: Routledge.

Balzacq, Thierry. ed. 2011. *Securitization Theory: How Security Problems Emerge and Dissolve*. Abingdon, UK: Routledge.

Bartlett, F. C. 1932. *A Theory of Remembering: A Study in Experimental and Social Psychology*. Cambridge, UK: Cambridge University Press.

Behrend, Heike. 1999. "Power to Heal, Power to Kill. Spirit Possession and War in Northern Uganda (1986–1994)." In *Spirit Possession, Modernity, and Power in Africa*, edited by Ute Luig and Heike Behrend, 20–33. Madison, WI: University of Wisconsin Press.

Bellamy, Alex J. and Ruben Reike. 2010. "The Responsibility to Protect and International Law." *Global Responsibility to Protect* 2 (3): 267–286.

Betancourt, Theresa S., Ivelina I. Borisova, Marie De la Soudiere, and John Williamson. 2011. "Sierra Leone's Child Soldiers: War Exposures and Mental Health Problems by Gender." *Journal of Adolescent Health* 49 (1): 21–28.

Bleiker, Roland, and Emma Hutchison. 2008. "Fear No More: Emotions and World Politics." *Review of International Studies* 34 (S1): 115–135.

Cameron, Adrian Colin, and Pravin K. Trivedi. 2010. "Microeconometrics Using Stata." www.stata.com/stata-news/statanews.23.4.pdf.

Chime, Chimelu. 1977. *Integration and Politics among African States: Limitations and Horizons of Mid-Term Theorizing*. Uppsala: The Scandinavian Institute of African Studies.

Chomsky, Noam. 1957. *Syntactic Structure*. The Hague: Mounton Publishers. www.linguist.univ-paris-diderot.fr/~edunbar/ling499b_spr12/readings/syntactic_structures.pdf.

Cockburn, Cynthia. 2010. "Gender Relations as Causal in Militarization and War." *International Feminist Journal of Politics* 12 (2): 139–157.

Collier, Paul. 2000. "Rebellion as a Quasi-Criminal Activity." *Journal of Conflict Resolution* 44 (6): 839–853.

Collier, Paul, and Anke Hoeffler. 2004. "Greed and Grievance in Civil War." *Oxford Economic Papers* 56 (4): 563–595.

Crawford, Neta C. 2000. "The Passion of World Politics: Propositions on Emotion and Emotional Relationships." *International Security* 24 (4): 116–156.

Deleuze, Gilles, and Michel Foucault. 1977. "Intellectuals and Power." In *Language, Counter-Memory, Practice: Selected Essays and Interviews*, edited by D. F. Bouchard, 205–17. Ithaca, NY: Cornell University Press.

Downes, William. 1998. *Language and Society*. Cambridge, UK: Cambridge University Press.

Doyle, Michael W. 2005. "Three Pillars of the Liberal Peace." *American Political Science Review* 99 (3): 463–466.

Dugdale, Eric, and Loramy Gerstbauer. 2017. "Forms of Justice in Aeschylus' Eumenides." *Polis: The Journal for Ancient Greek Political Thought* 34 (2): 226–250.

Fillmore, Charles J. 1976. "Frame Semantics and the Nature of Language." *Annals of the New York Academy of Sciences* 280 (1): 20–32.

Fisher, Kathryn Marie. 2015. *Security, Identity, and British Counterterrorism Policy*. Basingstoke, UK: Palgrave Macmillan.

Floyd, Rita. 2011. "Can Securitization Theory Be Used in Normative Analysis? Towards a Just Securitization Theory." *Security Dialogue* 42 (4–5): 427–439.

Floyd, Rita. 2016. "Extraordinary or Ordinary Emergency Measures: What, and Who, Defines the 'Success' of Securitization?" *Cambridge Review of International Affairs* 29 (2): 677–694.

Foucault, Michel. 2005. "The Discourse on Language: From 'Truth and Power.'" In *Truth: Engagements across Philosophical Traditions*, edited by José Medina and Wood, 315–335. Malden, MA: Blackwell Publishing.

Franke, Benedikt. 2009. *Security Cooperation in Africa: A Reappraisal*. Boulder, CO: FirstForumPress.

Galtung, Johan. 1987. "Language and War: Is There a Connection?" *Current Research on Peace and Violence* 10 (1): 2–6.

Gamson, William A. and Andre Modigliani. 1987. "The Changing Culture of Affirmative Action." In *Research in Political Sociology*, edited by Richard G. Braungart and Margaret M. Braungart, 137–77. Greenwich, CT: Jai Press.

Garfinkel, Michelle R. and Stergios Skaperdas, eds. 1996. *The Political Economy of Conflict and Appropriation*. Cambridge, UK: Cambridge University Press.

Gates, Scott. 2002. "Recruitment and Allegiance: The Microfoundations of Rebellion." *Journal of Conflict Resolution* 46 (1): 111–130.

Gimenez-Salinas, Andrea. 2004. "New Approaches Regarding Private/Public Security." *Policing and Society* 14 (2): 158–174.

Gledhill, John. 2008. "Anthropology in the Age of Securitization." *Annual Joel S. Kahn Lecture, Latrobe University*. Melbourne. Australia. http://jg.socialsciences.manchester.ac.uk/Conferences/Anthropology%20in%20the%20Age%20of%20Securitization.pdf.

Goffman, Erving. 1974. *Frame Analysis: An Essay on the Organization of Experience*. Cambridge, MA: Harvard University Press.

Goldstein, Daniel M. 2016. "Some Thoughts on the Critical Anthropology of Security." *Etnofoor, Humour* 28 (1): 147–152.

Goodenough, Ward Hunt. 1981. *Culture, Language, and Society*. Menlo Park, CA: Benjamin-Cummings Publishing Company.

Hale, Katherine. 1998. "The Language of Cooperation: Negotiation Frames." *Mediation Quarterly* 16 (2): 147–162.

Hansen, Lene. 2011. "Theorizing the Image for Security Studies: Visual Securitization and the Muhammad Cartoon Crisis." *European Journal of International Relations* 17 (1): 51–74.

Hirshleifer, Jack. 1988. "The Analytics of Continuing Conflict." *Synthese* 76 (2): 201–233.

Hirshleifer, Jack. 2001. *The Dark Side of the Force: Economic Foundations of Conflict Theory*. Cambridge, UK: Cambridge University Press.

Holbraad, Martin, and Morten Axel Pedersen, eds. 2013. *Times of Security: Ethnographies of Fear, Protest and the Future*. New York, NY: Routledge.

Holdcroft, David. 1991. *Saussure: Signs, System and Arbitrariness*. Cambridge, UK: Cambridge University Press.

Howard, Steve. 2012. "Towards Researching Peace." *African Conflict & Peacebuilding Review* 2 (2): 1–4.

Huysmans, Jef. 2011. "What's in an Act? On Security Speech Acts and Little Security Nothings." *Security Dialogue* 42 (4–5): 371–383.

Jacobsen, Michael Hviid, and Soren Kristiansen. 2015. *The Social Thought of Erving Goffman*. Thousand Oaks, CA: Sage Publications.

Johnston, Hank, and Pamela E. Oliver. 2000. "What a Good Idea! Frames and Ideologies in Social Movement Research." *Mobilization: An International Quarterly* 5 (1): 37–54.

Kaplow, Jeffrey M. 2015. "The Negotiation Calculus: Why Parties to Civil Conflict Refuse to Talk." *International Studies Quarterly* 60 (1): 38–46.

Ke, Changxia, Kai A. Konrad, and Florian Morath. 2013. "Brothers in Arms: An Experiment on the Alliance Puzzle." *Games and Economic Behavior* 77 (1): 61–76.

Kelsall, Tim. 2005. "Truth, Lies, Ritual: Preliminary Reflections on the Truth and Reconciliation Commission in Sierra Leone." *Human Rights Quarterly* 27 (2): 361–391.

Keskinen, Suvi. 2017. "Securitized Intimacies, Welfare State and the 'Other' Family." *Social Politics: International Studies in Gender, State & Society* 24 (2): 154–177.

Lacomba, Juan A., Francisco Lagos, Ernesto Reuben, and Frans van Winden. 2014. "On the Escalation and De-Escalation of Conflict." *Games and Economic Behavior* 86: 40–57.

Lakoff, George. 2016. "Language and Emotion." *Emotion Review* 8 (3): 269–273.

Lane, Frederic C. 1958. "Economic Consequences of Organized Violence." *The Journal of Economic History* 18 (4): 401–417.

Lawrence Butler, C. T. and Amy Rothstein. 1987. *On Conflict and Consensus: A Handbook on Formal Consensus Decisionmaking*. Portland, ME: Food Not Bombs Publishing.

Léonard, Sarah, and Christian Kaunert. 2011. "Reconceptualizing the Audience in Securitization Theory." In *Securitization Theory: How Security Problems Emerge and Dissolve*, edited by Thierry Balzacq, 57–76. Abingdon, UK: Routledge.

Lindquist, Kristen A. and Maria Gendron. 2013. "What's in a Word? Language Constructs Emotion Perception." *Emotion Review* 5 (1): 66–71.

Makoa, Francis K. 2005. "Managing Conflict in an Integrating Southern Africa: Peace, Security and Stability in Lieu of Democracy?" *Monitoring Regional Integration in Southern Africa Yearbook* 5 (1): 1–25.

McNay, Lois. 2013. *Foucault and Feminism: Power, Gender and the Self.* Cambridge, UK: Polity Press.

Mercer, Jonathan. 2006. "Human Nature and the First Image: Emotion in International Politics." *Journal of International Relations and Development* 9 (3): 288–303.

Miller, Kenneth E. and Andrew Rasmussen. 2010. "War Exposure, Daily Stressors, and Mental Health in Conflict and Post-Conflict Settings: Bridging the Divide between Trauma-Focused and Psychosocial Frameworks." *Social Science & Medicine* 70 (1): 7–16.

Miller, Sarah Clark. 2009. "Moral Injury and Relational Harm: Analyzing Rape in Darfur." *Journal of Social Philosophy* 40 (4): 504–523.

Mollica, Richard F., B. Lopes Cardozo, Howard J. Osofsky, Beverley Raphael, Alastair Ager, and Peter Salama. 2004. "Mental Health in Complex Emergencies." *The Lancet* 364 (9450): 2058–2067.

Montgomery, Martin. 2008. *An Introduction to Language and Society*. London, UK: Routledge.

Nelson, Thomas E., Rosalee A. Clawson, and Zoe M. Oxley. 1997. "Media Framing of a Civil Liberties Conflict and Its Effect on Tolerance." *American Political Science Review* 91 (3): 567–583.

Nguyen, Minh Cong. 2010. "XTSUR: Stata Module to Estimate Seemingly Unrelated Regression Model on Unbalanced Panel Data." *Statistical Software Components*. https://ideas.repec.org/c/boc/bocode/s456953.html.

Odobo, Samuel Osagie, Amos Musa Andekin, and Kingsley Udegbunam. 2017. "Analysis of ECOWAS Institutional Framework for Conflict Management." *Mediterranean Journal of Social Sciences* 8 (6): 143–153.

Ong, Walter J. 1979. "Literacy and Orality in Our Times." *Profession*, 1–7.

Ong, Walter J. 1982. *Orality and Literacy: The Technologizing of the Word.* London, UK: Methuen & Co. Ltd.

Ong, Walter J. 2015. *Orality and Literacy*. Abingdon, UK: Routledge.

Park, Augustine SJ. 2010. "Community-Based Restorative Transitional Justice in Sierra Leone." *Contemporary Justice Review* 13 (1): 95–119.

Pedersen, Duncan. 2002. "Political Violence, Ethnic Conflict, and Contemporary Wars: Broad Implications for Health and Social Well-Being." *Social Science & Medicine* 55 (2): 175–190.

Pfeiffer, James. 2005. "Commodity *Fetichismo*, the Holy Spirit, and the Turn to Pentecostal and African Independent Churches in Central Mozambique." *Culture, Medicine and Psychiatry* 29 (3): 255–283.

Pruitt, Dean G. 2007. "Readiness Theory and the Northern Ireland Conflict." *American Behavioral Scientist* 50 (11): 1520–1541.

Putnik, Nenad, and Mladen Milošević. 2018. "Trends in Peace Research: Can Cyber Détente Lead to Lasting Peace?" In *Handbook of Research on Examining Global Peacemaking in the Digital Age*, edited by Bruce L. Cook, 1–18. Hershey, PA: IGI Global.

Romaine, Suzanne. 2000. *Language in Society: An Introduction to Sociolinguistics*. Oxford, UK: Oxford University Press.

Salter, Mark B. 2008. "Securitization and Desecuritization: A Dramaturgical Analysis of the Canadian Air Transport Security Authority." *Journal of International Relations and Development* 11 (4): 321–349.

Sampson, Geoffrey. 1980. *Schools of Linguistics: Competition and Evolution*. London, UK: Hutchinson & Co Ltd.

Schelling, Thomas C. 1960. *The Strategy of Conflict*. New York, NY: Oxford University Press.

Silver, Morris. 1974. "Political Revolution and Repression: An Economic Approach." *Public Choice* 17 (1): 63–71.

Skaperdas, Stergios. 1991. "Conflict and Attitudes toward Risk." *The American Economic Review* 81 (2): 116–120.

Stritzel, Holger. 2007. "Towards a Theory of Securitization: Copenhagen and Beyond." *European Journal of International Relations* 13 (3): 357–383.

Summerfield, Derek. 2002. "Effects of War: Moral Knowledge, Revenge, Reconciliation, and Medicalised Concepts of 'Recovery.'" *BMJ: British Medical Journal* 325 (7372): 1105.

Sylvester, Christine. 1994. *Feminist Theory and International Relations in a Postmodern Era*. Vol. 32. Cambridge, UK: Cambridge University Press.

Taurek, Rita. 2006. "Critical Approaches to Security: Telling the Story of Securitization Theory." In *Proceedings of the Central and Eastern European Studies Association Convention*, 25–26.

Torres-Reyna, Oscar. 2007. "Panel Data Analysis Fixed and Random Effects Using Stata (v. 4.2)." Data & Statistical Services, Princeton University. https://pdfs.semanticscholar.org/f70f/9754bc51b1eb2e74dc7dc4e47549910730ed.pdf.

Vuori, Juha A. 2008. "Illocutionary Logic and Strands of Securitization: Applying the Theory of Securitization to the Study of Non-Democratic Political Orders." *European Journal of International Relations* 14 (1): 65–99.

Watson, Scott. 2011. "The 'Human' as Referent Object? Humanitarianism as Securitization." *Security Dialogue* 42 (1): 3–20.

Whitrow, Gerald James, and Marlene P. Soulsby. 2003. *What Is Time?* Oxford, UK: Oxford University Press.

Williams, Michael C. 2003. "Words, Images, Enemies: Securitization and International Politics." *International Studies Quarterly* 47 (4): 511–531.

Zartman, I. William. 1989. *Ripe for Resolution: Conflict and Intervention in Africa*. 2nd edition. Oxford, UK: Oxford University Press.

Part II

Child labor

Thematic indicators and interventions

5 Child labor, poverty and fragility

Introduction

Child labor has a strong positive relationship with fragility, in general, and with all the 12 fragility indicators (UCW 2017), which implies that state fragility places children at a greater risk of child labor. Evidence shows that large shares of child laborers live in fragile states and in countries that have experienced armed conflicts (ILO 2017a). The other side to this picture is the short- and long-term effects of child labor on the victims, their families and the larger society. This is depicted in how child labor activities have the potential to cause underdevelopment in children, perpetuate poverty, widen inequality gaps, create tension between the rich and poor, and fuel the mechanisms that drive countries into a state of fragility. According to UCW (2017), not only does child labor undermine the basic rights of children in the acquisition of labor and academic skills needed for the future, but it impedes national development through losses in productivity, competitiveness and income. This notwithstanding, child labor has received little attention in the fragility discourse. Requiring much attention in the fragility literature/discourse are the drivers of the surge in the prevalence of child labor in Sub-Saharan Africa.

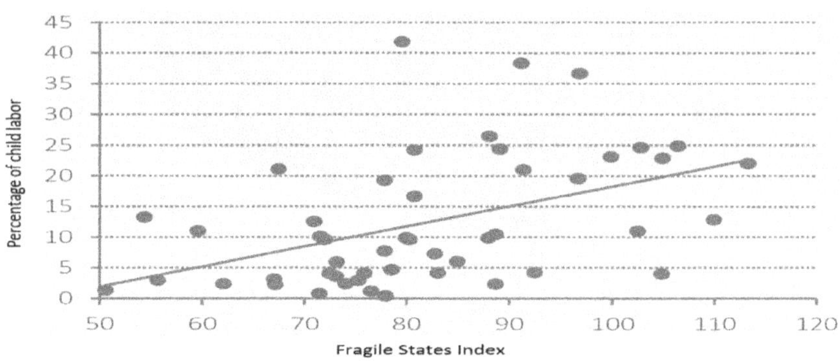

Figure 5.1 The link between fragility and child labor in fragile states, multiple countries.
Source: Understanding Children's Work (2017).

The number of children involved in child labor worldwide in 2016 was estimated at 152 million, of which boys accounted for 88 million (58%) and girls 64 million (42%). Put another way, one in ten children worldwide is involved in child labor. Globally, Africa ranks highest for the prevalence of child labor, accounting for 72 million (47%) of the world total (ILO 2017a), while within sub-Saharan Africa (SSA), at 70 million, is predominant. Although the 47% represents Africa's proportion of the total number of child laborers worldwide, the incidence of child labor in Africa is 20%—measured as the percentage of children classified as child laborers out of the total number of children aged 5–17 years within the continent.

Although the incidence of child labor declined from 2012 to 2016 in other major regions of the world, SSA experienced an increase in the number (and incidence) of child laborers, from about 59 million (with an incidence of 21.4%) to 70 million (with an incidence of 22.4%) within the same period. In 2017, SSA's incidence of child labor again increased to 29% for children aged 5–17 years. The gender breakdown of these figures shows that girls are as likely as boys to be engaged in child labor (Figure 2B). This upward trend in the incidence of child labor was experienced despite SSA governments' implementation of policies aimed at combating child labor (ILO 2017b), with these efforts including increased resources for criminal law enforcement to combat the worst forms of child labor; policies to increase the capacity of law enforcement; and

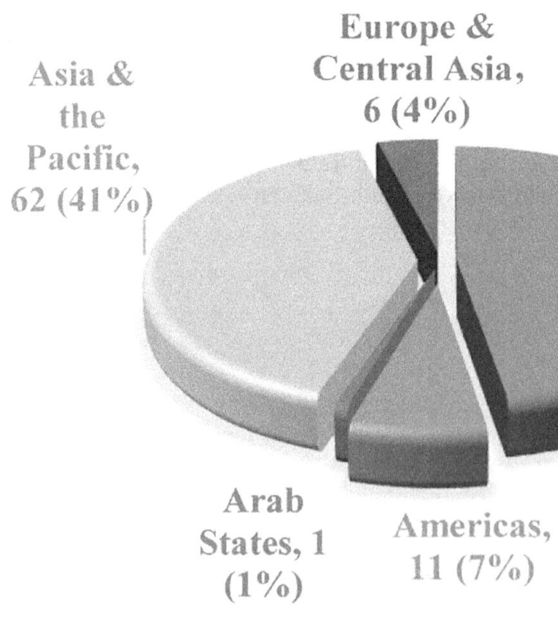

Figure 5.2 Child labor across the regions of the world.

Source: Global estimates of child labor: Results and trends, 2012–2016. Geneva (ILO 2017a).

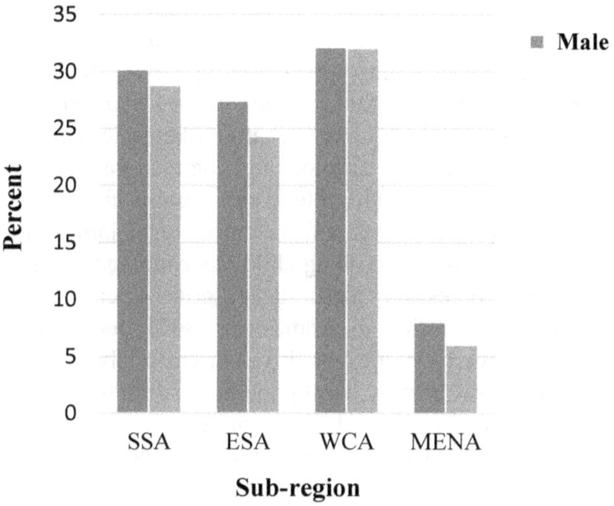

Figure 5.3 Child labor by gender in Africa (SSA, ESA, WCA, MENA).[1]

Source: UNICEF global databases, 2017, based on DHS, MICS and other nationally representative surveys, 2010–2016 (data.unicef.org).

Note

1 SSA = sub-Saharan Africa, ESA = Eastern and Southern Africa, WCA = West and Central Africa, MENA = Middle East and North Africa

new or expanded social programs to prevent or eliminate child labor (USDOL 2017a). That the incidence of child labor in SSA increased after such efforts suggests the core drivers of child labor, and their linkages to other phenomena, deserve further examination.

Despite the efforts described above, SSA is still bedeviled by the problem of child labor. The United States Department of Labor's report *2016 Findings on the Worst Forms of Child Labor* reveals that children continue to be engaged in mining and extraction activities, street hawking, drug trafficking; recruited and used in armed conflicts; and, for some girls, trapped in exploitative commercial sex activities (USDOL 2017a). The negative consequences for the prospects of affected children—as the majority are not in school—set in motion a vicious cycle of poverty that becomes characteristic of the wider society/economy. According to Acaroğlu and Kutlu (2015), child labor (in both rural and urban areas) causes a loss in the accumulation of human capital, which reduces productivity and perpetuates poverty. Lopez-Calva (2001) also notes that, under some circumstances, child labor can put downward pressure on average wages and trigger a cycle of poverty. As individual or household economic units more generally become poorer and more vulnerable, so will the country become increasingly fragile within the international political economy. Poverty is a primary cause of fragility (European Communities 2009), since those who feel marginalized as a result of poverty may resort to destructive tactics (such as conflict) to project their frustration.

Among the reasons cited for the persistence of child labor in SSA is that Africa more broadly is among the regions most affected by crises of all forms, which increases the risk of child labor. Other factors noted in the Department of Labor report are that many African countries have not ratified key international conventions on child labor, that government inspectors lack the resources necessary to enforce child labor laws, and that social protection programs are insufficient to address the scope of the problem. Apart from macro-level indicators, other factors linked to the lack of progress in curbing child labor include broader socio-economic and demographic forces that work against government efforts (ILO 2017a), including poverty. According to Admassie (2002), Jensen and Nielsen (1997) and Ray (2002), poverty is one key driver of child labor, along with a poorly developed agricultural sector, high population growth/fertility rates and low levels of educational attainment and participation.

This chapter seeks to draw linkages between poverty, child labor and state fragility by drawing on theoretical and empirical evidence from Ghana and Tanzania. SSA is the focus given it has the highest incidence of child labor in the world; the International Labor Organization (ILO) has also indicated that a breakthrough in Africa would be critical to ending child labor worldwide. The relevance of the child labor discourse is reflected in the pledges by governments in SSA to take pragmatic steps in achieving the United Nations Sustainable Development Goals (SDGs) by 2030; the seventh target of SDG8 calls on countries to

> take immediate and effective measures to eradicate forced labor, end modern slavery and human trafficking and secure the prohibition and elimination of the worst forms of child labor, including recruitment and use of child soldiers, and by 2025 end child labor in all its forms.
>
> (United Nations 2015, 20)

The rest of this chapter proceeds as follows. Section two deals with child labor activities in SSA and is followed by a section on definitions of child labor. Section four discusses the child labor–poverty nexus, while section five provides a discussion on the cycle of poverty in fragile states. Section six examines the prospects of child laborers and its implications on society while section seven outlines the methodology used in the data analyses. Here, we talk about the data source and theoretical and empirical models and the estimation technique employed in the data analyses.

Child labor activities in SSA countries

In SSA, child labor is likely to be exploitative in character and fall into the worst category of child labor, with children performing dangerous activities in mining, agriculture and domestic work as well as being forced into commercial sexual exploitation (Admassie 2002; USDOL 2017). Child laborers in commercial sex exploitation can be found in countries such as Cote d'Ivoire, Liberia, Tanzania, Nigeria, Cameroon, Zimbabwe and in some unlisted countries. Others are forcibly recruited into non-state armed groups; and yet others deal in illicit drugs (USDOL 2017). Child labor activities exhibit similar characteristics across countries, especially among countries that are geographically close. In Ghana, children are forced into fishing and cocoa harvesting. Some are also found in quarrying and small-scale mining (known locally as 'galamsey'), where they use mercury and dig deep pits, crush stones, operate machines and carry heavy loads. In Cote d'Ivoire, children are mainly involved in cocoa production, clearing and burning fields and harvesting, fermenting and drying cocoa seeds. These children break pods using sharp tools, transport heavy loads of cocoa pods and water and are involved in the spraying of pesticides (USDOL 2017).

In Liberia and Sierra Leone, children engage in dangerous activities in agriculture, cultivating cassava, cocoa, palm oil, rice, coffee and peanuts while others engage in in deep-sea fishing. Other children are into quarrying and stone crushing, and in diamond and gold mining (locally known as 'half shovel'), where they sometimes carry sacks on their heads. Children in Tanzania process coffee, cloves, tobacco and tea crops for cultivation and are also engaged in ploughing, weeding and harvesting. In other parts of the agricultural sector, children are involved in herding livestock and fishing (USDOL 2017). In Ethiopia, child labor is used to plant and harvest apples, cotton, bananas, coffee and khat, and in fishing and cattle herding while some are into gold mining and stone quarrying, digging, carrying of heavy loads, and in making of pottery products and traditional hand-woven textiles. Some of the Ethiopian child laborers provide unpaid household services, carrying firewood and heavy loads of water. Some are shoe-shiners, vendors, potters and beggars, while others provide assistance to taxi drivers (USDOL 2017).

Nigerian children also work in the agricultural sector, growing cassava, rice, tobacco and cocoa. Other children work in fishing and nomadic cattle herding. Besides operating as bus conductors, begging on the streets and scavenging, children are also caught in the trap of commercial sex exploitation and are used by non-state armed groups for domestic work while others are involved in armed conflicts (USDOL 2017). Similarly, Children in Cameroon work in rubber, banana, tea, coffee, onion, cocoa and palm oil production in the agricultural sector. In doing so, they handle pesticides, use machetes, climb trees and lift heavy loads. Children are also used in fishing and raising livestock. Some of the services these children provide include commercial sex exploitation (mainly due to child trafficking) and forced recruitment into non-state armed groups, where some are used as suicide bombers or concubines (USDOL 2017).

In South Africa and Zimbabwe, children are found in the agricultural sector, where they work growing and harvesting grapes, lychees, bananas, citrus fruits, of cocoa, tea, cotton, corn, sugarcane and mangoes. The services children provide include street vending and begging, drug trafficking, home burglaries and gang-related activities. Some children are involved in drug trafficking, gambling and in commercial sex exploitation (usually after being trafficked from Zimbabwe into South Africa) (USDOL 2017).

Definitions of child labor

There is no single accepted definition of child labor, nor is there any unanimously recognized activity that qualifies a participant as being a child laborer. Existing studies have tried to define child labor by focusing on some aspects of the construct and have, over time, provided a general understanding of myriad of activities and specific characteristics that qualify as child labor. These notwithstanding, the key idea that cuts across all attempted definitions has been the welfare of the child—whether the activity is harmful to the child. The ILO defines child labor as work that deprives children of their childhood, their potential and their dignity, and work that is harmful to physical and mental development. These forms of work (i) are mentally, physically, socially or morally dangerous and harmful to children, and (ii) interfere with their schooling by (iii) depriving them of the opportunity to attend school; (iii) obliging them to leave school prematurely; or (iv) requiring them to attempt to combine school attendance with excessively long and heavy work (ILO 2004). This definition is offered in the context of the ILO Minimum Age Convention 1973 (No. 138), which sets the age below which children should not be economically employed at 15 years (13 for light work). The age set for hazardous work is 18 (16 under certain strict conditions). For countries where the economy and educational facilities are insufficiently developed, the convention makes room for setting the general minimum age at 14, or 12 for light work (ILO 2004).

The Uganda Bureau of Statistics (2003) defines child labor as comprising economically active children aged 5–17 years. The Ghana Statistical Service (GSS) adopts ILO Convention No. 138, defining child laborers as children under the age of 15 who are economically employed for wages/salaries (GSS 2003, 2014). The Central Statistical Agency (CSA) of Ethiopia also relies on ILO Convention No. 138—and adds Convention No. 182 (defining the worst category of child labor)—to define child labor as the employment of children in prohibited work and, more generally, in types of work considered as socially and morally undesirable as stipulated by national legislation (CSA and ILO 2018). Under the CSA's operational definition, child labor includes (i) children aged 5–13 years engaged in any economic activity for at least one hour during the reference week, and (ii) children aged 5–17 years engaged in hazardous work in the reference week. This shows that countries can sometimes combine international conventions with government legislation to tailor their definition of child labor to reflect country-specific goals.

Due to the complex nature of this construct, empirical studies across countries have mainly defined child laborers as children aged 10–14 years who are economically active (Dehejia and Gatti 2005; Hussain and Maskus 2003; Neumayer and De Soysa 2005). Frempong and Stadelmann (2018) and Koomson and Asongu (2016) also define child labor as covering children aged 5–14 who are economically active. Frempong and Stadelmann (2018) also include children aged 5–11 engaged in domestic activities that have the potential to negatively affect key child welfare variables such as education. This extended definition is grounded in the assertion by Edmonds (2008) and the ILO (2011) that there may be no significant difference between children's domestic and commercial activities, especially with regard to the potential impact on schooling.

Knowing the definitions of child labor, we need to explore its various dimensions to understand the determinants of this social menace; as discussed in the following sections, many researchers consider poverty to be the dominant driver.

Child labor–poverty nexus

There are three main theoretical approaches to the linkages between poverty and the incidence of child labor: the altruistic model, the non-altruistic model and the inverted-U model. Basu and Van's (1998) altruistic model, which is supported by Bhasker and Gupta (2012), considers poverty (or, conversely, wealth) as the key driver of child labor. In other words, parents come to rely on their children's income, or increase the extent to which they subject their children to child labor, if they experience a deterioration in their economic status. In Rosati and Tzannato's (2003) altruistic model, parents are seen as having control over their children's time when they are young and are the ultimate decision-makers regarding the use to which that time is put—school or be commercial activity. Parents also have control over all income inflows to the household, which includes incomes from work by both adults and children. Also known as the luxury axiom, the altruistic model incorporates the quantity and quality of children into the households' (parents') utility function, so a child's time allocated to work or in school is considered an investment meant to maximize the market value of the household. A parent may find other investments more profitable than investing in the child when the avenues for investment are either not available or under-developed. For most of SSA (mainly made up of developing countries that lack well-structured or developed financial systems), the opportunity costs of holding financial assets are considered very high. For this reason, parents may consider land holdings and other durable assets as yielding greater and more attractive rates of return.

According to Brown, Deardorff and Stern (2002), if parents consider the return on children's education to be low, and that of land to be high, the household tends to maximize its wealth by having more child laborers. Another dimension to this is where parents are motivated to have more children to use as insurance in economic systems with underdeveloped insurance markets because they can fall back on their children's income and economic productivity (Pörtner 2001). Like Basu and Van (1998), Admassie (2017) also posits that poverty is the major determinant of child labor. By inference, if households had greater wealth, children's education and economic employment would not be considered as substitutable investment portfolios.

The non-altruistic model (wealth paradox), on the other hand, explains how some parents continue to increase their household's supply of child labor when household wealth increases. Other proponents argue that the poor have fundamental problems of self-control and are unlikely to reduce the extent to which they exploit the labor hours of their children as a result of improved wealth. A possible explanation for this is that parents usually will use child laborers' income as a risk-coping mechanism and will continue to exploit such labor because they are unable to predict their future income stream (Banerjee and Mullainathan 2010; Lima, Mesquita, and Wanamaker 2015). For non-altruistic parents, there is no significant differences in outcome whether the children work domestically or in the labor market (Rosati, Tzannatos, and others 2003). Other authors have posited that non-altruism is not necessarily an issue of active selfishness on the part of parents but, rather, the existence of a very low degree of parental altruism (Dumas 2007; Kruger 2007).

A third group of studies embraces a non-linear relationship between household income and child labor. This reflects what is termed an inverted-U relationship and can be conceptualized as a combination of the altruistic and non-altruistic models playing out in some households, countries and sub-regional blocs, depending on the analytical scope of the researcher. Such evidence has been found by Basu et al. (2010); Lima et al. (2015) and Koomson (2017) for cross-sectional studies. In a time-dimensional study, Kambahampati and Rajan (2006) found a child labor-Kuznets curve (that is, an inverted-U). The studies by Basu et al. (2010) and Lima et al. (2015) focused on agricultural households and captured household wealth using land size, while Koomson (2017) extended the scope of the research to include child laborers in urban and non-farm households by considering household income from six different sources. The rationale for the inclusion of a range of income sources is that most farm households have embarked on income diversification as a result of climate change and unstable income flows from agricultural activities; this causes them to push children into more non-farm economic activities. A second reason is that child laborers have been found to contribute more to households through non-farm income than farm income. The key message of inverted-U theories is that households need child laborers at relatively lower levels of income/wealth but that the need for child laborers will diminish as the household income approaches a threshold at which there are sufficient funds to employ external labor. Beyond this threshold, the opportunity cost of children's time spent on education no longer outweighs the value of that education for the household. Even for parents who may consider increasing their land holdings as a better investment, such assets can be acquired without being traded off against investment in their children's future through education.

The policy message to be taken from these three theories is that governments within SSA must seek to reduce income inequality so that the average household will be financially stable, resulting in decreasing demand for child labor to augment household income. Even for agricultural households, the labor of children will not be considered as a key input in their quest to diversify their income portfolios. The poverty–child labor nexus has the effect of perpetuating the poverty of the victims of child labor, and the multiplier effect on the wider society and economy cannot be overemphasized. Such an effect is evident in the vicious cycle of poverty at both household and country levels, and the likelihood of the poor and disadvantaged becoming agents of social instability has been well documented.

The vicious cycle of poverty in fragile states

We have already explained in Chapter 2 that fragility of a country can be indicated by a range of dysfunctional behaviors (or incapacities): the government's inability to provide essential services to its people; the existence of persistent and extreme poverty; unstable and weak governance structures; lack of territorial control; and high propensity to conflict and civil wars (see also, Bertocchi and Guerzoni 2012, 1). In addition, the World Bank considers fragile states to be those in which state policies and institutions are weak, leaving the state vulnerable in its capacity to deliver services to its citizens, control corruption, or provide for sufficient voice and accountability (World Bank 2005, quoted in Ferreira 2015, 34). From the economic perspective, we can refer to a bi-directional relationship between state fragility and the level of economic development (European Communities 2009). Poverty has been identified as the key driver of fragility, although not all poor countries are fragile. Fragility has been linked to primary drivers such as economic and social exclusion, economic collapse and worsening forms of poverty, lack of good governance, religious extremism, state weakness and collapse, and ideological exclusion. Secondary drivers include the 'natural resource curse,' youth bulges and demographic stresses, proliferation of small arms and weapons, and superpower rivalry.

We focus on the economic drivers to shed light on how economic and social exclusion creates two sets of groups—the "haves and have nots" or the "we-versus-them"—where the dominated group relentlessly seeks to change the status quo and become the controllers of the resources. In addition, low levels of economic output dominated by low agricultural productivity and a small industrial sector (common among states in sub-Saharan Africa) has been cited as another root cause of fragility (Ncube and Jones 2013). The consequences of these economic characteristics of fragile states are increasing rate of youth (particularly graduate) unemployment, and low standards and high costs of living. The victims of these economic and political failures come to feel disenfranchised and become the source of uprisings and upheavals (Ncube and Jones 2013) that push the country(s) to further levels of poverty, creating a vicious cycle of poverty.

The vicious cycle of poverty can be understood from the broader perspective of the interconnections of factors that reinforce each other to cause poverty. The basic understanding of this concept (in Nurkse's words) is that "a country is poor because it is poor" (Bauer 1965). The Nurkse model (1953, 1957) views the vicious cycle of poverty as emanating mainly from the low level of capital formation within economies, while Kindleberger (1958) sees poverty as being a consequence of the smaller size of markets. Combining the Nurkse and Kindleberger models, the vicious cycle can be explained from both the supply and demand sides. On the supply side, we can say that low income (poverty) results in lower savings and investment, which in turn results in low productivity and hence, low income (real income). The demand side is explained by considering the low investment in production due to lower demand for goods and services within an economy. The low level of investment leads to low productivity and to reduced income (or poverty). These models and what they represent are highly symptomatic of SSA. A 2015 World Bank report shows that poverty is declining in all regions of the world with the exception of Africa, with that finding driven largely by trends in sub-Saharan Africa (World Bank 2015). Evidence also shows that countries in SSA are unable to adequately translate income into wealth and consumption due to inability to save and invest to accumulate wealth (particularly in rural areas).

These economic characteristics of countries in SSA, and the resulting likelihood of those countries remaining trapped in a vicious cycle of poverty, form the link between fragility and poverty. To reiterate, those who perpetually remain poor become frustrated with their current status and resort to the use of unconventional means to change their fortunes, thereby creating chaos and tension in society. Child labor is both a symptom and a driver of poverty, with children engaged in such labor more likely to remain poor. The future of child laborers is discussed in the next section.

The future of child labor and its societal implications

The high incidence of child labor in SSA is a conspicuous indication of parents' under-investment in children's education. Evidence generally shows that higher levels of education are associated with higher income levels, and parents who forego short term economic gain to push their children into education enjoy future benefits that outweigh the immediate sacrifices by the family. Research has shown that entering the labor market at an earlier age potentially reduce overall years of education and decreases average hourly future earnings by as much as 20%. Studies also suggest that the future household income of such children suffers by an even larger margin (Ilahi, Orazem, and Sedlacek 2009). It is also known that schooling provides a child with the skills needed to operate effectively within the workplace; thus, the lack of skills as a result on engagement in child labor rather than education means being a less efficient, and therefore less productive employee and consequently earning less income. In the current global economic context, where job market prospects increasingly require some level of computer skills, child laborers stand the risk of missing out even on the menial jobs they currently can secure.

Apart from reduced income, there are other short- and long-term effects of child labor on the victims, their families and society. The decision to push children into economic activities before they are sufficiently mature to enter the labor market may be narrowly informed by the economic needs of their families but largely ignores the impact on the child and society. Once school enrolment or the educational attainment of the child is affected, there are attendant health and psychological implications that may affect the child throughout their life (Knaul 2001).

The activities typical of child labor in SSA also negatively affect children's physical development. For example, children in SSA are involved in mining activities in which they are directly exposed to chemicals (cyanide) used for washing the minerals. These chemicals have long-term impacts on their physical health, leaving them weaker as adults. Similarly, exposure to pesticides and activities where children carry heavy loads imply a higher risk of poorer future health (Faria 2010). Those whose health is affected make a reduced contribution to society; their productivity levels are lower and so are their income levels. As a result, their tax contributions are low and the economy suffers a reduction in revenue. Other active members of society must sometimes abandon their own economic activities to care for the more seriously affected, compounding the loss of productivity and negative effects for the economy.

Emotionally, children may develop low self-esteem and lack confidence (Faria 2010) because of exploitative conditions under which they work. This is likely to be the case for many of the child laborers in SSA, who are usually isolated from their family and friends for either a significant portion of their childhood or for a large part of each day. Socially isolated children may suffer delays or other adverse impacts on their personality development due to limited interaction. Self-development theories place a great emphasis on social interaction as a key element in this process. Herbert Mead's theory of self-development points out that children take on characteristics from their significant others (such as teachers, nurses etc.) in the "play stage" (ages two to six), while they learn to integrate rules and regulations at the "game stage", from age seven upwards. (Bolton 1981; Watson 2010). Unfortunately, these formative years are the same years children (including those in SSA) are typically driven into child labor. The broader implication is that these children will usually lack iconic, socially responsible figures on whose lives they model their own development. Not going through the game stage properly also means that these children will grow up failing to recognize and abide by rules and regulations, and are more likely to become social delinquents. Social delinquents either work to destroy what has been produced or their potential contributions are lost due to incarceration, premature death or ill health.

Methodology

The methodology for this chapter covers data sources, measurement of child labor, estimation technique and theoretical and empirical models. These specific aspects of the methodology are itemized in the subsections that follow.

Data sources

The empirical analyses were performed using two secondary datasets from Ghana and Tanzania. A detailed description of the datasets is provided below.

The data from Ghana is the sixth round of the Ghana Living Standards Survey (GLSS6), which covered every region of the country and comprised many sections (modules), including child labor, health, employment, housing conditions, migration, tourism, access to financial services and asset ownership, education, agriculture and non-farm enterprise. The data was collected over a 12-month period between 2012 and 2013 using a multi-stage sampling approach. The number of households covered in this nationally representative survey was 18,000, but with a response rate of 93.2% the sample included 16,772 households. Since we used a regression analysis, which uses a square matrix in its algorithm, missing observations for rows and columns resulted in a further reduction of the sample size to 5,051 households, but this does not affect the representativeness of the final sample and analyses.

The second dataset is drawn from the Tanzania National Child Labor Survey (NCLS) 2014, which was conducted by the International Labor Organization (ILO) and the Tanzania National Bureau of Statistics (NBS). The NCLS was part of the 2014 Intergraded Labor Force Survey (ILFS), which sought to obtain and provide comprehensive data on the labor market in Tanzania. Apart from providing information on child labor characteristics and its effect on health, education and the development of children aged 5–7 years, the ILFS covers topics and concepts such as current and usual economic activities, employment and unemployment, labor under-utilization, hours or work, branches of economic activity and productivity, and low pay and the working poor. The survey used the sampling frame derived from the 2012 Population and Housing Census and employed a stratified three-stage sampling design. The first stage involved the selection of 480 enumeration areas (EAs), 360 representing rural areas and 120 representing urban areas. The second stage used a systematic sampling approach to select 11,520 households from the EAs, with 4,800 coming from Dar es Salaam, 3,840 from other urban areas and 2,880 from rural areas. The response rate for the survey was 99.6% (NBS and ILO 2016).

Measurement of child labor

Child labor in the GLSS6 data was captured using ILO Convention No. 138, which has been adapted by the Ghana Statistical Service to include economically employed children aged 5–14 years. After identifying the number of children who fit this description, we derived the total number of hours worked by child laborers in each household. This served as the dependent variable for our analyses (GSS 2003, 2014).

From the 2014 NCLS, we defined a child laborer as one who is aged 5–17 years and is economically employed or performed household chores for at least one hour during the one-week reference period. We excluded children whose household chores did not add up to one hour. The household chores included were: shopping for household; repairing household equipment; cooking; cleaning utensils/house; washing clothes; caring for children or old/sick family members; and other household tasks (CSA and ILO 2018; NBS and ILO 2016).

Estimation technique

An ordinary least squares (OLS) approach was used in deriving the average difference in the number of hours worked by children in poor and non-poor households and in determining the marginal effect of household income on child labor hours. This choice of method was motivated by the dependent variable, which is continuous and is normally distributed. Post-estimation tests such as the link-test for model specification and variance inflation factor (VIF) for multicollinearity were all conducted.

Theoretical and empirical models

The theoretical model adopted for this study works within the framework of the altruistic model proposed by Basu and Van (1998). Other researchers (Abdul-Mumuni, Vijay, and Camara 2018; Coon 2016; Rosati, Tzannatos, and others 2003) who used this model imposed a basic assumption that it is the parent or the household head who presides over child labor decisions within the household. In other words, it is the parent who decides the use of the child's time. From the studies above, the child labor supply function is specified in equation (5.1), where *Clhrs* is the number of child labor hours, *H* represents all possible household-level variables, α and η are parameters to be determined and υ is an error term.

$$Clhrs_i = \alpha_0 + \sum_{i=0}^{n} \eta_i H_i + \upsilon_i \tag{5.1}$$

From equation (5.1), we structure our empirical models as indicated below:

Model 1 (Ghana): effect of poverty on child labor

$$\begin{aligned} Clhrs_i &= \beta_0 + \beta_1 Poor_i + \beta_2 rural_i + \beta_3 female_i + \beta_4 age_i + \\ &\beta_5 Hhsize_i + \beta_6 employed_i + \beta_7 edu_i + \beta_8 nojobs_i + \beta_9 region_i + \varepsilon_i \end{aligned} \tag{5.2}$$

Model 2 (Tanzania): effect of household income on child labor

$$\begin{aligned} Clhrs_i &= \alpha_0 + \alpha_1 \ln inc_i + \alpha_2 rural_i + \alpha_3 female_i + \alpha_4 age_i + \\ &\alpha_5 Hhsize_i + \alpha_6 employed_i + \alpha_7 edu_i + \alpha_8 mstat_i + \alpha_9 region_i + \upsilon_i \end{aligned} \tag{5.3}$$

Where (beginning from the Model 1), *Clhrs* represents the total number of child labor hours for all child laborers within a household; *Poor* is a binary variable for poverty status, which is 1 for poor and 0 otherwise. The poverty measurement here is consumption poverty. The *rural* variable is also binary and represents location of the household. It is captured as 1 for rural and 0 for urban; *age* is the age of the household head; *hhsize* is the household size; *employed* represents the household head's employment status and is captured as 1 for employed and 0 for unemployed; *edu* is the educational status of the household head;

nojobs is the number of jobs done by the head of the household; *region* is a structural variable representing regional dummies; *lninc* is the natural log of household income from older members of the household; and *mstat* is the marital status of the household head. Note that while *regions* for Ghana represents all ten regions in the dataset, we found 25 regions in the Tanzania dataset and paired them to arrive at 12 combinations, with Dar es Salaam standing alone. We left Dar es Salaam out because of its population and similar sample representation in the NCLS.

Empirical results and discussion

The analysis is done for both estimations because they both seek to provide empirical evidence for the effect of household wealth on child labor outcomes. Household wealth is represented in Table 5.1 with consumption poverty, while in Table 5.2 it is represented with household income of older household members (aged 18 and above). The rationale for this is to prevent possible bi-causality between child labor hours and income. For post-estimation tests, the linktest has the _hat and _hatsq being significant and insignificant respectively and signifies that the model is correctly specified, while the variance inflation factor (VIF) also falls below the threshold of 10 and indicates that the models do not suffer from multicollinearity. We proceed with the analysis in the next paragraph.

From Table 5.1, we compare the total number of hours child laborers in poor and non-poor households work within a week. The findings show that child laborers in poor households work an average of eight hours more than their counterparts in non-poor households. This supports multiple findings in the extant literature that identify poverty as one of the key drivers of child labor. Following the altruistic model, we can infer that parents subject their children to more hours of economic and non-economic activities because of their poverty, with the additional child labor income augmenting the household income. Put differently, the child will be made to work and take responsibility for some of his/her own financial needs so that he/she does not become a burden to the head of the household. The other side to this argument is that the children take over non-economic household activities so that the adult members of the household can spend more time in their productive activities.

The analysis from Table 5.2 is no different from that of Table 5.1; again, the regression output depicts an inverse relationship between household income and hours of child labor. This means that a household that faces a reduction in its income generated by adult members will subject its children to more hours of child labor activities. Figure 5.3 enlightens us on children's perception of what they feel will happen if they stop being economically active. Apart from those who felt nothing will happen, 42% of them felt their parents will lose assistance. Others said they will be unable to provide financial support to their families.

Table 5.1 OLS estimation for the effect of poverty on number of child labor hours within a household

	Ghana	*Location*	
Total hours of child labor		*Rural*	*Urban*
Poor (not poor = 0; poor = 1)	8.107***	10.766***	–2.199
	(0.000)	(0.000)	(0.449)
Rural (urban = 0; rural = 1)	1.606		
	(0.409)		
Female (male = 0; female = 1)	2.137	–0.452	0.872
	(0.315)	(0.867)	(0.686)
Age of household head	–3.613***	–3.774***	–2.454***
	(0.000)	(0.000)	(0.000)
Household size	5.621***	6.060***	4.112***
	(0.000)	(0.000)	(0.000)
Worked	3.903	–2.361	25.374**
	(0.379)	(0.600)	(0.016)
Educational level (Base = not educated)			
BECE/MSLC	–0.794	–0.530	–2.350
	(0.645)	(0.803)	(0.342)
SSS/VOC/Tertiary	–5.993***	–6.030**	–12.421***
	(0.009)	(0.043)	(0.000)
Number of jobs	2.331***	2.463***	1.630***
	(0.000)	(0.000)	(0.000)
Region (Base = Volta)			
Western	–9.905*	–3.589	–30.617**
	(0.090)	(0.504)	(0.018)
Central	–2.408	2.384	–28.062***
	(0.624)	(0.644)	(0.001)
Greater Accra	3.536	–0.306	–15.249*
	(0.538)	(0.963)	(0.092)
Eastern	–4.931	1.833	–29.521***
	(0.295)	(0.714)	(0.000)
Ashanti	–5.798	–4.315	–23.579***
	(0.238)	(0.419)	(0.003)
Brong Ahafo	–7.420	–3.637	–29.390***
	(0.145)	(0.522)	(0.000)
Northern	–5.435	–3.742	–33.038***
	(0.414)	(0.608)	(0.000)
Upper East	–9.733**	–8.755*	–19.111**
	(0.042)	(0.100)	(0.031)
Upper West	–2.906	–2.926	–23.941**
	(0.564)	(0.598)	(0.011)
Constant	–6.341	–6.703	6.515
	(0.446)	(0.443)	(0.659)
Observations	5,051	4,190	861
R-squared	0.619	0.624	0.661

continued

Table 5.1 continued

Total hours of child labor	Ghana	Location: Rural	Location: Urban
Linktest (*p*-value)			
_hat	0.012		
_hatsq	0.522		
VIF	1.43		

Source: Sixth round of the Ghana Living Standards Survey (GLSS6).

Notes
***$p<0.01$;
**$p<0.05$;
*$p<0.1$;
VIF = variance inflation factor.
Robust P-values in parenthesis.

Table 5.2 OLS estimation for the effect of household income on number of child labor hours within a household

Total hours of child labor	Tanzania	Location: Rural	Location: Urban
ln(Total household (≥18 years)	–0.9585***	–0.3204	–1.3079***
	(0.0016)	(0.5494)	(0.0006)
Rural (urban = 0; rural = 1)	2.8286***	—	—
	(0.0007)	—	—
Female (male = 0; female = 1)	0.7229	3.0501	–1.1627
	(0.4983)	(0.1511)	(0.3234)
Age of household head	–0.0390	0.0060	–0.0499
	(0.1821)	(0.9040)	(0.1580)
Household size	2.0768***	2.2981***	1.9040***
	(0.0000)	(0.0000)	(0.0000)
Employed (no = 0; yes = 1)	0.2319	1.6279	–0.3609
	(0.8126)	(0.3582)	(0.7584)
Educational level (Base = dropped out)			
Never attended	4.2921***	6.9036***	2.5076
	(0.0010)	(0.0008)	(0.1107)
Completed	2.3762***	3.5569**	1.9231*
	(0.0070)	(0.0194)	(0.0838)
Attending	8.2781	—	7.6037
	(0.1720)	—	(0.2110)
Marital status (Base = living together)			
Single	5.7864***	3.0988	6.5382***
	(0.0013)	(0.4067)	(0.0009)
Married	6.3981***	7.9381***	5.2992***
	(0.0000)	(0.0005)	(0.0000)

Total hours of child labor	*Tanzania*	*Location*	
		Rural	*Urban*
Widowed	5.0196***	3.9739	6.0969***
	(0.0004)	(0.1730)	(0.0001)
Divorced/separated	5.9267***	4.0798	7.0228***
	(0.0000)	(0.1499)	(0.0000)
Region (Base = Mbeya and Rukwa)			
Lindi and Mtwara	7.6817***	4.7145**	11.1195***
	(0.0000)	(0.0252)	(0.0000)
Ruvumaand Njombe	1.2849	0.6486	1.0229
	(0.3826)	(0.7932)	(0.5708)
Dodoma and Iringa	–1.1171	–1.5225	–0.7571
	(0.2941)	(0.4460)	(0.5296)
Morogoro and Pwani	8.9274***	6.5156***	10.5087***
	(0.0000)	(0.0084)	(0.0000)
Tanga and Manyara	5.7454***	7.8788***	2.8825*
	(0.0003)	(0.0032)	(0.0799)
Singida and Tabora	1.2236	1.8337	–0.6055
	(0.3700)	(0.4156)	(0.7105)
Kigoma and Katavi	4.8894***	5.6567*	3.5742
	(0.0055)	(0.0538)	(0.1081)
Kagera and Geita	12.5537***	12.6373***	12.5653***
	(0.0001)	(0.0071)	(0.0022)
Mwanza and Mara	3.8960**	5.0464*	3.4742*
	(0.0189)	(0.0756)	(0.0928)
Shinyanga and Simiyu	–0.5077	–4.3013**	1.6185
	(0.7059)	(0.0410)	(0.3719)
Arusha and Kilimanjaro	6.1721***	6.9231***	4.8528**
	(0.0001)	(0.0016)	(0.0377)
Dar es Salaam	3.5938***		3.7917***
	(0.0001)		(0.0001)
Constant	4.4869	–7.2146	12.2643**
	(0.2885)	(0.3596)	(0.0129)
Observations	2,715	786	1,929
R-squared	0.1218	0.1614	0.0906
Linktest (*p*-value)			
_hat	0.000		
_hatsq	0.813		
VIF	2.16		

Source: Tanzania National Child Labor Survey (NCLS) 2014

Notes
***$p<0.01$;
**$p<0.05$;
*$p<0.1$;
VIF = variance inflation factor.
Robust P-values in parenthesis.

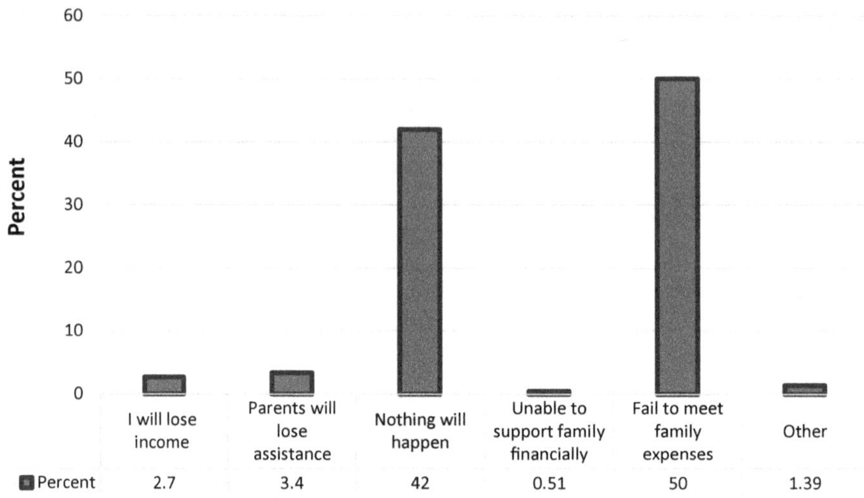

Figure 5.4 What will happen if you stop working?

Source: Tanzania National Child Labour Survey (NCLS) 2014.

The key link we draw from the synthesis of the literature and empirical evidence is that poverty drives child labor, which in turn perpetuates a country's long-term underdevelopment (through low productivity) and ends up fueling the mechanisms that drive countries into a state of fragility. First, we consider the low adult incomes that result from the early introduction of children into the labor market as exposing these children and their future households to higher vulnerability to poverty. We also link such potential vulnerabilities to the kind of economic activities that child laborers are currently engaged in (in Tanzania, Nigeria, Ghana, Liberia etc.) and infer that most of them will likely remain in the agricultural sector, using less advanced or no technology and producing on a lower scale. The lower levels of production imply lower GDP for the countries and a continuous struggle by governments to increase national income and provide government transfers to the potentially vulnerable who require government assistance to live meaningful lives. The inability of the government to adequately provide a social safety net may leave the most vulnerable feeling disenfranchised and, hence, result in social unrest—including, in its most extreme form, the emergence of rebel groups fighting against the state for a fair share of the national resource.

Second, the reduced education of child laborers, or their total disengagement from the educational system, connotes their low prospects in securing jobs as a result of lacking the skills needed to take advantage of the dynamic employment market. Fewer job opportunities means lower income and, in turn, lower productivity across the wider economy. This perpetuates poverty and can directly be linked to fragility, given that poverty has been found to be one of the primary drivers of state fragility.

Finally, child labor in SSA includes some of the most exploitative forms, with some children trapped in commercial sex exploitation (Côte d'Ivoire, Liberia, Tanzania, Nigeria, Cameroon, Zimbabwe and in some unlisted countries); others forcibly recruited into non-state armed groups; and yet others dealing in illicit drugs. These forms of child labor are also mainly driven by poverty, but their implications for society are of even deeper concern. Such children are more likely to die early or become physically incapacitated, stripping the country of the potential benefits from their labor, or to contract diseases that make them weaker and, thus, less productive members of society. Those who survive such activities physically unscathed may end up becoming security threats to their immediate social environments and to the country at large. Threats to political security is a characteristic of state fragility, and curbing such threats diverts economic resources that could have been invested in productive sectors of the economy. Given the strong link between child labor and fragility, we advocate that child labor should be given much attention among the fragility indicators.

References

Abdul-Mumuni, Abdallah, Bhasin K. Vijay, and Obeng K. Camara. 2018. "Remittances and Child Labour in Ghana: Does the Gender of the Household Head Matter?" *Development Southern Africa* 36 (1): 1–16.

Acaroğlu, Hakan, and Erol Kutlu. 2015. "The Human Capital Vicious Cycle Created by the Child Labor Issue in Turkey." *Journal of Business and Economics*, 500.

Admassie, Assefa. 2002. "Explaining the High Incidence of Child Labour in Sub–Saharan Africa." *African Development Review* 14 (2): 251–275.

Banerjee, Abhijit, and Sendhil Mullainathan. 2010. "The Shape of Temptation: Implications for the Economic Lives of the Poor." National Bureau of Economic Research. www.nber.org/papers/w15973.

Basu, Kaushik, and Pham Hoang Van. 1998. "The Economics of Child Labor." *American Economic Review*, 412–427.

Basu, K., Das, S., and Dutta, B., 2010. "Child Labor and Household Wealth: Theory and Empirical Evidence of an Inverted-U." *Journal of Development Economics* 91 (1): 8–14.

Bauer, Peter T. 1965. "The Vicious Circle of Poverty." *Weltwirtschaftliches Archiv*, 4–20.

Bertocchi, Graziella, and Andrea Guerzoni. 2012. "Growth, History, or Institutions: What Explains State Fragility in Sub-Saharan Africa?" *Journal of Peace Research* 49 (6): 769–783.

Bhaskar, Venkataraman, and Bishnupriya Gupta. 2012. "Parental Altruism and Child Labor: Examining the Historical Evidence from the United States." *Cliometrica* 6 (3): 249–266.

Bolton, Charles D. 1981. "Some Consequences of the Meadian Self." *Symbolic Interaction* 4 (2): 245–259.

Brown, Drusilla K., Alan V. Deardorff, and Robert Mitchell Stern. 2002. *The Determinants of Child Labor: Theory and Evidence*. School of Public Policy, University of Michigan. www.academia.edu/download/33242469/child_labor_as.pdf.

Coon, Michael. 2016. "Remittances and Child Labor in Bolivia." *IZA Journal of Migration* 5 (1): 1.

CSA and ILO. 2018. "Ethiopia National Child Labour Survey 2015." Central statistical Agency (CSA) and International Labour Organization (ILO). www.ilo.org/ipec/Informationresources/WCMS_IPEC_PUB_28475/lang-en/index.htm.

Dehejia, Rajeev H. and Roberta Gatti. 2005. "Child Labor: The Role of Financial Development and Income Variability across Countries." *Economic Development and Cultural Change* 53 (4): 913–931.

Dumas, Christelle. 2007. "Why Do Parents Make Their Children Work? A Test of the Poverty Hypothesis in Rural Areas of Burkina Faso." *Oxford Economic Papers*. http://oep.oxfordjournals.org/content/early/2007/01/06/oep.gpl031.short.

Edmonds, Eric V. 2008. *Defining Child Labour: A Review of the Definitions of Child Labour in Policy Research*. International Programme on the Elimination of Child Labour (IPEC), International Labour Organization.

European Communities. 2009. "Overcoming Fragility in Africa: Forging a New European Approach." Robert Schuman Centre for Advanced Studies, European University Institute, San Domenico di Fiesole.

Faria, Cassandra Fernandes. 2010. "Why Is Child Labour Detrimental for Children?" *Nurture, Aga Khan University, Institute for Educational Development, Karachi*, no. 9: 18.

Ferreira, Ines Afonso Roque. 2015. "Defining and Measuring State Fragility: A New Proposal." In, 39. Berkeley, CA. http://cega.berkeley.edu/assets/miscellaneous_files/109__ABCA_2015_Ines_Ferreira_Defining_and_measuring_state_fragility__A_new_proposal_May15.pdf.

Frempong, Raymond Boadi, and David Stadelmann. 2018. "The Effect of Food Price Changes on Child Labour: Evidence from Uganda." *The Journal of Development Studies* 55 (7): 1–16.

GSS. 2003. "Ghana Child Labour Survey."

GSS. 2014. "Ghana Living Standards Survey Round 6 (GLSS 6): Child Labour Report." Ghana Statistical Service, Accra. www.statsghana.gov.gh/docfiles/glss6/GLSS6_Labour%20Force%20Report.pdf.

Hussain, Mahmood, and Keith E. Maskus. 2003. "Child Labour Use and Economic Growth: An Econometric Analysis." *The World Economy* 26 (7): 993–1017.

Ilahi, Nadeem, Peter F. Orazem, and Guilherme Sedlacek. 2009. "How Does Working as a Child Affect Wages, Income, and Poverty as an Adult?" In *Child Labor and Education in Latin America*, 87–101. Springer.

ILO. 2004. *Child Labour: A Textbook for University Students*. Geneva: International Labour Office.

ILO. 2011. *Children in Hazardous Work: What We Know, What We Need to Do*. Geneva: International Programme on the Elimination of Child Labour (IPEC), International Labour Office.

ILO. 2017a. "Global Estimates of Child Labour: Results and Trends, 2012–2016." Geneva. www.ilo.org/wcmsp5/groups/public/-dgreports/-dcomm/documents/publication/wcms_575499.pdf.

ILO. 2017b. "Global Estimates of Modern Slavery and Child Labour." ILO. www.ilo.org/wcmsp5/groups/public/@ed_norm/@ipec/documents/publication/wcms_597869.pdf.

Jensen, Peter, and Helena Skyt Nielsen. 1997. "Child Labour or School Attendance? Evidence from Zambia." *Journal of Population Economics* 10 (4): 407–424.

Kambhampati, Uma S. and Raji Rajan. 2006. "Economic Growth: A Panacea for Child Labor?" *World Development* 34 (3): 426–445.

Kindleberger, Charles Poor. 1958. *Economic Development*. New York, NY: McGraw Hill.

Knaul, Felicia Marie. 2001. "The Impact of Child Labor and School Dropout on Human Capital: Gender Differences in Mexico." *The Economics of Gender in Mexico: Work, Family, State, and Market*, 46–84.

Koomson, Isaac. 2017. "Examining Child Labour and Parental Altruism from the Rural-Urban Divide: Extending the Inverted-U Empirics." *NESRA – WP/17/003*. http://nesranetwork.com/admin/images/pdf/20170421043933child%20labour%20and%20parental%20altruism%20from%20the%20rural-urban%20divide.pdf.pdf.

Koomson, Isaac, and Simplice A. Asongu. 2016. "Relative Contribution of Child Labour to Household Farm and Non-Farm Income in Ghana: Simulation with Child's Education." *African Development Review* 28 (1): 104–115.

Kruger, Diana I. 2007. "Coffee Production Effects on Child Labor and Schooling in Rural Brazil." *Journal of Development Economics* 82 (2): 448–463.

Lima, Luiz Renato, Shirley Mesquita, and Marianne Wanamaker. 2015. "Child Labor and the Wealth Paradox: The Role of Altruistic Parents." *Economics Letters* 130: 80–82.

Lopez-Calva, Luis F. 2001. "Child Labor: Myths, Theories and Facts." *Journal of International Affairs*, 59–73.

NBS and ILO. 2016. "Tanzania National Child Labour Survey 2014: Analytical Report." International Labour Organization (ILO) and the Tanzania National Bureau of Statistics (NBS). ttp://www.ilo.org/ipec/Informationresources/WCMS_IPEC_PUB_28475/lang-en/index.htm.

Ncube, Mthuli, and Basil Jones. 2013. "Drivers and Dynamics of Fragility in Africa." *African Development Bank, Africa Economic Brief* 4 (5): 1–16.

Neumayer, Eric, and Indra De Soysa. 2005. "Trade Openness, Foreign Direct Investment and Child Labor." *World Development* 33 (1): 43–63.

Nurkse, Ragnar. 1953. *Problems of Capital Formation in Underdeveloped Countries*. Oxford: Oxford University Press.

Nurkse, Ragnar. 1957. *Problemas Da Formação de Capital Em Países Subdesenvolvidos*. Rio de Janeiro: Editora Civilização Brasileira.

Pörtner, Claus Chr. 2001. "Children as Insurance." *Journal of Population Economics* 14 (1): 119–136.

Ray, Ranjan. 2002. "The Determinants of Child Labour and Child Schooling in Ghana." *Journal of African Economies* 11 (4): 561–590.

Rosati, Furio Camillo, Zafiris Tzannatos, and others. 2003. "Child Work: An Expository Framework of Altruistic and Non-Altruistic Models." The World Bank. http://ideas.repec.org/p/wbk/hdnspu/25984.html.

UCW. 2017. "Understanding Trends in Child Labour." UCW Working Paper Series, Rome. www.ucw-project.org/attachment/04122017609Understanding__child_labour_trends.pdf.

Uganda, B. O. S. 2003. *Uganda National Household Survey, 2005/2006: Report on the Socioeconomic Survey*. Entebbe, Uganda: Uganda BOS.

United Nations. 2015. "Transforming Our World: The 2030 Agenda for Sustainable Development." 2015. www.un.org/ga/search/view_doc.asp?symbol=A/RES/70/1&Lang=E.

USDOL. 2017. "2016 Findings on the Worst Forms of Child Labour." Bureau of International Labour Affairs, U.S. Department of Labour. https://businessandhumanrights.uconn.edu/wp-content/uploads/sites/1850/2017/11/US-Dept-of-Labor-2016-Worst-Forms-of-Child-Labor.pdf.

Watson, Rod. 2010. "Symbolic Interactionism." *Society and Language Use* 7: 304–313.

World Bank. 2015. "'World Development Indicators', World Bank Publications." www.gopa.de/fr/news/world-bank-release-world-development-indicators-2015.

6 Regional and country-level interventions to end child labor

Making economic development child-friendly by eradicating child labor is, and should be, at the core of politically legitimated and socially resonant economic development policies. It requires expanding the economic reach of governments to the downtrodden, to children in households that are below the poverty line (of U.S.$1.9 a day). The extent of this reach, the United Nations Development Program's (UNDP) Human Development Report of 2016 suggests, should not be limited to a few such households. It should extend to "all, in every corner of the world [should] be able to realize their full potential now and in the future" (UNDP 2017). It was this understanding that spurred the UN in December 2015 to issue the Sustainable Development Goals (which replaced the Millennium Development Goals, MDGs). The goals relating to children have a single message: "leave no child behind." While impressive progress has been made in the development of democratic best practice to resolve political problems—such as civil wars and election-related tensions—in sub-Saharan Africa, the past quarter-century has also witnessed a rise in the incidence of child labor. In Chapter 5 we employed a series of statistical models to explain the link between child labor, income, poverty and fragility. More profound, however, is the trivialization of the "child factor" in the theorization of the legal and institutional aspects of the econometrically informed indexes used by other scholars and think tanks to study the unevenness of development in micro-communities—households—in sub-Saharan Africa.

It is an established fact that, while economic development is one of the surest means to reverse state fragility, the value a society places on the rights and welfare of its children is a reflection of that society's character. The devaluation of people's worth—their being and knowing—that arises from deprivation run deep in the discourse of economic and social empowerment in the 'fragile' spaces of sub-Saharan Africa (Chauvet and Collier 2008; Potts 2007; Bryceson 2006). While deprivation has also been an outcome of nature's wrath, such as famine and drought, man-made artefacts—exclusionary social norms, violence, discriminatory laws, imbalances in political participation, unequal distribution of opportunities and the conflicts they generate—play a major role in the disappearance of the category of "children" in the discourse of state fragility. Thus, the value society places on, say, economic growth *should* go beyond satisfying basic human needs and the elimination of wants (and greed and grievance). It should encompass the voice of the voiceless (the children) in an expanded space for experimentation with economic, sociocultural and political models of human development. To recommend the right of children to 'self-determine' the development trajectory of nations would invite the rebuttal that children are not mature and, therefore, lack the requisite independence of thought. Nonetheless, we can safely remark that children's agency, and their right to be the focus of development policies, should determine the policy choices of development experts and governments, and shape the political, legal and economic outcomes of their interventions. To accomplish this requires, to borrow the words of the UNDP, a refocusing of "some aspects of the human development approach—collective capabilities, not only individual capabilities; voice and autonomy, not only well-being; and inclusion, not only diversity. It also needs focusing on assessment perspectives going beyond averages and quantitative achievements" (UNDP 2017).

To that end, this chapter attempts to authenticate the argument that the rights and welfare of the African child are central to the African peace, development and human rights architecture developed to guide states in sub-Saharan Africa in a collective venture to make development work for children, and, in tandem, escape the fragility trap. By collectivizing their efforts, first, through the Organization of the African Unity (OAU) and, after 2002, through the African Union (AU), most sub-Saharan African governments—and especially those that have ratified the *African Charter on the Rights and Welfare of the Child* (ACRWC)—are defying those who argue that child labor has little to do with the causes of state fragility.

The first part of this chapter traces the political and legal histories of anti-child labor regimes in sub-Saharan Africa, demonstrating that the discourse on the need for a strong national plan or policy to combat the worst forms of child labor is supported by regional institutional and legal advances within a broader, multidimensional international human rights regime. It is this argument that provides the basis for the second part of the chapter, which addresses the politics of re-affirmation of the global child protection regime created by the ACRWC. From there, we examine, using frame theory, country-level progress in the elimination of the worst forms of child labor. We scrutinize the national plans of five sub-Saharan African countries, selected from five sub-regional economic blocs in the region: **Cameroon** (from the Economic Community of Central African States (ECCAS) sub-region); **Kenya** (the Intergovernmental Authority for Development, IGAD); **Ghana** (the Economic Community of West African States, ECOWAS); **Tanzania** (the East African Community, EAC); and **Zimbabwe** (the Southern African Development Community, SADC). We examine how the construct of 'intervention' (which seeks to promote the fundamental aspects of international human rights law and the emergent doctrine of an international responsibility to protect) is structured through 15 sub-frames within the three themes of (1) social programming, (2) legal proactivity, and (3) institutional interventions, monitoring, and evaluation. We look at the similarities in the framing of risk management as it relates to medical, social, nutritional, judicial and educational interventions. While frame theory is the overarching discourse used to understand subject matter similarities, for the judicial section, we employ French and Raven's *The Basis of Social Power Theory* (1959) to assess the impact of national laws on child labor. On the issue of institutional intervention, we also draw from the various behavioral and child-development theories of Sigmund Freud, Erik Erikson, Jean Piaget, John Bowlby and Lev Vygotsky.

An historical overview of the development of regional anti-child labor legal regimes

The desire to use a multi-prong anti-child labor framework to end state fragility—and, in tandem, promote economic development—is integral to states' commitment to uphold international human rights law and labor standards. In Africa, the pedigree of this commitment can be traced back to the meeting of the OAU Assembly of Heads of State and Government held in Monrovia, Liberia, in July 1973. It was at this meeting that the leaders of postcolonial African states decided to adopt a resolution titled *The Guidelines and Measures for National and Collective Self-reliance in Social and Economic Development for the Establishment of a New International Economic Order* (hereafter, the Monrovia Declaration) (Harris 1994, 7:124). Endorsed by the 11th Ordinary Session of the OAU council of ministers of economic development in Addis Ababa on 25 May 1974, the Monrovia Declaration expresses, in its preamble, OAU member countries' commitment to creating space for sustainable development and economic growth in Africa by the year 2000, to coincide with the OAU's planned announcement of the start of Africa's development decade (2000–2010) (Ofodile 2010, 45). The Monrovia Declaration did not explicitly identify empowerment of children as a core economic priority; however, the wording of clause 4(a) accorded children an important place, with its call on states to take steps to eliminate illiteracy among their youth—a sure means, as section 4(j) of the Declaration affirmed, to achieve sustainable socioeconomic transformation at the sub-regional level, which would culminate in the establishment of dynamic sub-regional economic integration and common market regimes (ECCAS, ECOWAS, EAC, IGAD, SADC) in sub-Saharan Africa.

But a sub-regional common market regime that lacks ethical benchmarks for the treatment of children in the economic and social sectors of member states is inimical to the idea of economic development. To curtail the impact of "child-insensitive development," at least in principle, the OAU Assembly of Heads of State and Government, during its 16th ordinary meeting in Monrovia, which took place between 17 and 20 July 1979, adopted the *Declaration on the Rights and Welfare of the African Child* (DeRWAC). In practice, DeRWAC was a reminder to OAU member states of their responsibility to prioritize the general advancement of the children of Africa. In fact, with 1979 also being United Nations International Year of the Child, DeRWAC was a conscious move to recognize the place of the rights and welfare of the African child in international law (DeRWAC 1979; quoted in Kaime 2009, 21).

In the main, the framers of the DeRWAC were receptive to international partnerships. They realized many countries, only recently emerged from European colonial rule, would still be experiencing a steep learning curve; still in the processes of becoming self-reliant. Against this backdrop, the DeRWAC recommended member states to partner with other countries (both within and outside their respective sub-regional blocs), as well as with non-governmental and community-based organizations, to develop programs that would promote the rights and welfare of children. The framers of the DeRWAC were convinced that, through this declaration, states would succeed in curbing "'unnecessary' child labor, especially [that] affecting the girl child" (Freeman 2007, 20). Interestingly, however, the use of the word 'unnecessary' (implying acceptance of some other 'necessary' forms of child labor) in the preamble of DeRWAC suggests the framers of the DeRWAC were mindful of cultural and economic forces within OAU member states that rendered the immediate, complete elimination of child labor impracticable—within communities, for example, where, without child labor, families would starve; in communities where vulnerable children had assumed the responsibility of providing for low income families—a responsibility that should have been that of the governments of their countries. If we are to deconstruct the word 'unnecessary,' our conclusions is that while the DeRWAC, in theory, rejects hazardous forms of child labor, it did, in practice, recognize, if not endorse, other unspecified forms of child labor. Perhaps it was in recognition of the role child labor plays in the sociocultural continuity of families (as a sub-unit of the political legitimacy of the state) that led the OAU Secretariat to say (during the session at which the DeRWAC was tabled for member state approval) that it recognized

> the deep concern [of member states] about the future of African children as inheritors and keepers of African cultural heritage; bearing in mind that the welfare of the African Child is inextricably bound up with that of its parents and other members of its family, especially the mother.
>
> (Organisation of African Unity 1979, quoted in Van Bueren 1998, 31)

With the rights of female children, and their freedom to self-determine their reproductive rights, not a priority for individual members states in the 1970s, the OAU Secretariat was essentially affirming the existence of politically motivated and culturally regulated platforms wherein the social, economic and political plight of governments was indirectly tied to familial aspects of gender relationships that are disempowering to the women and the child.

That notwithstanding, the DeRWAC (ibid., 32) called on states to develop and strengthen "their own activities in co-operation with national organs set up in the framework of the IYC [International Year of the Child]." It further called for those countries yet to develop their intervention models to give preferences to programs directly connected to the health, nutrition and education of the child. Policy and intervention strategies in these three priority areas were to be measured by the extent to which (1) they were mainstreamed into national development plans, with the aim of making them universally accessible to all children, including the vulnerable and disabled; and (2) their impact on basic accessible services for children and economically disadvantaged families, and on the expansion of those services within the shortest possible timeframe.

Once the 1979 Monrovia Declaration was adopted, however, the drive to mainstream children's rights and welfare within development activities quickly dissipated. It remained largely dormant until 1990, when the OAU adopted the *African Charter on the Rights and Welfare of the Child* (otherwise known as the African Children's Charter). Even then, it took another nine years for the African Children's Charter to come into force, on November 29, 1999. The reasons for this delay are many, but the most prominent ones are as follows. First, the OAU lacked the power to compel member states to ratify its declarations, conventions and protocols, and to adhere to their provisions. Using competing conceptual theories on state behavior and decision-making with respect to treaty ratification, Tiyanjana Maluwa (Maluwa 2012, 1), concludes that, like its successor (the AU), the OAU was a respecter of the sovereign 'entitlement' of member states. By focusing on the "basic ratification–signature correlation of these treaties," Maluwa shows how sovereign entitlements raise procedural, constitutional and legislative obstacles that prevent states from expediting the treaty ratification process. The general outcome was (and still is, for the AU) low treaty commitment. Although Maluwa understands how the sovereign rights of states constrain regional and international legal regimes, however, he is of the view that, the treaties of regional organizations in Africa "do not create any tension with the domestic legal regime and structure" (Maluwa 2012, 1).

Maluwa's point is valid, and we can assume that—since the ambassadors of the OAU member states at the time understood Maluwa's point (given he was the legal counsel for the OAU in the 1990s)—the lack of action to ratify the African Children's Charter was caused by other, non-legal debates. This leads us to the second point: the crisis of armed conflict in sub-Saharan African between 1989 (with the eruption of the civil war in Liberia) and 1999 (the signing of the Lomé Peace Accord that brought the civil war in Sierra Leone to an end, and the start of the final phase of South Sudan's war for independence). The years between the African Children's Charter's adoption (1990) and its coming into force (1999) thus coincided with a decade of internecine civil war throughout sub-Saharan Africa. Against this backdrop, the question of children's rights and welfare was a lower priority; even where their rights mattered, it was merely implied in the international efforts to de-militarize the "governable spaces," where children can play. This is not to say that, during these years, nothing was done for children. The institutional design of the child protection regime during this troubled era depended, on the economic front, on International Labour Organization (ILO) interventions; on the political, the UN Committee on the Rights of the Child (CRC); on the cultural, the interventions of the United Nations Educational, Scientific and Cultural Organization (UNESCO); on the security front, the humanitarian interventions authorized by the UN Security Council (UNSC); and, on the general socio-educational and developmental front, on the United Nations Children's Fund (UNICEF). Taken together with the progressive responses of some governments at the time, the active roles of these international institutions suggests that "getting it right" for the children" was integral to peace and security, and economic development during the turbulent decade of the 1990s.

The politics of international (re-)affirmation in a post-ratification era: the African Charter on the Rights and Welfare of the Child (ACRWC)

Spurred on by the understanding that until the child labor crisis was addressed fragility in sub-Saharan Africa would persist, in 2016, the African Union (AU) committed itself to achieving sustainable development for the sake of the children by 2063. Two years later, on June 16, 2018, during the commemoration of the 'Day of the African Child,' the AU further pledged to "leave no child behind for Africa's development" by 2040. Both declarations seek to mainstream the developmental and human rights needs of the 'African child,' particularly those living in conditions of fragility and poverty. These declarations are also part of AU member states' strategic roadmap to the United Nations Sustainable Development Goal 8.7 (ACERWC 2018b), which calls on UN member states to

> take immediate and effective measures to eradicate forced labour, end modern slavery and human trafficking and secure the prohibition and elimination of the worst forms of child labour, including recruitment and use of child soldiers, and by 2025 end child labour in all its forms.

The steps proposed in Goal 8.7 are in keeping with the ratification and implementation of fundamental ILO labor "standards and compliance in law and practice towards … sustainable, inclusive and sustainable economic growth, full and productive employment and decent work for all."

Despite its inability to make "development work for the continent's children" before it was disbanded, and replaced by the AU on July 9, 2002, the OAU deserves recognition for laying the groundworks for its successor. In 1990 the OAU, in partnership with the ILO and the CRC, adopted the *African Charter on the Rights and Welfare of the Child* (ACRWC) (ACERWC 2018a, 2). The primary objective of the ACRWC, as the OAU Secretariat envisaged it, was to lead all OAU member states to centralize the needs and concerns of children, recognizing that not all children were benefiting from the 'trickle-down' economics of growth and development in the continent. The Charter was intended to motivate member states to prioritize children and children's rights in their implementation of poverty reduction interventions funded by the World Bank and the International Monetary Fund (IMF), and to develop national strategies for monitoring and evaluating these poverty reduction strategies. The Charter also called on these states to emphasize the annual celebration of the Day of the African Child,[1] as a means of encouraging OAU member states to accord children an active role in planning and implementing policies that affect them directly, and of reminding states of their obligation to create national children's protection mechanisms (ACERWC 2018b, 3).

The *African Charter on the Rights and Welfare of the Child* states, in Article 15 (the 'Child Labor' clause), that:

1 Every child shall be protected from all forms of economic exploitation and from performing any work that is likely to be hazardous or to interfere with the child's physical, mental, spiritual, moral, or social development.
2 States Parties to the present Charter take all appropriate legislative and administrative measures to ensure the full implementation of this Article which covers both the formal and informal sectors of employment and having regard to the relevant provisions of the International Labour Organization's instruments relating to children, States Parties shall in particular:
   a provide through legislation, minimum wages for admission to every employment;
   b provide for appropriate regulation of hours and conditions of employment;
   c provide for appropriate penalties or other sanctions to ensure the effective enforcement of this Article;
   d promote the dissemination of information on the hazards of child labour to all sectors of the community.

(Organization of African Unity (OAU) 1990)

From the standpoint of comparative politics, Article 15 aimed at giving a regional, Africanist cast to universalized neoliberal norms on children's rights and welfare, in an era in which 'exclusionary' postcolonial narratives of 'Africa's problems deserving an African solution' were losing their impetus. As such, it is arguable that Article 15 affirms the need for African states to move beyond acceptance to actually *doing* that which was called for under international norms such as the United Nations *Convention on the Rights of the Child* (UNCRC) of 1989; the *International Covenant on Economic, Social and Cultural Rights* (ICESCR) of 1966, the *International Covenant on Civil and Political Rights* (ICCPR) of 1976, the ILO *Convention No. 138* (the 'minimum age' convention) of 1973 and the ILO *Convention No. 182* (on the worst forms of child labor) of 1999.

Although the UNCRC has been criticized for the binary it created between "children's working rights" and the "child labor abolition" regimes (see Okyere 2013), it does define "hazardous work" as wealth-generation activities that are not in the best interest of the child (Lundy 2007). In Articles 32 (child labor), 33 (drug abuse), 34 (sexual exploitation) and 36 (other unspecified forms of exploitation that may impact the welfare and development of the child), the UNCRC emphasizes what the potential adverse impacts where children are subjected to harmful and exploitative work. In broader terms, the UNCRC imposes an obligation on states to take proactive steps to address the sociocultural, economic and political factors that compel families to subject their children to hazardous work (Invernizzi 2008, 135). For its part, the ICCPR states, in Article 24, that

> [e]very child shall have, without any discrimination as to race, colour, sex, language, religion, national or social origin, property or birth, the right to such measures of protection as are required by his status as a minor, on the part of his family, society and the State.
>
> (ICCPR, Art. 24; 1976, quoted in Langlois 2005, 417)

The ICESCR contains clauses that recognize the rights of families and the child. These clauses are noted in Articles 6–7 (on the right to work), Article 10 (on protection of and assistance to the family), Article 11 (the right to adequate standards of living) and Articles 13–14 (on the right to education) (UN General Assembly 1966). Most important of these clauses occurs at Article 10(3), which states:

> Special measures of protection and assistance should be taken on behalf of all children and young persons without any discrimination for reasons of parentage or other conditions. Children and young persons should be protected from economic and social exploitation. Their employment in work harmful to their morals or health or dangerous to life or likely to hamper their normal development should be punishable by law. States should also set age limits below which the paid employment of child labour should be prohibited and punishable by law.
>
> (ICESCR, quoted in Nilsson 2013, 13)

The ICESCR Committee reaffirmed, particularly in paragraphs 22 and 23 of its General Comment No. 14 (adopted in 2000), the need to protect children from all forms of work that are likely to interfere with their development or physical or mental health. The Committee emphasized states' obligations to protect children from all forms of economic exploitation and forced labor, to enable them to pursue their full development and acquire a technical and vocational education (as indicated in Article 6(2)). Moreover, the Committee, in General Comment 13 (on the right to education), outlined essential and interrelated elements that States Parties are to use as measurement indicators when fulfilling their obligations under Article 12. These elements are availability, adaptability, acceptability and accessibility. "Availability" signifies that functioning education facilities are present; "adaptability" that the modes of knowledge delivery are flexible and responsive to the changing needs and circumstances of the children and their communities; "acceptability" (in pursuance of Article 13(1), 13(3) and 13(4)) is about ensuring that the substance of knowledge delivery is of high quality and culturally sensitive; and "accessibility" reflects the discrimination to which vulnerable groups (children and women) are often subject, with one way of ending such discrimination being to make schooling (primary, secondary and higher) economically accessible to the poor—noting that, under Article 13(2) of General Comment No. 14, it is the responsibility of governments, not the private sector, to ensure that the poor are able to afford schooling. Put another way, the clause on "accessibility" is aimed at reminding governments that higher school fees lead to illiteracy, and that illiteracy increases the incidence of child labor in poverty-stricken communities (Committee on Economic, Social and Cultural Rights 2000).

The ACRWC is also an affirmation of the ILO's 'Minimum Age' Convention (*Convention No. 138*). This convention requires ratifying states to set a minimum age for employment (Article 2(3)), which should not be below 16 or the age required to complete secondary schooling (whichever comes first) (Article 2(1)). In recognition of lack of education as a driver of child labor, *Convention No. 138* calls on States Parties to emphasize the education, health and physical well-being of children; as part of its recommendations for ending child labor, the framers of *Convention No. 138* emphasized the establishment of national policies on child labor and child welfare regulatory institutions. For its part, ILO *Convention No. 182* (on the worst forms of child labor) observes that most child laborers in poor, fragile states are compelled to work by circumstances such as poverty, family needs and social settings. Therefore, it calls on governments to identify the 'push' and 'pull' factors of poverty and take steps to resolve them. In fact, the context in which 'identify' and 'resolve' are used in *Convention No. 182* places them under the broader responsibility of states to ensure that the family unit enjoys its fundamental, inalienable rights under in Appendix 5 of the *Universal Declaration of Human Rights*: the rights to equality (Article 1), freedom from discrimination (Article 2), life, liberty and personal security (including the right to food and shelter) (Article 3), freedom from slavery (Article 4) and freedom from torture and degrading treatment (Article 5).

On the whole, what unites these international legal regimes is their call for state parties to establish anti-child labor regulatory institutions. Although the AU is not a state, it nonetheless understands that these international instruments place an obligation on regional bodies to continually reaffirm their commitment to the UN Charter and all other conventions and protocols relevant to international peace and security (OAU 1990). In pursuance of this obligation, and in light of its self-imposed duty of care to the children of Africa (as noted in the Monvoria Declaration of 1979), the OAU established the 'African Committee of Experts on the Rights and Welfare of the Child' (ACERWC) (see Appendix One of the *Declaration on the Rights and Welfare of the African Child*). The ACERWC is an autonomous body. Article 32 explains its relevance and functions; Article 33 addresses its composition; Article 34, the election of its members; Articles 35 and 36, the process of nomination of members; Article 37, members' term of office; Article 38 outlines its bureaucratic rules of procedure; Article 39, the advertisement and filling of a vacant position; Article 40, the functions of its secretariat; and Article 41, its privileges and immunities—which, it should be noted, also come with employees' responsibilities in the performance of their duties.

Demonstrably, the renewed attention to the fight against child labor by the ACERWC constitutes, on the one hand, a continuation of efforts to make political aspects of regional integration child-sensitive; while, on the other hand—and most importantly—a new effort to achieve what can best be described as the '*childification*' of human rights standards that would, directly and indirectly, influence economic development in the sub-region. This 'childification' of politics, economic and law, in this instance, denotes the development of bureaucratic principles, rules and decision-making procedures that circumscribe the policy preferences of states to ensure outcomes that are not detrimental to the future of the children. As the ACERWC pursues its work through a specific set of international norms, guiding principles and policies, we can classify it as a supranational institution. Moreover, as its methodical way of promoting the mainstreaming of the needs and concerns of children has the potential to depoliticize the lived experiences of children, we can classify it as a social organization in the quest to create an 'affective community,' wherein the social and cultural markers of society are sensitive to children.

For once, rather than calling for non-child responsive governments to be expunged, the affective communities of children's right advocacy are now emotively calling on governments to 'learn' the art of 'good parenting'—thanks to the work of the ACERWC. With the ACRWC and the ACERWC to guide them through this 'learning curve,' most of the sub-Saharan African states are gradually moving beyond the mere ratification of regional and international instruments. They are creating formal anti-child labor regimes anchored on three principles that capture the fundamental aspects of international human rights law and the emergent doctrine of an international responsibility to protect: prevent, react and rebuild. It is these three aspects of human rights law and responsibility that create the necessary conditions for a proactive turn (away from inaction) in the discourse of human rights norms in sub-Saharan Africa. Some sub-Saharan African countries—arguing from the relativist character of 'human rights'—have resisted the ACERWC's model, especially with regards to such questions as: *who is a child: should the definitional age limit of 18 (as stated in the African Charter on the Rights and Welfare of the Child) be revoked because it conflicts with the age limit of 16 set by the UN Convention on the Rights of the Child? Who should determine what becomes of the 'African Child': the African country where the 'African child' lives, or the neoliberal international organizations, whose activities are seen (by cultural relativists) as attempts to regulate the family structures in post-colonial Africa?* Notwithstanding the negative impact of such misgivings over ulterior motives, the ACERWC—and its partners, the ILO and CRC)—have set in motion standards that could enable sub-Saharan African countries to make development work for children.

Comparing sub-Saharan African country-level institutional and legal advances to end the worst forms of child labor

The rate at which states have ratified the Charter and its commitments has continued to rise, notwithstanding intermittent periods of stagnation. For example, between 1990 and 1999 the Charter accumulated 16 state signatories, while between 2000 and 2009, a further 29 state signatures were added.[2] As of the time of writing this chapter, 13 sub-Saharan Africa countries had yet to fully accept the Charter (that is, to move beyond merely signing to actually ratify and domesticate the Charter's provisions). These countries (with the dates of signature in brackets) include the Central African Republic (February 4, 2003), Guinea-Bissau (March 8, 2005), Liberia (May 14, 1992), Swaziland (August 23, 1990) and Zambia (February 28, 1992). Countries that have neither signed nor ratified the charter include the Democratic Republic of the Congo, São Tomé and Príncipe, and South Sudan[3] Further, Botswana, Mali and Mauritania, which have ratified the Charter, in 2015 recorded a reservation, stating that they would not be bound by the Charter's inflexible upper age limit for childhood of 18 years (African Union 2016, 3). They reiterated, however, that they would abide by the United Nations' Convention on the Rights of the Child, since its age limit of 16 was consistent with their respective cultural and economic interests. Interestingly, Sudan—which has neither signed nor ratified the Charter—also entered a reservation, stating that it did not consider itself bound by Article 21(2), which calls for "the abolition of child marriage and further made reservations in respect of the right to education of pregnant girls (article 11(6)) and to privacy (article 10)" (African Union 2016, 3). However, with a clear majority of regional states having endorsed the Charter, there has been a shift in the way children are imagined, understood and represented in the discourse of peace, security and economic development in sub-Saharan Africa.

Case studies

This chapter does not address the statistical prevalence and sectoral distribution of child labor, which have already been addressed in Chapter 5. Instead, as outlined at the start of the chapter, frame theory is employed in an examination of the policy documents of five sub-Saharan African countries, Cameroon, Ghana, Kenya, Tanzania and Zimbabwe (see Table 6.1).

Methods

Readers are reminded, first, that this group of countries was selected from a list of equally eligible countries, due, in part, to the fact that they have not (at the time of writing this book) entered contentious caveats to the *African Charter on the Rights and Welfare of the Child.* Second, the focus on only one document (published between 2009 and 2016) for each country, with the understanding that these national policies can only be built upon by the successive policies of the government.

Third, our methodology takes note of the non-uniformity of these documents, in terms of their headings and subheadings, contents and projected outcomes. That notwithstanding, we tried to find parallel themes that are present in all these documents. These themes are constructed around 'protection,' 'prevention' and 'reaction' (the last in the context of rebuilding the broken lives of child laborers).

Table 6.1 Anti-child labor policies and institutional/operational/legal frameworks of case study countries

Country	*Title of national policy and author*	*Year adopted*	*Institutional framework (implementing agencies)*	*Legal frameworks that meet international standards*
Cameroon	**Name of national policy:** The National Plan of Action to Combat Child Labor and Trafficking in Children (PANETEC) **Author(s):** Government of Cameroon **Internet link:** Hard copy used for this study	2016	• Ministry of Labor and Social Security (MINTSS) • National Committee to Combat Child Labor (CNLCTE) • National Committee for Child Protection • Ministry of Justice (MOJ). • Ministry of Social Affairs (MINAS) • Ministry of Women's Empowerment and Family (MINPROFF)	• **The minimum age for work:** Section 86 of the Labor Code (3, 9, 31) • **The minimum age for hazardous work:** Articles 9–23 of Law No. 017; Sections 86 and 87 of the Labor Code (3, 31, 32, 55, 56) • **Identification of hazardous occupations or activities prohibited for children:** Article 9–23 of Law No. 017 (32, 56) • **Prohibition of forced labor:** Article 4 of the Constitution; Law No. 2011/024; Articles 11, 341–1,353, 292 and 293 of the Penal Code; Section 2 of the Labor Code (31, 33–36, 55, 57, 58)
Kenya	**Name of national policy:** The Framework for the National Child Protection System for Kenya **Author(s):** National Council for Children's Services, Government of Kenya **Internet link:** https://resourcecentre.savethechildren.net/sites/default/files/documents/5429.pdf	2011	• Ministry of Labor, Social Security, and Services (MLSSS) • National Police Service • Office of the Director of Public Prosecutions • National Council for Children's Services (NCCS) • National Council for Children's Services • National Steering Committee on Child Labor	• **The minimum age for work:** Section 56 of the Employment Act; Section 10.4 of the Children Act; Section 12 of the Employment (General) Rules (43, 49, 50) • **The minimum age for hazardous work:** Sections 2 and 53.1 of the Employment Act; Sections 2 and 10.1 of the Children Act (43, 49)

continued

Table 6.1 continued

Country	*Title of national policy and author*	*Year adopted*	*Institutional framework (implementing agencies)*	*Legal frameworks that meet international standards*
			• National Labor Board • Counter-Trafficking in Persons Advisory Committee. • Local, Advisory, and District Child Labor Committees	• **Identification of hazardous occupations or activities prohibited for children:** Section 12 and the Fourth Schedule of the Employment (General) Rules; Section 10.1 of the Children Act (43, 50) • **Prohibition of forced labor:** Article 30 of the Constitution; Sections 4.1 and 53.1 of the Employment Act; Sections 174 and 254–266 of the Penal Code; Article 3 of the Counter-Trafficking in Persons Act; Article 13 of the Sexual Offences Act; Section 13.1 of the Children Act (43, 49, 51–54)
Ghana	**Name of national policy:** The National Plan of Action (Phase II) for The Elimination of the Worst Forms of Against Child Labor (NPA II) (2017–2020): Towards Achieving Sustainable Development Goal (SDG) 8.7 **Author(s):** Ministry of Employment and Labour Relations, Government of Ghana **Internet link:** www.unicef.org/ghana/NPA_(II)_EWFCL.pdf	2016	• Ministry of Gender, Children, and Social Protection (MOGCSP) • National Steering Committee on Child Labor (NSCCL) • Community Child Protection Committees (CCPCs) • Community Child Protection Committees (CCPCs) • Ministry of the Interior (MOI)	• **The minimum age for work:** Section 89 of the Children's Act (59) • **The minimum age for hazardous work:** Section 91 of the Children's Act (59) • **Identification of hazardous occupations or activities prohibited for children:** Articles 16.1 and 16.2 of the Constitution; Articles 116 and 117 of the Labor Act; Sections 1–3 and 42 of the Human Trafficking Act; Sections 1 and 2 of the Human Trafficking Prohibition Legislative Instrument (53, 60, 62, 63) • **Prohibition of forced labor:** Articles 16.1 and 16.2 of the Constitution; Articles 116 and 117 of the Labor Act; Sections 1–3 and 42 of the Human Trafficking Act; Sections 1 and 2 of the Human Trafficking Prohibition Legislative Instrument (53, 60, 62, 63)

Tanzania	**Name of national policy:** National Action Plan for the Elimination of Child Labor **Author(s):** Ministry of Labor, Employment, and Youth Development **Internet link:** www.ilo.org/dyn/natlex/docs/MONOGRAPH/94604/111054/F347421111/TZA94604.pdf	2009	• Ministry of Labor and Employment (MOLE) (mainland & Zanzibar)–Child Labor Unit • Ministry of Community Development, Gender, and Children (mainland & Zanzibar) • Ministry of Labor, Economic Empowerment, and Cooperatives—Labor Commission (Mainland) • Ministry of Social Welfare and Youth Development (Zanzibar)—Child Protection Unit • Police (mainland & Zanzibar)	• **The minimum age for work:** Article 5 of the Employment and Labor Relations Act, 2004; Article 77 of the Law of the Child Act, 2009 (38, 39, 48, 49) • **The minimum age for hazardous work:** Article 6 of the Zanzibar Employment Act, 2005; Articles 2 and 98 of the Zanzibar Children's Act, 2011 (50–52) • **Identification of hazardous occupations or activities prohibited for children:** Article 5 of the Employment and Labor Relations Act, 2004; Article 82 of the Law of the Child Act, 2009; Articles 8 and 9 of the Zanzibar Employment Act No. 11 of 2005; Article 100 of the Zanzibar Children's Act, 2011 (48, 49, 51, 52) • **Prohibition of forced labor:** Article 5 of the Employment and Labor Relations Act, 2004; Article 82 of the Law of the Child Act, 2009; Articles 8 and 9 of the Zanzibar Employment Act No. 11 of 2005; Article 100 of the Zanzibar Children's Act, 2011; List of Hazardous Child Labor (7, 48, 49, 51, 52)

continued

Table 6.1 continued

Country	*Title of national policy and author*	*Year adopted*	*Institutional framework (implementing agencies)*	*Legal frameworks that meet international standards*
Zimbabwe	**Name of national policy:** National Action Plan for Orphans and Vulnerable Children (Phase II 2011–2015) (Annex IV; supplement of the National Action Plan to Combat Child Labor) **Author:** Ministry of Labour and Social Service, Government of Zimbabwe **Internet link:** www.unicef.org/zimbabwe/ZIM_resources_Natactionovc.pdf	2010	• Ministry of Public Service. • Labor, and Social Welfare (MPSLSW) • Ministry of Justice and Legal Affairs • Zimbabwe Republic Police (ZRP) • Ministry-Level Committee on Children's Issues • National Steering Committee to Address the Worst Forms of Child Labor • Child Protection Committees National Task Force on Street Children Anti-Trafficking Inter-Ministerial Committee	• **The minimum age for work:** Section 3 of the Labor Amendment Act (20) • **The minimum age for hazardous work:** Section 11(4) of the Labor Act (20) • **Prohibition of forced labor:** Sections 54 and 55 of the Constitution; Section 4A of the Labor Act (20, 22) • **Identification of hazardous occupations or activities prohibited for children:** Section 11(4) of the Labor Act; Section 10A of the Children's Act (20, 21); Section 87 of the Criminal Law Act; Section 3 of the Sexual Offenses Act; Section 8(2) of the Children's Protection and Adoption Act; Section 3 of the Trafficking in Persons Act (7, 10, 21, 23, 24) • **Prohibition of forced labor:** Sections 54 and 55 of the Constitution; Section 4A of the Labor Act (20, 22)

Source: institutional and legal frameworks US Department of Labor's Bureau of International Labor (BIL). *2016 findings on the worst forms of child labor*. Bureau of International Labour Affairs, U.S. Department of Labour. Retrieved from www.dol.gov/sites/default/files/documents/ilab/reports/child-labor/findings/TDAMagazine.pdf

We then compare the framing of 15 subframes of risk management, and how they inform the linear constructs of the themes: (1) social programming, (2) legal proactivity, and (3) institutional interventions, monitoring, and evaluation. We verify the stance of the governments of the case study countries by context-specific readings of their respective country-level responses (in the year following the adoption of the national plan) to the questionnaires issued annually to these governments by the UN Commission on the Rights of the Child. Although we do not cite these response here, they enabled us to confirm or reject the framing of the phenomenon of (the worst forms of) child labor in the five national policies examined.

To reiterate, we are only interested in 'institutional' (i.e., the implementing bodies) and the legal framework-based interventions. By legal framework, we are referring to the national laws on child labor that meet international standards—as defined by the ILO's anti-child labor regime, the UN *Convention on the Rights of the Child* and the *African Charter on the Rights and Welfare of the Child*, among others. Our "international standards" threshold includes the domestication and incorporation of international norms into the national laws of the country through an act of parliament. In this respect, we relied on the U.S. Department of Labor's (USDOL) simplified documents, which list the institutional and legal frameworks of each of these countries. These USDOL country documents are not the same in terms of their length due, in part, to the issues and typologies of child labor within each country; consequently, some reports contained seven pages, others nine pages and yet others 13 pages.[4] In any case, these documents contain abridged summaries of legal frameworks and multi-level institutional reflections on who does what and how.

Review of the five national plans on the worst forms of child labor

We recognize that each country developed its own national policy based on its individual circumstances. However, the outcomes of our review (and other supporting/reviews) reveal that while the governments of these select sub-Saharan African countries have individual responsibilities to the children-citizens, they are not alone in the fight to end the worst forms of child labor. From a sociological standpoint, with an emphasis on organizational isomorphism and collective rationality of norm regulation, and from a legal (tort law) perspective, it can be argued that the move by the governments of these countries to ratify and domesticate the *African Charter on the Rights and Welfare of the Child* is an example of mimetic isomorphism, the institutionalization of global norms that are constructed by, and diffused through, transnational associational processes.

It is true that the countries under review are 'copycat' countries, and their national reports cannot be said to be, in the strict sense, national policies with authenticated local characteristics. That notwithstanding, it should be noted that they only replicated the best practices of one another. The intent, we suggest, is to create a micro-phenomenological discourse (or discourses) around the possibilities of regional change—from worse to better; from political legitimation of economic wrongs (the use of child labor) to legal legitimation of the processes that enable the sub-region to escape the category of the 'worse-off' in the UNDP's Human Development Index (HDI) (Grimm et al. 2008; Elu 2000).

In this respect, readers are reminded that since these national policies are based on 'shared obligations' by all ratifying states, the isomorphic trajectories to combat the worst forms of child labor are channeled through a series of mimetic constitutional processes that highlight state responsibility, on the one hand; and, on the other, the civil duties of adults—parents, the private sectors and consortia—towards children. Thus, while the global norms on the elimination of child labor account for global trends in the problem, the implementation of national norms in communities with high incidences of child labor is an outcome of the infusion of acceptable rules and actual sociocultural and economic practice. In this respect, our research finds that the most significant challenges to the elimination of child labor are (1) poverty (the economic) and (2) familial aspects of cultural narratives (the cultural) that see the child as part of the family with a designated set of nurtured roles and responsibilities).

A "Subject matter similarities"

The country-level national policies/documents we reviewed (excluding those of the USDOL) varied in length (Kenya's policy is 36 pages long, Tanzania's 53 pages, Cameroon's 60 pages, Zimbabwe's 76 pages, and Ghana's policy is 80 pages long). While the headings and sub-headings differ, these documents all have two main 'subject matter' similarities. First, they are developed by the governments of the countries under review, with technical support from specialized international organizations (the ACERWC, UNICEF, UNCRC, UNDP and World Bank, among others). Second, they have national legitimacy and authority (power) because they are products of the legislature. What this means (at least to political scientists and scholars of legalism) is that the legitimacy of these national policies gives implementing agencies the right to demand recognition and acceptance of their work from the cultural relativist, economic and political forces that are opposed to the neoliberal international standards. These international standards also explain, in part, the stance of governments on anti-child labor global platforms, where the 'pro-child' recognition they achieve enhances the authority of the anti-child labor crusaders within their national legal and institutional frameworks.

B "Legal matter" similarities

Legal frameworks are not all constant, relative to the issues and people they seek to influence. Our reviews revealed context-specific variations, albeit less profound than the similarities they exhibit in terms of their impact on the social and political uses of the law. We identified four key aspects in the fight against child labor that are defined by international labor law: (a) the legal minimum age for work, (b) the legal minimum age for hazardous work, (c) the identification of hazardous occupations or activities prohibited for children, and (d) law's prohibition of forced labor.

To understand the impact of what the legal framework says about these aforementioned issues, we applied John R. P. French's and Bertram Raven's *The Basis of Social Power Theory* (1959). According to this theory, there are six forms of power with social consequences:

- reward power, which entails the granting of rewards for compliance;
- coercive power, the capacity to punish non-compliance;
- referent power, which entails the behavioral aspects of reliance of the reactions of one party (in this case, the general public, as the inferential audience for political speech acts) to legitimate the actions of the other (the government, as the actor who uses actions/laws to persuade the audience to accept its securitization move to end the problem of child labor);
- legitimate power, otherwise known as 'positional authority.' This type of social power is neither linear nor rational (at least, not in all situations). It is about the power of the 'office.' Take, for example, the person working as a child protection officer in Kenya or Zimbabwe. The person holding this office may change, but the title, roles and responsibilities of the office remain;
- expert power—this implies the areas and source of expertise (which are also sources of power), and the scientific processes involved in the development of expertise knowledge; and
- informational power, the most transient form of social power. The seeker of the information (people and institutions) is less powerful than the giver of the information, but the moment the giver provides the information, he/she becomes powerless, and the seeker becomes powerful.

By fusing frame theory and the basis of social power theory with our lived experiences in sub-Saharan Africa, we discovered that, with regards to the "legal minimum age for work" and "the legal minimum age for hazardous work," the impact of the law is driven by two forms of power: 'legitimate' and 'informational' power. With regard to the legitimate form of power, it is the government that decides the age for work, not the parents or other social units. Regarding informational power, the government relies on the general public for information about the age of the child who is working in hazardous conditions. This is especially the case for situations where the government does not have the birth details of all the children in the country.

With regards to the "the identification of hazardous occupations or activities prohibited for children," the impact of the law is measured by the 'expert' and 'referent' power of the regulatory institutions. What is considered hazardous is determined through methodical studies by an expert community; and where the reach of the government is limited (in sub-Saharan African countries, mostly beyond the urban and peri-urban areas), the institutions regulating child labor become information-seekers (and, therefore, powerless). To become powerful, they rely on the information-givers (the general public) to provide them with the necessary information on location (where children are being used to perform "hazardous" work) and identity (of those who employ children in such work).

With regards to the "legal prohibition of forced labor," the legal frameworks associated with the national policies project a frame of coercive powers—the capacity to inflict punishment for non-compliance or for violating laws regulating the use of children in hazardous work. Our reviews also revealed that this 'capacity' to inflict punishment does not always positively influence the behavior of the general public. Depending on the character and goals of the political leadership, the relationships between the governed and the governors, the resources at the disposal of the government, and the needs of the people, there are cases where the application of the law to protect children has resulted in outcomes that worsened the problem.

C "Operational/intervention matter" similarities

iSocial programming

Prior to the rise of national policies to combat child labor in sub-Saharan Africa, a common way of dismissing the relevance of social programming for child protection interventions was to refer to the uncertainties of household income poverty. We found that all national plans attribute the uncertainties of poverty, and its impact on "inadequacies in social protection measures" (see, for example, *the Tanzania National Plan*, p. 50), to the ineffective economic modeling of national income distribution. This consequence of this focus on the problem (poverty) rather than the structures that create it (poor governance, among others) is limited success in combating the worst forms of child labor. This is also connected to the way in which the framers of these national plans may have imagined, understood and situated the problem of donor fatigue towards social programs in the context of stringent donor conditionalities on peacebuilding activities. It is usually the case that, where external donor funding is unavailable, governments would 'ration' their welfare support to vulnerable groups, especially children and women. Notably, also, at the conclusion of civil or other wars, policy changes—consistent with the country-specific poverty reduction strategy papers (or PRSPs, developed under the Bretton Woods system for Heavily Indebted Poor Countries (HIPC))—have also led to the introduction of economic strategies that lacked social programming for children. Even where these strategies (in line with the guiding principles of the Bretton Woods system) purport to be pro-child with the long-term goal of ending poverty, the outcomes are sector-defined and children's empowerment—across all sub-Saharan countries—receives the smallest share of allocated funds.

On the sociocultural front, the exclusion of the social knowledge about the plight of children in conditions of economic fragility has also led to the misrepresentation of the binary between the psychosocial aspects of child labor prevention and poverty reduction. The unhelpful anti-neoliberal cultural narrative that has created an asymmetrical impact of social programming (aimed at using social interventions to change societal narratives that support child labor) has been criticized by feminist theorists. Judged against the allocation of resources to augment the already asymmetrical power of the law to inflict punishment for non-compliance, the meagre allocation of resources to social programs aimed at using non-punitive methods to promote the rights and welfare of children seems to serve a dual function. On one hand, it ensures that cultures and traditions are not challenged by child protection workers trained in the theories and models of western formal institutions. On the other hand, it seeks to transform women (as mothers) into a 'mothering' space, where it is believed children, neglected by governments, can find solace and resilience. As has been observed by Loretta Elizabeth Bass (2004), in her research on the sociocultural aspects of the political economy of child labor in 18 countries in Africa, mothers' nurtured roles include the use of their lived experiences to develop, through fostering, life lessons for the children. As Bass puts it,

> the fostering of children is an African cultural tradition that lends itself to the socialization and training of children ... such training [provided mostly by the mothers though informal means] sees children's work as education and social reproduction during childhood.
>
> (Bass 2004, 22)

But this cultural aspect of social reproduction, engendered by inadequate funding of social programs, also has a negative impact, especially for the child. As observed in the Tanzania National Plan, these socio-cultural practices

> include the cultural practices that influence gender-biased households' investment decisions against girls. Households' investment decisions, especially in rural areas, favor boys than girls. This leads to weak capability creation on girls, as they are denied education, which is a critical element in capability creation in addition to health. Girls are forced to remain at home early in their tender ages to help their mothers in household chores and in taking care of their siblings. They eventually end up in child labor as domestic workers.
>
> (Government of Tanzania 2009, 11)

The consequences of this common practice of "socially" projecting ambiguity or forgetfulness on issues regarding the children's psychosocial development go beyond the trivialization of the negative impact of culture on the psychosocial education of the girl child. It also affects the economic framing of poverty reduction, which, directly or indirectly, compromises the financial earnings and household income of disadvantaged families. That notwithstanding, the trend is gradually changing for the better since the coming into force of the African Children's Charter. Through the Charter, social programming of anti-child labor interventions has gained traction. In the words of the Tanzania National Plan:

> The realization of the rights of the child and the elimination of WFCL requires advancement of the social development agenda to protect and restore children's dignity and wellbeing of children by creating new openings to help fulfil children's rights to survival, development, and protection. This requires a collective effort from government, business sector, civil society and the strengthening of community responses. This is the cornerstone of this Plan of Action for the Elimination of Worst Forms of Child Labor in Tanzania. To this end, we will continue to foster inter-governmental cooperation and also enlist the support of donors and of both local and international development agencies and Civil Society Organization (CSOs). These partnerships will ensure that policies and plans are being translated into realities that will benefit orphans and vulnerable children in their communities.[5]
>
> (Government of Tanzania 2009, viii)

In line with the recognition of the "most vulnerable children" category, the Tanzanian government has developed several social projects. Among them is the Wekeza Project (2012–2017), developed to "support local efforts to reduce child labor in Tanzania through an area-based approach in the regions of Tanga and Kigoma, where there is a prevalence of child labor in agriculture production and domestic service" (U.S. Department of Labor 2016, 1). The expected outcomes (with the evaluation report yet to be released by the Government of Tanzania) were: (1) On children-at-risk: the outcomes should be to achieve increased enrolment in formal and non-formal education; improved teaching and learning outcomes; engaged community, and government capacity, contributions, and accountability. (2) On household income: that households have increased income and asset accumulation from their agriculture livelihoods; households have increased access to alternative livelihood options; household resources and ability to withstand shocks are increased through savings and access to credit; youth have the necessary skills to access or create employment opportunities; youth access market-relevant vocational training and apprenticeship opportunities; youth own and operate their own micro-franchise businesses. (3) That children at risk of or engaged in child labor and their families have increased access to national social protection services, and improved linkages with national social protection services. (4) On institutional capacity building to address child labor: improved local government capacity to address child labor; and a functioning child labor monitoring systems at the national and district level to inform policies and programs to address child labor; increased awareness on child domestic labor at the local level; and, increased understanding at the national level of the issues related to child domestic labor (U.S. Department of Labor 2016, 1–3).

For its part, the Zimbabwe National Plan has three main social programs targeted at orphans and vulnerable children. The first

> includes a focus on equity and access to quality education for children and provides child protection services. Provides a cash transfer program that encourages families to keep children in school … During the year, cash transfers reached at least 52,000 poor households in 19 districts and provided child protection and welfare services to 35,460 children in 37 districts.
>
> (U.S. Embassy, Harare 2017; quoted in U.S. Department of Labor 2017d, 5)

The second social program is called the "Stop Child Labor Program." This program seeks to create

> child labor-free zones throughout the country. The program includes the Ministry of Labor, Coalition Against Child Labor in Zimbabwe, African Network for the Prevention and Protection Against Child Abuse and Neglect, Progressive Teachers Union of Zimbabwe, Zimbabwe Teachers' Association, and the General Agriculture and Plantation Workers Union [quoting the January 15, 2017 report of the U.S. Embassy, Harare, to the U.S. Department of Labor]. Teachers, labor inspectors, police officers, and other stakeholders support this initiative by sending child laborers back to school [quoting the 9 May 2016 report of the U.S. Embassy, Harare to the U.S. Department of Labor]. During the year, the program developed a social responsibility project to address child labor in plantations, resulting in 178 children being withdrawn from child labor and sent back to school.
>
> (U.S. Department of Labor 2017d, 5)

The final program is called "Basic Education Assistance Module." Through this, the Zimbabwe government "provides basic financial assistance to families for education costs, such as tuition and examination fees … [It a]ims to keep children in school and to enrol children who lack access to school as a result of economic hardship" (Herald.co.zw [online] March 5, 2014, quoted in U.S. Department of Labor 2017d, 5).

The Cameroon National Plan contains two social projects. Project 559 (or the project to combat the phenomenon of street children) offers free healthcare, education and psychosocial care. In 2016, for instance, it provided "shelter to 92 children removed from Boko Haram elements, identified and provided reintegration or reinsertion services to 265 street children, and facilitated primary education for 5,250 indigenous Baka children" (U.S. Department of Labor 2017a, 6). The Country Program Action Plan (2013–2017, 2017–2021), funded entirely by the government of Cameroon, seeks to improve social protection services to children at risk (Government of Cameroon 2013). This support ranges from preventative healthcare and psychosocial support to free primary schooling. It considers children displaced by the conflict between the Cameroon military and Boko

Haram insurgents in northern Cameroon as at-risk children. Through this program, the government of Cameroon provides psychosocial support and reintegration services for these displaced children (U.S. Department of Labor 2017a, 6).

The Kenya National Policy involves a series of social programs to combat child labor (of the worst forms, such as commercial sexual exploitation of children) and increase children's enrolment in formal primary schooling. Accordingly, it has opened several child protection and rescue centers for vulnerable children. As of 2016, the Kenyan government had spent U.S.$2 million on the construction of these centers. One such center is the Kitui County Child Rescue Center, which is helping to address the problem of an estimated 600,000 street children, many of whom are victims of the child sex industry and child trafficking rings (U.S. Department of Labor 2017c, 6).

The Ghana National Policy focuses mostly on the cocoa-growing and mining communities. In this regard, there are several projects that have emerged out of the National Plan, among them the Livelihood Empowerment Against Poverty (LEAP) initiative and the Mobilizing Community Action and Promoting Opportunities for Youth in Ghana's Cocoa-Growing Communities (MOCA) 2015–2019. LEAP seeks to supplement the incomes of poorer families so that parents will allow their children to go to school and receive their vaccinations. To date, the project has achieved moderate success in 28 districts (with more than 43,368 new participants added for the year 2016 alone) (U.S. Department of Labor 2017b, 7). MOCA aims to eliminate the use of children in cocoa production sector through research, monitoring, and enforcement of the anti-child labor laws of Ghana. It is also engages in sensitizing the public to the issue of exploitation of children in the sex industry, through an education and public awareness program using various media including television, public events, radio talk shows, newspapers, and billboards (Government of Ghana 2016, 34). Through its Ghana Cocoa Board's Child Education Support Program, the Ministry of Gender, Children, and Social Protection (MOGCSP) is rehabilitating old schools and building new ones in cocoa-growing communities. Under its Free Compulsory, Universal Basic Education (F-CUBE) program, the Ministry of Education has established (1) a school meal program to reduce malnutrition and attract under-fed children), (2) a Capitation Grant Scheme to pay for the primary schooling of children, and (3) a girls education program that targets girls in more impoverished communities.

iiFrames of intervention—protection, prevention and reaction

At the core of anti-child labor policy framing is the construction of interventions, and the question of which standpoint to adopt when looking at the historical and spatial developments of the crisis in sub-Saharan Africa. Depending on the theoretical perspective one applies to child development, the frame of intervention can be modeled in different ways. If the policy framers are influenced by Freudian psychosexual development theory, they will be biased towards aspects of the worst form of child labor, commercial sex work, reflecting the Freudian psychoanalytical perspective on the sexual development of girls.[6] If they are influenced by Erik Erikson's psychosocial development theory, they will frame interventions with reference to the manner in which children are mistreated in their homes prior to becoming street children; in Erikson's eight developmental stages, children are in constant inner conflict over integrity vs. despair, trust vs. mistrust, shame vs. guilt, superiority vs. inferiority, identity (as given) vs. identity (as self-assumed), intimacy vs. isolation, and mental progress vs. stagnation.[7] If they are influenced by Jean Piaget's cognitive development theory,[8] they will focus on the role of "informal education" (which is culture-centric and delivered through unstructured means at home, with the lived experiences of the everyday as the template for knowledge generation) and "formal education" (delivered using established sets of skills: reading, writing and speaking) in the making (and unmaking) of child labor. Thus, if their theoretical leaning was toward Piaget's theory, the framers would suggest various methods (such as the use of school meal programs or cash incentives for poorer parents) to get children and parents to accept schooling as the surest means to escape the poverty trap. If they are influenced by Bowlby's attachment theory,[9] they will focus their interventions on trying to disconnect at-risk children from their parents, where those parents' occupation is in hazardous activities like commercial sex work. If, however, the framers of the national policy are influenced by Vygotsky's sociocultural theory,[10] they will design their interventions to draw at-risk children to skilled individuals who can help them to construct best practices out of their sociocultural environment—or, in Vygotskyian parlance, into a 'zone for cognitive proximal development' (Day 1983, 156), where social interactions play a role in shaping a child's cognitive development.

Of course, these theoretical influences do not provide the complete story of how governments formulate their anti-child labor intervention strategies. Our examination of the various national plans revealed that biases in the frames of intervention could have been outcomes of pre-existing trends in the most prevalent form of child labor at the time those national policies were developed. Say, for example, that at the time of writing its policy a government was faced with higher numbers of children in the commercial sex industry and fewer children in artisanal mining. In such circumstances, the government would naturally make the rational decision to focus most of its intervention resources on the sex industry.

That said, with reference to our illustration of the sub-frames in Table 6.2, we discovered that the framing of the key intervention words—protect, prevent, react and rebuild—were also determined by the social and political worldviews of both local (government) and external (donor) actors regarding the impact of culture, poverty, economic disempowerment, and disease on the crisis of child labor.

We did not rely solely on data from the national policies to design Table 6.2 but substantiated our findings by employing a data de-mining technique. This entailed crosschecking the information with information published on the websites of international agencies such as the World Food Programme (on the school feeding program), the UNCRC (on the national policies' claims of providing

Table 6.2 The framing of child interventions through 12 themes in the five National Policies[1]

Theme	*Framing*	*Cameroon*	*Ghana*	*Kenya*	*Tanzania*	*Zimbabwe*
Detach at-risk children from abusive families	As an 'emergency' prevention and reactive move			x		
	At-risk children identified but detachment not recommended or prioritized	x	x		x	x
Commercial sex work intervention phrases	Phrases based on 'emergency' intervention		x		x	
	Intervention include medical assistance for those infected with sexually transmitted diseases		x			
Expert social workers (with cultural orientation) phrases	Framing based on the local sociological understanding of culture	x			x	x
	Framing based on the local political understanding of culture		x			x
Expert social workers (with cultural orientation) phrases	Framing based on the external (donor preference) cultural sensitivity	x				
	Framing based on the external (donor preference) political sensitivity					
Expert social workers (with anti-culture cognitive orientation) phrase	Framing based on the local social understanding of culture			x		
	Framing based on the local political understanding of culture	x	x	x		
Expert social workers (with anti-culture cognitive orientation) phrase	Framing based on the external (NGO-level preference) social understanding of culture			x	x	
	Framing based on the external (country-level donor's preference) political understanding of culture					

Child's psychosocial support phrase	Framing psychosocial support as depending on the behavior of the child	x				x
	Framing psychosocial support as depending on societal (adult) behavior	x		x		x
Challenges posed by societal cultural beliefs	Discourage retrogressive cultural practice to protect at-risk children			x	x	
	Interventions include protection of children from cultural beliefs			x	x	
Benefits of social cultural beliefs	Cultural beliefs as essential for society's fight to end child labor (role of parent)	x	x	x		x
	Interventions include protection of progressive cultural values	x	x	x		
School feeding program	Targeting only some select school communities (poorer communities only)	x	x	x	x	x
	Targeting all school communities nationwide					
School meal program	Framed on the basis of donor intervention from either WFP or the Comprehensive African Agricultural Development Programme (CAADP)	x		x	x	x
	Framed on the basis of direct government intervention		xx	x	x	
Financial support to families with child laborers	Support reflective of donor funding	x	x	x	x	x
	support reflective of government's direct investment		x			
Combating forced labor	Vulnerable groups are defined independent of ILO's Convention No. 182 (definition of worst forms of child labor) and No. 105 (steps to eradicate forced labor), UNCRC, and ACRWC					

continued

Table 6.2 continued

Theme	*Framing*	*Cameroon*	*Ghana*	*Kenya*	*Tanzania*	*Zimbabwe*
	Vulnerable groups defined in line with ILO's convention No. 182 and No. 105, UNCRC, and ACRWC	x	x	x	x	
Risk management (vulnerability)—social intervention	Framing vulnerability as socio-cultural issue			x	x	x
	Social interventions has top priority	x	x	x		
Risk management (vulnerability)—medical intervention	Child laborers are defined medically				x	
	Medical interventions has top priority	x	x	x	x	x
Risk management (vulnerability)—economic intervention	Child labor define as economic poverty	x	x	x	x	x
	Economic empowerment intervention has top priority	x	x	x	x	x
Risk management (vulnerability)—educational intervention	Child labor define as an outcome of illiteracy	x	x			
	Educational intervention (compulsory primary schooling) has top priority		x	x	x	x
Risk management (surveillance and enforcement)—legal intervention	Worst forms of child labor (commercial sex work) define as criminal	x	x	x	x	x
	Legal intervention (formulation and enforcement of the law against the worst forms of child labor) has top priority	x	x	x	x	x

Note

1 An 'x' denotes subframes for action under the National Plan; A double 'xx' denotes the existence of a national law (or a bill on the final stages of parliamentary deliberations).

compulsory primary education) and the International Bureau of the U.S. Department of Labor (on the claim of criminal laws and enforcement mechanism against the worst forms of child labor,[11] especially commercial sex work).

It is evident that there are more similarities than variations across the select country case studies in the processes of framing interventions. Local ownership of the institutional framework is emphasized. There are also multi-dimensional formulations of, and interventions against, vulnerability framing in risk management. Vulnerability has attracted five frames of formulation: the social (cultural), medical, educational, economic and legal. We did not desegregate the social and the education frames given the compulsory nature of one (formal education) and the spatialized non-compulsory nature of the other (culture-centric informal education). Concerning the medical intervention frame, while there is ambiguity regarding the possibility of defining child labor medically, the five national plans hold as sacrosanct the prioritization of medical interventions targeting children (especially girls) with the aim of mitigating early childhood pregnancy and the spread of sexually transmitted diseases. Another area of similarity is in the legal frameworks' source of legitimacy. While they are adopted by the national parliaments of these countries, our observations reveal that they owe their direction to the international and regional conventions and norms that underpin them. This, we suggest, will lead to the strengthening of the legal frame against cultural relativist objections—that is, if the political and social pull and push factors (such as the political misuse of identity politics) that give cultural belief systems political relevance are controlled. Framing of intervention based on the political preferences of external donor communities is not evident in the national plans, but there is evidence in the national policies of Kenya and Tanzania that the social sensitivities of international non-governmental organizations (INGOs) sway the framing of interventions. These similarities of frames could serve as a platform for the construction of a secure regional child protection database for the exchange of ideas and the development of a regional child offender registry system.

Notes

1 This day, which is celebrated every June 16, was developed in 1991 to honor the children who took part and died during the Soweto Uprising in Apartheid South Africa in 1979 (see, Rwezaura 1998, 85).

2 Between 2010 and 2018, however, only four additional countries ratified the Charter.

3 ACHPR Newsletter, title: "*Ratification Table: African Charter on the Rights and Welfare of the Child.*" www.achpr.org/instruments/child/ratification/ (accessed June 10, 2018).

4 U.S. Department of Labor's Bureau of International Labor (BIL). *2016 Findings on the Worst Forms of Child Labour*. Bureau of International Labour Affairs, U.S. Department of Labour. Retrieved from www.dol.gov/sites/default/files/documents/ilab/reports/child-labor/findings/TDAMagazine.pdf.

5 The Tanzania National Plan goes on to extend the definition of poverty to include the lack of psychosocial support for the child:

> Child poverty, which is the deprivation of a range of both material and social supports and services that are considered essential to ensure children's well-being is inadequately addressed in the implementation of the existing policies. In essence, social protection measures must take into consideration the multi-dimensional and interrelated nature of child poverty and vulnerability. This includes addressing issues of social exclusion, which are currently not adequately addressed by the existing social insurance measures through the provision of the [unrestricted] cash and in-kind transfers to the Most Vulnerable Children (MVC) and their caregivers. Social policy and provisioning in Tanzania does not address inequalities and enhance access to basic services of all children and adolescents; mitigation of poverty on families; strengthening of families in their childcare role and providing special services to children who live outside a family environment. This is mainly due to the fact social provisioning is not statutorily guaranteed.
>
> (Government of Tanzania 2009, 6)

6 For more on the historical constructions of the feminine psychosexual development in Freudian theory, see Zenia Odes Fliegel (1973).

7 For more on the inventory model for examining Erikson's stages of psychosocial development see, Doreen A. Rosenthal, Ross M. Gurney and Susan M. Moore (1981).

8 For more on Piaget's theory of cognitive and affective development: Foundations of constructivism, see Barry J. Wadsworth (1996).

9 For more on Bowlby's theory see, *The Handbook of Attachment: Theory, Research, and Clinical Applications*, edited by Jude Cassidy and Phillip R. Shaver (1999).

10 For more on the contributions of Vygotsky's sociocultural theory on social relations, see Alex Kozulin et al. (2003).

11 We observe that, the national plans did not treat the crisis of child labor the same way it treats incidences like armed insurgency, pandemic, famine and flooding. We believe this did contribute to creating the missing link that have made it less likely for to the crisis of child labor to be included as a stand-alone indicator of state fragility.

References

ACERWC (African Committee of Experts on the Rights and Welfare of the Child). 2018a. "Concept Note Day of the African Child 2018 – Leave No Child Behind for Africa's Development." An Africa Fit for Children. www.acerwc.org/download/concept-note-day-of-the-african-child-2018/?wpdmdl=10329.

ACERWC (African Committee of Experts on the Rights and Welfare of the Child). 2018b. "Day of the African Child 2018." 2018. www.acerwc.org/ourevents/day-of-the-african-child-2018/.

African Union. 2016. *African's Agenda for Children 2040: Fostering an Africa Fit for Children.* Addis Ababa, Ethiopia: African Union (AU). https://au.int/sites/default/files/newsevents/agendas/africas_agenda_for_children-english.pdf.

Bass, Loretta Elizabeth. 2004. *Child Labor in Sub-Saharan Africa*. Boulder, CO: Lynne Rienner Publishers.

Bryceson, Deborah Fahy. 2006. "Fragile Cities: Fundamentals of Urban Life in East and Southern Africa." In *African Urban Economies: Viability, Vitality or Vitiation?*, edited by Deborah Fahy Bryceson and Deborah Potts, 3–38. New York, NY: Palgrave Macmillan.

Cassidy, Jude, and Phillip R. Shaver, eds. 1999. *Handbook of Attachment: Theory, Research, and Clinical Applications*. New York, NY: The Guilford Press.

Chauvet, Lisa, and Paul Collier. 2008. "What Are the Preconditions for Turnarounds in Failing States?" *Conflict Management and Peace Science* 25 (4): 332–348.

Committee on Economic, Social and Cultural Rights. 2000. *General Comment 14, The Right to the Highest Attainable Standard of Health (Twenty-Second Session, 2000)* [Reprinted in Compilation of General Comments and General Recommendations Adopted by Human Rights Treaty Bodies, U.N. Doc. HRI/GEN/1/Rev.6 at 85 (2003)]. http://hrlibrary.umn.edu/gencomm/escgencom14.htm.

Day, Jeanne D. 1983. "The Zone of Proximal Development." In *Cognitive Strategy Research*, vol 3, issue No 1, 155–175. Springer.

Elu, Juliet. 2000. "Human Development in Sub-Saharan Africa: Analysis and Prospects for the Future." *Journal of Global South Studies* 17 (2): 53.

Fliegel, Zenia Odes. 1973. "Feminine Psychosexual Development in Freudian Theory: A Historical Reconstruction." *The Psychoanalytic Quarterly* 42 (3): 385–408.

Freeman, Michael. 2007. *Article 3: The Best Interests of the Child*. Leiden, The Netherlands: Martinus Nijhoff Publishers.

French, J. R. and Bertram Raven. 1959. "The Bases of Social Power." *Classics of Organization Theory* 7: 311–320.

Government of Cameroon. 2013. *Plan d'Action National Pour l'Elimination Des Pires Formes de Travail Des Enfants Au Cameroun (PANETEC)* [The National Plan of Action to Combat Child Labor and Trafficking in Children] (2014–2016). Yaoundé, Cameroon: Ministere du Travail et de la Securite Sociale (MINTSS).

Government of Ghana, Ministry of Employment and Labour Relations (MELR). 2016. *The National Place of Action (Phase II) for the Elimination of the Worst Forms of Child Labor in Ghana (2017–2012: Towards Achieving Sustainable Development Goal (SDG) 8.7*. Accra, GH: Ministry of Employment and Labour Relations (MELR), Government of Ghana. www.unicef.org/ghana/NPA_(II)_EWFCL.pdf.

Government of Tanzania. 2009. *National Action Plan for the Elimination of Child Labor*. Arushia, TZ: Ministry of Labor, Employment and Youth Development. www.ilo.org/dyn/natlex/docs/MONOGRAPH/94604/111054/F347421111/TZA94604.pdf.

Grimm, Michael, Kenneth Harttgen, Stephan Klasen, and Mark Misselhorn. 2008. "A Human Development Index by Income Groups." *World Development* 36 (12): 2527–2546.

Harris, Gordon. 1994. *The Organization of African Unity*. Vol. 7. Oxford, UK: Clio Press Ltd.

Invernizzi, Antonella. 2008. "Everyday Lives of Working Children and Notions of Citizenship." In *Children and Citizenship*, edited by Antonella Invernizzi and Jane Williams, London: Springer, 131–142.

Kaime, Thoko. 2009. *The African Charter on the Rights and Welfare of the Child: A Socio-Legal Perspective*. Pretoria, South Africa: Pretoria University Press.

Kozulin, Alex, Boris Gindis, Vladimir S. Ageyev, and Suzanne M. Miller, eds. 2003. *Vygotsky's Educational Theory in Cultural Context*. Cambridge University Press.

Langlois, Anthony. 2005. "International Covenant on Civil and Political Rights (ICCPR)." In *Encyclopedia of International Relations and Global Politics*, edited by Martin Griffiths, 416–418. Abingdon, UK: Routledge.

Lundy, Laura. 2007. "'Voice' Is Not Enough: Conceptualising Article 12 of the United Nations Convention on the Rights of the Child." *British Educational Research Journal* 33 (6): 927–942.

Maluwa, Tiyanjana. 2012. "Ratification of African Union Treaties by Member States: Law, Policy and Practice." *Melbourne Journal of International Law 636* 13: 1–49.

Nilsson, Ann-Charlotte. 2013. *Children and Youth in Armed Conflict*. Leiden, The Netherlands: Martinus Nijhoff Publishers.

Ofodile, Uche Ewelukwa. 2010. "Universal Declaration of Human Rights and the African Child Today: Progress or Problems." *American University International Law Review* 25 (37): 37–76.

Okyere, Samuel. 2013. "Are Working Children's Rights and Child Labour Abolition Complementary or Opposing Realms?" *International Social Work* 56 (1): 80–91.

Organization of African Unity (OAU). 1990. *African Charter on the Rights and Welfare of the Child (1990)*. http://hrlibrary.umn.edu/africa/afchild.htm.

Potts, Deborah. 2007. *The State and the Informal in Sub-Saharan African Urban Economies: Revisiting Debates on Dualism (Working Paper No. 18 – Cities and Fragile States)*. Working Paper. London, UK: LSE Development Studies Institute. https://assets.publishing.service.gov.uk/media/57a08beee5274a31e0000ea6/wp18.2.pdf.

Rosenthal, Doreen A., Ross M. Gurney, and Susan M. Moore. 1981. "From Trust on Intimacy: A New Inventory for Examining Erikson's Stages of Psychosocial Development." *Journal of Youth and Adolescence* 10 (6): 525–537.

Rwezaura, Bart. 1998. "The Duty to Hear the Child: A View from Tanzania." In *Law, Culture, Tradition, and Children's Rights in Eastern and Southern Africa*, edited by Welshman Ncube, 57–94. Aldershot, UK: Ashgate Publishing, Ltd.

UN General Assembly. 1966. "International Covenant on Economic, Social and Cultural Rights." *United Nations, Treaty Series* 993 (3).

UNDP, United Nations Development Programme. 2017. *Human Development Report 2016: Human Development for Everyone*. United Nations Publications. New York, NY: United Nations Development Programme. http://hdr.undp.org/en/2016-report.

U.S. Department of Labor, International Labor Affairs Bureau. 2016. *Technical Cooperation Project Summary – Wekeza: Wezesha Ustawi, Endeleza Kiwango Cha Elimu Kuzia Ajira Kwa Watoto/Invest: Supporting Livelihoods And Developing Quality Education To Stop Child Labor*. Washington, DC: U.S. Department of Labor. www.dol.gov/ilab/projects/summaries/Tanzania_WEKEZA.pdf.

U.S. Department of Labor, International Labor Affairs Bureau. 2017a. *2016 Findings on the Worst Forms of Child Labour (Cameroon)*. Washington, DC: U.S. Department of Labor. Retrieved from www.dol.gov/sites/default/files/images/ilab/child-labor/Cameroon2016.pdf.

U.S. Department of Labor, International Labor Affairs Bureau. 2017b. 2016 *Findings on the Worst Forms of Child Labour (Ghana)*. Washington, DC: U.S. Department of Labor. Retrieved from www.dol.gov/sites/default/files/images/ilab/child-labor/2016 Ghana.pdf.

U.S. Department of Labor, International Labor Affairs Bureau. 2017c. "2016 Findings on the Worst Forms of Child Labour (Kenya)." Washington, DC: U.S. Department of Labor. Retrieved from www.dol.gov/sites/default/files/images/ilab/child-labor/Kenya2016.pdf.

U.S. Department of Labor, International Labor Affairs Bureau. 2017d. "2016 Findings on the Worst Forms of Child Labour (Zimbabwe)." Washington, DC: U.S. Department of Labor. www.dol.gov/agencies/ilab/resources/reports/child-labor/zimbabwe.

Van Bueren, Geraldine. 1998. *International Documents on Children*. The Hague, The Netherland: Martinus Nijhoff Publishers.

Wadsworth, Barry J. 1996. *Piaget's Theory of Cognitive and Affective Development: Foundations of Constructivism*. White Plains, NY: Longman Publishing.

Part III

Food (in)security

Contextual indicators and interventions

7 The Ebola pandemic and household food insecurity

Since the onset of the Ebola virus diseases (EVD) in 2013, the estimated number of related deaths in the three affected countries (Guinea, Liberia and Sierra Leone) is more than 11,000 (out of 27,000 reported cases by June 2015). Of the affected countries, Sierra Leone reported the highest number of cases (12,901, with 3,915 deaths). The nature of the pandemic and the resulting death toll have socioeconomic and food insecurity implications for affected households. This chapter examines socioeconomic determinants of food insecurity at the household level in Sierra Leone using six indicators of food insecurity. Data for the chapter are derived from the three rounds of the High Frequency Cell Phone Survey jointly collected by Statistics Sierra Leone (SSL) and Innovations for Poverty Action (IPA). Empirical techniques include random-effects Poisson and population-averaged Poisson models. We generate an index of food insecurity from six household coping strategies that indicate food insecurity, using principal component analysis and employing the household unitary model (since the data used for the analyses were generated by focusing on the household head). Findings indicate that households that engage only in agriculture have a higher risk of being food-insecure. In contrast, households that have diversified their income portfolios experience a reduction in their levels of food insecurity, as incomes from their non-farm enterprises experienced a boost. We also find that households in Freetown are less food-insecure than their counterparts in other urban areas (the provinces). In specific terms, we find that incomes from non-farm enterprises significantly reduce the intensity at which households restrict adult consumption to ensure access to food for children. Similar reductions in food insecurity intensities can be identified for households that rely on less preferred or expensive food, as well as those that reduce number of meals eaten in a day. These are the grounds on which we recommend that households in fragile states engage in income diversification to mitigate food insecurity in times of pandemic disease.

Synoptic overview

Food insecurity and pandemics are closely related, but the sub-Saharan African discourse has usually been linked to HIV/AIDS. The intuition is that the morbidity and mortality associated with HIV/AIDS creates household labor shortages, reductions or slowdowns in households' accumulated assets and special skills. It also leaves existing relatives with a burden of care for affected adults and orphaned children (De Waal and Whiteside 2003; Himmelgreen et al. 2009; Naysmith, de Waal and Whiteside 2009). On the one hand, the reduction in the household size and in the number of economically active members causes a reduction in the volume of food production (for agricultural households) and general productivity (for non-agricultural households). On the other hand, the depletion of resources (assets and income) used in either taking care of the sick or lost through economic inactivity has a debilitating effect on the quantity of food acquisition by households. The Ebola Virus Disease (EVD), more than most other pandemics, has the potential to cause or worsen food insecurity problems within a very short space of time by completely disrupting socioeconomic and geopolitical activities, making it difficult to mitigate its food insecurity impacts. This was the experience during and following the 2013–2016 EVD pandemic in Guinea, Liberia and Sierra Leone.

The estimated death toll from the EVD pandemic in the three affected countries was more than 11,000 people, out of 27,000 reported cases between December 2013 and June 2015. Sierra Leone reported the highest number of cases (12,901) with 3,915 deaths. The nature of the pandemic, and the resulting deaths, had significant socioeconomic—including food insecurity—implications for affected households and for the countries as a whole (Himelein et al., 2015). Apart from the direct health impact, the EVD had indirect effects on market chains, resulting in food insecurity in affected and neighboring countries. The fear and panic caused, and the restrictions imposed on social gatherings and movement of goods and people, had social implications far beyond the usual sickness and mortality issues. The reactionary public policies implemented to control the spread of the disease also had effects on trade and commerce (Figuié 2016).

Studies on food insecurity have produced findings and projections that have been a matter of policy concern. A study conducted during the outbreak in 2014 projected that rates of malnutrition in Guinea, Liberia and Sierra Leone had the potential to increase by 1.72%, 5.80% and 4.12% respectively by 2016 (with Guinea noticeably less affected than Liberia and Sierra Leone) (UNDP, 2015). At the peak of the Ebola pandemic in February 2015, about 67% of households in Sierra Leone adopted at least one of six forms of coping strategies that connote food insecurity. Approximately 52% of households resorted to eating less preferred or less expensive foods, with 43% reducing the number of meals per day. About 51% limited portion sizes at meal times, while 37% restricted consumption by adults in order for small children to eat. Some households (30%) had to sell assets to buy food and 30% borrowed food or relied on help from friends and relatives. In the case of Guinea, Liberia and Sierra Leone, the impact of the EVD was a matter of grave concern as the outbreak coincided with their gradual recovery from civil war and political unrest. Thus, the epidemic affected fragile states, with mass poverty and poor health infrastructure (UNDP 2015; UNECA 2014; World Bank 2014).

Food insecurity and fragility have a bi-directional relationship. A society bedeviled by food insecurity, resulting in undernourished inhabitants, is associated with lower levels of productivity, as undernourished people exhibit weakened physical and cognitive abilities. Thus, as expressed by the Food and Agriculture Organization (FAO), 'societies with undernourished people cannot progress' (FAO 2000, 3). The other side of this argument is the evidence of food insecurity in countries that have become fragile due to long periods of conflict. Examples in sub-Saharan Africa (SSA) include the Democratic Republic of Congo (DRC), Somalia and Sudan. From 1991 to 2002, during a period of heightened conflict within SSA, the number of undernourished people increased by 37%, with the events in war-torn countries accounting for 78% of this increase. The number affected by food insecurity in the DRC, for example, tripled from 12 million to 36 million, with the prevalence rate increasing from 31% to 72% of the population (Alinovi, Hemrich, and Russo 2007). The FAO's 2017 Africa Regional Overview of Food Security and Nutrition report also shows an increase in the prevalence of undernourishment in SSA (from 20.8% to 22.7%) from 2015 to 2016. In 2016, undernourished people in SSA accounted for 25% of the 815 million people undernourished world-wide (FAO, 2017). The report also indicates a growing number of people who have experienced severe food insecurity due to their inability to access food. Among the drivers of such food insecurity in SSA are adverse climatic conditions, conflicts and the difficult global economic environment, which also resulted in reduced economic growth and falling prices for the primary commodities largely traded by countries in the sub-region (FAO, 2017). The revelations of food insecurity in SSA can be directly traced to the countries that experienced the EVD outbreak from 2013 to 2016 due mainly to their fragile economic and political systems.

Although the three countries under consideration were experiencing food insecurity issues (affecting an estimated 1.6 million people) prior to the EVD outbreak, the onset of the pandemic worsened the situation for households within these countries. Per evidence of a simulated study by the World Food Programme (WFP) and Trends and Analysis Service (VAM) in 2015, there were high risks of food insecurity across the three EVD-affected countries. The study estimated that, by the third quarter of 2015, the number of food-insecure people in Guinea, Liberia and Sierra Leone combined would reach 6.2 million, representing 27% of the total population of these countries. Put differently, one in every four households was expected to be food-insecure. This resulted from reduced household income and hikes in seasonal food prices. The reduction in incomes was also driven by the slowdown in economic activities. For the same period, it was estimated that households in Guinea would be the most food insecure, followed by Sierra Leone and Liberia respectively (WFP and VAM 2015). In Guinea, areas vulnerable to high levels of food insecurity included Kindia and Labé. Similarly, areas at risk of food insecurity in Liberia included Bomi, Montserrado, River Gee, River Cess, Grand Kru and Sinoe. In the case of Sierra Leone, the vulnerable places were Port Loko, Tonokilili, Mayamba and Pujehum. At the household level, residents in rural areas, with high dependence on agricultural produce but very low incomes, were projected to experience the highest risk of becoming food-insecure (WFP and VAM 2015). This links the problem directly to smallholder households that rely heavily on agricultural activities but have very low incomes to serve as risk-coping mechanisms. For such households to mitigate the risk of food insecurity, they need to diversify their income-generating activities.

Studies in Ethiopia have called on smallholder households to embark on income diversification by adding on non-farm economic activities. To support this, policy-makers have also been encouraged to provide an enabling environment by making credit easily accessible and providing training and community education (Mentamo and Geda 2016). It has been observed that Ethiopian farmers' engagement in non-farm activities provides them with extra income that makes it possible for them to spend more on basic needs such as food, education, clothing and healthcare (Adem, Tadele, Mossie[,] and Ayenalem 2018; Zerai and Gebreegziabher 2011). Another study in Nigeria showed that households that had diversified their income were better able to withstand the shocks of food insecurity. Income from such ventures is used to cater for expenses in times of emergency, such as sickness, and for children's education, while farm produce mainly supplies food and other cash requirements (Agbola et al., 2008). In Ghana, farmers' reasons for diversifying their incomes include food security, payment of fees and saving so that they can better cope with risks (Agyeman, Asuming-Brempong[,] and Onumah 2014).

Evidence from the extant literature shows that studies applying rigorous regression analyses to determine the effect of income diversification on food insecurity have been carried out in countries or regions not affected by EVD. Those undertaken in EVD-affected countries have employed descriptive analysis to draw inferences. Such inferences have been drawn without simultaneously accounting for the effect of other socioeconomic indicators that have the potential to influence food insecurity. Some of these studies have also been carried out on other indicators and have considered, only in passing income, diversification as a solution to food insecurity. This gap in the literature calls for studies that employ robust econometric techniques to ascertain the effect of income diversification on household food insecurity from an EVD-affected country perspective.

To provide evidence of the income diversification–food insecurity nexus from an EVD-affected country, the case of Sierra Leone is used in this chapter. For Sierra Leone, the drivers of household food insecurity have been identified as low agricultural productivity, lack of income generation diversification, poverty and a lack of resilience, gender inequality and poor road and market accessibility (AFDB et al. 2015).[1] Most Sierra Leoneans are known to be heavily reliant on agricultural activities for their livelihoods but, as of the period of the EVD, just 4% were found to have the capacity to grow enough rice to meet their yearly consumption needs. That notwithstanding, rice production was also found to have decreased considerably during the period of the EVD pandemic. In general, disruptions in economic activities due to the EVD caused a reduction in Sierra Leonean local food production. In 2014–2015, rice production declined by 15%

compared to 2013–2014, while cassava production declined by 26% (AFDB et al. 2015). If agricultural households and those who have not diversified their income portfolios are more likely to be food insecure, there is a need to examine the effect of income diversification (by means of operation of non-farm economic activities) on household food insecurity.

We fill the gap in the extant literature by employing econometrically robust techniques to examine the effect of income diversification strategies on household food insecurity in the period of the Ebola pandemic in Sierra Leone (2014–2015) and controlling for other socioeconomic covariates. We also explore the locational heterogeneities in the effect of income diversification on household food insecurity by estimating sub-sampled models for Freetown, other urban areas and rural areas. The data enables us to capture the time-effect of a diversification strategy adopted by households to mitigate the food insecurity risks that usually accompany the Ebola pandemic. The analysis provides grounds on which stakeholders can promote such livelihood strategies to benefit households in countries at risk of suffering pandemics or similar shocks. In addition, this strengthens the push for income diversification as a parallel policy prescription along with government policies aimed at curbing household food insecurity.

The second section of this chapter discusses food insecurity in Sierra Leone before and during the pandemic. The third section touches on methodology and includes data sources, measurement of food insecurity and estimation techniques. The fourth section is dedicated to analysis and discussion, while the final discussion concludes with some remarks on policy.

State of food (in)security in Sierra Leone before the pandemic

The impact of the EVD pandemic cannot be assessed in isolation from the prevailing state of food insecurity in Sierra Leone. At the time of the pandemic's eruption, Sierra Leone was ranked among the least food-secured countries, even though the agriculture, forestry and fishing sectors accounted for about 45.6% of the country's GDP (2012 figures by the African Development Bank's country level data portal). The consumption by product index for Sierra Leone for the year 2011, for example, shows a supply of 2,333 kcal per capita per day across all products. Of these, animal products (including rodents—the main transmitters of the Ebola virus to humans) was the second highest category, at 116 kcal per capita per day. The highest contributor to the grand total of food supply was cereals (excluding beer) at 1149 kcal per capita per day (see Table 7.1: Consumption by product (2011).

Of these figures, the proportion of consumption of rice for the previous year supplied through domestic production (as reported by the FAO's Food Balance Sheets for June 2010) was 719 tonnes (per 1,000 tonnes). The proportion of domestically supplied consumption for other staples was also very low: sugar (77 tonnes), maize (43) sorghum (36), tomatoes (31), onions (11), olives (zero),

Table 7.1 Consumption by product (2011)

	Food	*Feed*	*Seed*	*Processed*	*Other use*	*Food supply, quantity (kg/capita/yr)*	*Food supply, energy (kcal/capita/day*	*Protein supply g/capita/day)*
	% Domestic supply							
Cereals—excluding beer	81	2	5	0	0	128	1149	24
Maize	70	23	2			5	44	1
Wheat	96				0	12	97	3
Meat, total	100					9	33	3
Bovine meat	100					2	9	1
Pigmeat	100					1	6	0
Poultry meat	100					4	10	1
Fish, seafood	100	0			0	34	62	10
Animal products, total							118	15
Milk—excluding butter	95					7	11	1
Eggs	79		7			2	6	1
Fruits—excluding wine	91					38	46	1
Vegetables	91					56	34	2
Sugar and sweeteners	100				3	6	55	0
Alcoholic beverages	98				2	44	51	0
Grand total							2333	56

Domestic supply, exports, imports, net trade—quantity in 1000 tonnes

Source: African Development Bank (Open Data for Africa), http://sierraleone.opendataforafrica.org/nbkzqug/sierra-leone-agriculture-sheet

wheat (73), potatoes (2 tonnes), dates (zero), and barley (2 tonnes). To supplement the poor state of domestically produced food supplies, the government was forced to import from Asia (mostly from China and Vietnam) 176,000 tonnes of rice; 2000 tonnes of processed maize; 8000 tonnes of tomatoes; 11,000 tonnes of onions; 66,000 tonnes of wheat; and 2000 tonnes of barley. For a country of about six million people (2014 data), with a gross national income (GNI) of U.S.$1,690 and a gross domestic product registering an annual growth of 4%, with a projected increase in life expectancy from 40 years to 45 or even 50 (Lahai, 2017: 17), this record explains why Sierra Leone was consistently ranked among the least food secure countries for the years 2005 and 2014 by the United Nations Development Index. This was a dire situation when one takes into consideration the general indicators of food insecurity: unemployment, high population growth with little in the way of social safety net, and a limited land area under cultivation (see Tables 7.2 and 7.3). Sierra Leone was not self-sufficient. It was importing more than it was exporting (see Table 7.4). Amid all this, farmers' access to local markets was impeded by poor roads, with only 11,315 km of good road networks nationwide in 2014 (World Bank 2014).

Thus, the state of food (in)security in Sierra Leone prior to the pandemic exposed the poor state of the agriculture sector, which set the stage for food-insecure people to become vectors for the Ebola virus. As we see it, food *insecurity* went beyond food *unavailability*. It was a situation that explains the state's understanding (and the understanding of all pre-EVD governments in Sierra

Table 7.2 General indicators (2011–2014)

	Ave. 01–05	*Ave. 06–10*	*2008*	*2009*	*2010*	*2011*	*2012*	*2013*
Total population (millions)	4.7	5.5	5.5	5.6	5.8	5.9	6.0	6.1
Rural population (% of total population)	63.6	62.3	62.4	62.1	61.8	61.4	61.1	60.8
Rural population growth (annual %)	3.9	1.9	1.7	1.5	1.5	1.4	1.4	1.3
Agriculture, value added (% of GDP)	50.5	55.7	56.4	58.2	56.1	56.7		
Employment in agriculture (% of total employment)	67.9							
Population density (people per sq. km)	65.7	77.1	77.2	78.8	80.3	81.9	82.8	84.4

Sources: FAO—Production Statistics Aug. 2014; Food Balance Sheets 2014; African Development Bank (Open Data for Africa). http://sierraleone.opendataforafrica.org/nbkzqug/sierra-leone-agriculture-sheet

Table 7.3 Land area cultivated between 2008 and 2011

	Ave. 00–08	*Ave. 04–08*	*2010*	*2011*
Land area (1000 sq. km)	71.62	71.62	71.62	71.62
Agricultural land (% of land area)	46.48	49.37	47.96	47.96
Arable land (% of land area)	13.95	16.77	15.36	15.36
Permanent cropland (% of land area)	1.81	1.88	1.88	1.88
Land area per capita (sq. km per capita)	0.01	0.01	0.01	0.01

Source: African Development Bank (Open Data for Africa). http://sierraleone.opendataforafrica.org/nbkzqug/sierra-leone-agriculture-sheet

Table 7.4 Food self-sufficiency (import vs export and net trade as % of GDP)

	Ave. 00–08	*Ave. 04–08*	*2008*	*2009*	*2010*
Agricultural exports (US$ million)	13.17	18.46	25.65	32.31	31.37
Agricultural imports (US$ million)	150.96	150.49	242.48	175.59	184.04
Net agricultural trade (US$ million)	−137.79	−132.03	−216.83	−143.28	−152.67
Net agricultural trade (% of GDP)	−9.97	−6.83	−8.78	−5.97	−6.03

Source: African Development Bank (Open Data for Africa). http://sierraleone.opendataforafrica.org/nbkzqug/sierra-leone-agriculture-sheet

Leone) of human security—namely, that security, including 'food security', was that which guaranteed the militant relationship between the governed and the governors. What persisted as food insecurity, our reviews of the literature revealed, was an outcome of the 'predatory political re-engineering' of life following political independence from Britain in 1961.

> Sustaining a dysfunctional [agricultural] sector was a control mechanism of the one-party dictatorships of Presidents Stevens [1968–1984] and Joseph Saidu Momoh (1985–1992). Calculated against the incidence of political protests in countries with [well-fed] people, these dictators, oblivious of the long-term implications of their actions, were of the view that a poor, malnourished, and unhealthy population [was] a population that would be too weak to challenge their political authority by aspiring to join anti-government activities.
>
> (Lahai, 2017, 19)

Drawing on other scholars, such as William Reno, Krijn Peters and David Keen, it can be concluded that the kind of political system that emerged after 1961 can best be described as patrimonial' (ibid.). These conclusions are supported by various scholarly works on the origins and character of the rogue political economy of the pre-EVD era. This political economy was characterized by the worst form of the 'Dutch disease'—the destruction of the agriculture sector for the sustenance of the informal artisanal diamond mining sector (Smillie et al., 2000). Driven by a greed-based class system, food insecurity took root. At the top of this hierarchy were the 'well-fed', while the forgotten majority fell either below or outside of the predatory hierarchical system created by the patrons (the presidents) and militantly defended by a select group of rogue politicians and businessmen (the clientele). Through this system, governance was hijacked and the people's sense of ownership of the land, including for agricultural use, was lost as they become expendable peasants and serfs in a system that re-enacted feudalism on the platforms of neopatrimonialism and political autocracy.

On this platform, agricultural policies were put in place to ensure that only a few could access food. These policies, according to Paul Richards (1996, 34), were based on the principles of redistribution of agricultural produce—rice, maize and other products—as "marks of personal favour rather than to the institution [the whole state; the people] the leader [the president] represents." To get the food they needed to survive, people were obliged to "be seen to be worshipping those at the top of the political hierarchy" (Lahai 2017, 20). As part of their strategy to prevent any form of active opposition, the governments of Siaka Stevens and Joseph Momoh maintained firm control over the cultivation, purchasing and distribution of rice, the country's staple food. They gave a monopoly on retailing rice to powerful party-aligned women dubbed 'mammy queens,' among them Haja Dankeh Kabia, Haja Fatmata Saso, Nancy Steele and Kaindeh Bangura.

> To acquire rice, people were required to form queues every day in front of the houses of these women who, in turn, would select those to whom they would not sell rice to because of their political and ethnic connections. Consequently, as the government tightened its grip, political opponents were increasingly deprived of a basic amenity – rice – and, given the lack of sufficient locally produced alternatives, some joined the APC [All Peoples Congress; the party of the president]. Instead of solving the rice shortage, President Stevens was famous for his political antics and mockery of starving people in queues. As he drove by, he would stop his vehicle and shout: 'Unah see line, na so line long?!!' [you've seen the queue, is it that long]. The disgruntled people would helplessly reply back (after he was gone, of course): 'Leke bandelley eh nose' (meaning 'Like your nose') since the President, nicknamed 'Bandelley', had a very large, crooked nose.
>
> (Lahai, 2016: 75–76)

To maintain this system, these presidents actively negotiated with the international community to change the country's status, from the category of Newly Industrialized Countries (NIC) to that of Least Developed Countries (LDC) (Lahai 2016, 76; 2017, 21). The downgrading of the country's status within the international political economy contributed further to the decline of the agro-economic sector, and Sierra Leone became permanently donor-dependent in the face of plummeting domestic food production.

It was this situation that resulted in the eruption of civil war (1991–2003). During the conflict—which also resulted in the ousting of Joseph Momoh in a coup by young military men calling themselves the National Provisional Ruling Council (NPRC)—governments were forced to reduce spending in the agriculture sector; between 1991 and 1996, the sector was receiving just 9.4% of government expenditure. The reason for this was obvious; Sierra Leone was at war, and the people were unable to focus on farming activities because both rebel and government forces were known for attacking farms to steal produce and kill or abduct the farmers (Richards, 2005). Between 1997 and 1998, the agriculture sector (indeed, all sectors of the economy) had no financial allocation and did not feed into the GDP, after the rebels of the Revolutionary United Front (RUF) and renegade soldiers calling themselves the Armed Forces Revolutionary Council (AFRC) toppled the civilian government of President Tejan Kabbah. Following his return to power (with the help of the regional peace-keeping force, ECMOG) in the latter part of 1998, President Kabbah was focused on the peace process. This resulted in the Lomé Peace Accord, signed in July 1999, ending the civil war (although some fighting continued until March 2002). Following the end of the conflict, the Kabbah-led government increased the budgetary allocation to the agriculture sector, which rose to 12.5% in 2014. By 2007, with an increase in government intervention and donor assistance, agricultural production had surpassed expectations and was providing at least 40% of the country's annual GDP.

Notwithstanding the contribution of the agriculture sector to the 4% annual growth in the country's GDP, the people of Sierra Leone were still food insecure. This is not to say that the government of President Bai Koroma (who came to power in 2007 and led the country throughout the pandemic) made no effort to support the agriculture sector prior to the pandemic. It did, but the rent-seeking attitude of corrupt politicians undermined initiatives and contributed to the enduring fragility of the sector. For instance, the political preference for large-scale ethanol production and natural resource mining for export to European markets led to the displacement of farmers and accusations of land-grabbing by multinationals under the protection of politicians. With unemployment at its highest level, the years between 2007 and 2014, were years of lack: lack of money to buy food; lack of nutritionally balanced food to buy. According to the results of a survey conducted in April 2015 (a year after the start of the pandemic) by the Government of Sierra Leone in partnership with the World Bank and Innovations for Poverty Action, overall earnings among wage workers remained at pre-pandemic levels—with the exception of the non-agricultural private enterprise sector. The findings of the survey are worth quoting here.

> Only nine per cent of those who worked in LFS [Labor Force Survey] earned a wage income. Among wage earners, who comprise mostly

> (83 per cent) public sector employees and non-agricultural private enterprise workers, average earnings decreased from 680,000 Leones (approximately US$159) in the baseline to 583,000 Leones (approximately US$136) in Round 2. This decline was not statistically significant; however, there was a significant wage decline among non-agricultural private enterprise sector workers, whose wages were 544,000 Leones (approximately US 127) in Round 2, down 28 percent from LFS. This is consistent with the expectation that the business environment would experience more volatility than government and public sector employment due to EVD conditions such as transport disruptions and closure of large private enterprises. This decline is across the sector and not just caused by exit of high wage earners, as the pre-crisis wage level is not different between those who remained in this sector and those who left.
>
> (Himelein et al. 2015, 9)

The EVD and household food insecurity in Sierra Leone

The Ebola pandemic in Sierra Leone led to reduced agricultural productivity in two consecutive years. The pandemic-related restrictions on movement and trade, which occurred during the harvest season, caused post-harvest losses. Farmers who thus could not afford access to food were forced to consume the stored seeds meant for cultivation in the next planting season. Approximately 51% of Sierra Leonean households were negatively affected by the EVD outbreak with regard to their livelihoods, including food security. In rural areas, where 75% of households are engaged in agriculture as their main economic activity, food insecurity issues were even worse (AFDB et al., 2015). Households were forced to devise coping strategies to mitigate the food insecurity risks they faced. Looking at Figure 7.1, the information for all rounds of the survey shows that 52% of Sierra Leoneans were driven to consume on less preferred food or less expensive food; 51% had to limit portion size at meal times; 45% reduced the number of meals eaten in a day; 43% of households restricted adult consumption to ensure small children could eat; 32% sold assets to buy food; and 21% borrowed food or relied on help from friends/relatives.

From November 2014 (the first round of the survey) to April 2015 (third round), the food insecurity situation had improved and the number of households adopting such coping strategies had fallen, marginally for some strategies and considerably for others. In all, there was a 3% reduction in the number of households that had to rely on less preferred food or less expensive food; a 1% reduction in households that limited portion size; and a 4% reduction in households that reduced the number of meals eaten in a day. Most significant are the 9% reduction in the number of households that relied on help from friends/relatives, and the 7% reduction in the number that restricted adult consumption to ensure small children could eat. The exception was a 4% increase in the number of households that sold assets to buy food.

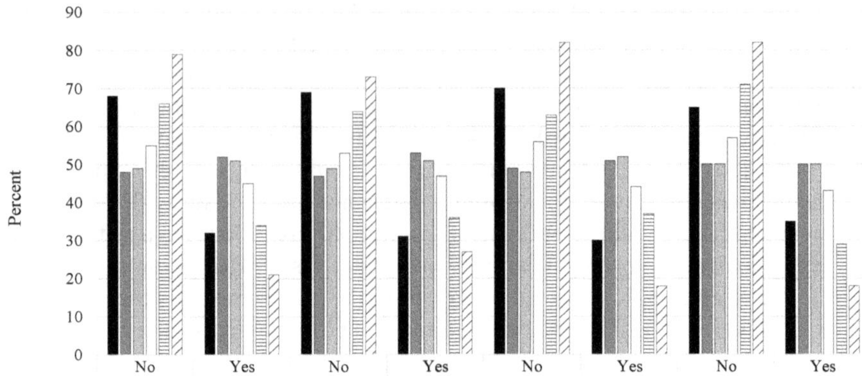

	No	Yes	No	Yes	No	Yes	No	Yes
	Full (All rounds)		Round 1 (Nov 2014)		Round 2 (Jan/Feb 2015)		Round 3 (APR 2015)	
SABF	68	32	69	31	70	30	65	35
RLP/EF	48	52	47	53	49	51	50	50
LP/SMT	49	51	49	51	48	52	50	50
RNMED	55	45	53	47	56	44	57	43
RACSME	66	34	64	36	63	37	71	29
BF/HF	79	21	73	27	82	18	82	18

SABF RLP/EF LP/SMT RNMED RACSME BF/HF

Figure 7.1 Food insecurity across three rounds of the survey.

Source: High Frequency Cell Phone Survey.

Notes

SABF: Sell assets to buy food. RLP/EF: Rely on less preferred or expensive food. LP/SMT: Limit portion size at meal times. RNMED: Reduce number of meals eaten in a day. RACSME: Restrict adult consumption for small children to eat.

BF/HF: Borrow food or rely on help from a friend/relative.

Methodology

Data

Data for this chapter are drawn from the three rounds of the High Frequency Cell Phone Surveys jointly conducted by Statistics Sierra Leone (SSL) and Innovations for Poverty Action (IPA), with funding from the World Bank. Round 1 of the data collection was undertaken from November 12 to 25, 2014; Round 2 data were collected from January 22 to February 4, 2015; and Round 3 from May 1 to 12, 2015. Respondents for the survey were mainly household heads whose cell phone numbers were recorded in July and August 2014, when the nationally representative Labor Force Survey (LFS) was conducted. Household heads comprised 93.6% of respondents in Round 1, 92.3% in Round 2 and 90.1% in Round 3. Any call answered by a person who was not an original household member was dropped and an 'incorrect number' was recorded for that house. Round 1, which formed the basis for subsequent rounds, included 2,764 households across all districts of the country. As the survey focused on the socioeconomic impact of the EVD, sections covered in Round 1 included employment and labor market conditions, non-agricultural business operations, agricultural activity, food security, health responses (covering only fever and pregnancy), remittances, travel, trust, and knowledge about Ebola. The only question on EVD was whether the respondent had heard of Ebola and, if so, the source of the information. In subsequent rounds, this question was dropped because the Round 1 data showed that information on the disease was widespread. In sum, the data for all the rounds represented repeated cross-sections and had information on some households that were represented in either one, two or all three rounds of the survey (Himelein et al., 2015).

The raw data represented 1,895 households in Round 1, 1,878 in Round 2 and 1,742 in Round 3. Since our objective was to generate panel data, we appended data for all rounds of the survey and maintained only data for households that were represented in at least two rounds. This left 1,757 households for Round 1, 1,794 for Round 2 and 1,491 for Round 3. Thus, a total 5,042 observations were used for the analysis and to generate the summary statistics. The regression analyses suffered further losses in the number of observations due to missing observations in the variables, which resulted in the deletion of rows and columns in the square matrices (Himelein et al. 2015). The limitation of this dataset is that it was collected at the household level and does not contain demographic information on the household head. This is why these variables are missing from the regression analysis.

Summary statistics

The summary statistics shows that 25.7% of the sample resided in Freetown 57.4% in other urban areas 16.9% in rural areas. Seventy-one percent of the sample were employed, with a majority (61.3%) being self-employed. It is worth noting that the mean and standard deviation for our income diversification variable (revenue from non-farm enterprise) suffers from outliers; to address this, we generated its natural log before using the variable in the regression analysis to prevent biased estimates.

Measurement of food insecurity

There are direct and indirect measures of food insecurity, including socioeconomic measures, food consumption, anthropometric measures and the coping strategy approach (Shariff and Khor 2008). This chapter employs the coping strategy approach, which has been adopted by many researchers due to its advantages of simplicity, lower cost and ease of comprehension (Himelein et al. 2015; Maxwell 1996; Oldewage-Theron, Dicks and Napier 2006; Shariff and Khor 2008). These coping strategies are adopted by households to alleviate food insecurity risks.

We employ principal component analysis (PCA) to generate an index of food insecurity based on six household coping strategies that connote food insecurity.

Table 7.5 Descriptive statistics of variables used in estimating the socio-economic determinants of household food insecurity

Variable	*Full*			*Round 1*			*Round 2*			*Round 3*		
	N	*Mean*	*Std. Dev.*	*N*	*Mean*	*Std. Dev.*	*N*	*Mean*	*Std. Dev.*	*N*	*Mean*	*Std. Dev.*
Food insecurity index	4,991	0.004	1.670	1,744	0.271	1.852	1,774	–0.019	1.614	1,774	–0.019	1.614
Location												
Rural	5,042	0.169	0.375	1,757	0.167	0.373	1,794	0.173	0.379	1,794	0.173	0.379
Freetown	5,042	0.257	0.437	1,757	0.252	0.434	1,794	0.271	0.445	1,794	0.271	0.445
Other urban	5,042	0.574	0.495	1,757	0.581	0.494	1,794	0.555	0.497	1,794	0.555	0.497
Employed (Yes = 1; No = 0)	5,003	0.712	0.453	1,749	0.651	0.477	1,781	0.688	0.463	1,781	0.688	0.463
revenue from non-farm enterprise	2,736	763060.90	2518575.00	1,079	602951.50	1833165.00	953	868518.10	2717735.00	953	868518.10	2717735.00
Engaged in agricultural activity	4,992	0.405	0.491	1,746	0.403	0.491	1,773	0.454	0.498	1,773	0.454	0.498
Status in employment												
Employee	4,081	0.308	0.462	1,391	0.305	0.460	1,459	0.300	0.458	1,459	0.300	0.458
Self employed	4,081	0.613	0.487	1,391	0.640	0.480	1,459	0.584	0.493	1,459	0.584	0.493
Cooperative/volunteer/apprenticeship	4,081	0.079	0.270	1,391	0.055	0.229	1,459	0.117	0.321	1,459	0.117	0.321
Remittance received (Yes = 1; No = 0)	4,992	0.152	0.359	1,745	0.162	0.369	1,774	0.156	0.363	1,774	0.156	0.363
New member joined household (Yes = 1; No = 0)	4,992	0.104	0.306	1,745	0.108	0.310	1,774	0.076	0.264	1,774	0.076	0.264

Attended community meeting (1 = yes; 0 = no)	4,992	0.386	0.487	1,745	0.364	0.481	1,774	0.374	0.484	1,774	0.374	0.484
Attendance to church/mosque	4,992	45.134	54.376	1,745	49.641	57.084	1,774	47.375	56.180	1,774	47.375	56.180
Market visits	4,991	5.953	11.711	1,745	5.790	10.917	1,773	5.728	9.864	1,773	5.728	9.864
Districts												
Kailahun/Pujehun	5,015	0.043	0.203	1,757	0.042	0.201	1,786	0.046	0.209	1,786	0.046	0.209
Kenema/Bo	5,015	0.217	0.412	1,757	0.216	0.411	1,786	0.213	0.410	1,786	0.213	0.410
Bonthe/Moyamba	5,015	0.092	0.289	1,757	0.090	0.287	1,786	0.091	0.288	1,786	0.091	0.288
Kono/Koinadugu	5,015	0.157	0.364	1,757	0.159	0.366	1,786	0.151	0.358	1,786	0.151	0.358
Port Loko/Kambia	5,015	0.059	0.235	1,757	0.058	0.234	1,786	0.061	0.239	1,786	0.061	0.239
Bombali/Tonkolili	5,015	0.106	0.308	1,757	0.106	0.308	1,786	0.107	0.309	1,786	0.107	0.309
Western Rural/ Urban	5,015	0.325	0.469	1,757	0.328	0.470	1,786	0.330	0.470	1,786	0.330	0.470

Source: Computed using the *High Frequency Cell Phone Survey*

These strategies are: (i) sell assets to buy food; (ii) rely on less preferred or expensive food; (iii) limit portion size at meal times; (iv) reduce number of meals eaten in a day; (v) restrict adult consumption for small children to eat; and (vi) borrow food or rely on help from a friend/relative. The PCA is used to generate a single variable (or index) from a set of variables that have high levels of correlation. The index combines the strength of all the variables together to generate the single indicator of interest and must be shown to possess adequate information or variation in the original dataset. We rely on the Kaiser (1974) and Jolliffe (2002) criteria to choose components that have eigen values greater than one. In this case, we maintain component 1 and 2, and it can be seen that they jointly explain 63% of the variations in the food insecurity index.

Based on the Bartlett test of sphericity, we reject the null hypothesis ($p<0.05$) of non-collinearity among the coping strategies (singular matrix). We then conclude that these coping strategies have their intercorrelation matrix being generated within households in which these strategies are highly correlated—linear combinations of the variables exist (Beavers et al. 2013). The Kaiser-Meyer-Olkin (KMO) measure of sampling adequacy is well above the 0.05 threshold considered suitable for PCA (Williams, Onsman and Brown 2010). In specific

Table 7.6 Eigen values from Principal Component Analysis (unrotated = principal)

Component	*Eigenvalue*	*Proportion*	*Cumulative*
Comp1	2.80	0.47	0.47
Comp2	1.20	0.16	0.63
Comp3	0.72	0.12	0.75
Comp4	0.63	0.10	0.86
Comp5	0.49	0.08	0.94
Comp6	0.38	0.06	1.00
Kaiser-Meyer-Olkin (KMO)			0.801
Bartlett test of sphericity (Chi2)			7512.66***

***p<0.01, **p<0.05, *p<0.1

Source: Computed using the *High Frequency Cell Phone Survey*

Table 7.7 Principal components (eigenvectors) rotated loadings

Variable (coping strategies)	*Comp1*	*Comp2*	*Unexplained*
Sell assets to buy food	0.31	0.56	0.42
Rely on less preferred or expensive food	0.46	–0.24	0.34
Limit portion size at meal times	0.46	–0.42	0.24
Reduce number of meals eaten in a day	0.46	–0.33	0.30
Restrict adult consumption for small children to eat	0.40	0.28	0.48
Borrow food or rely on help from a friend/relative	0.33	0.51	0.44

Source: Computed using the *High Frequency Cell Phone Survey*

terms, the value of 0.801 is considered meritorious among the stated bands for this test. In this case, the food insecurity index is appropriate and can be used to represent all six coping strategies. Looking at the rotated loadings (Table 7.7), we can see how each of the food insecurity indicators (coping strategies) load onto the principal components. In component 1, coping strategies such as reliance on less preferred or expensive food, limiting portion size at meal times and reducing number of meals eaten in a day all have equal weight (46%) in defining a household's food insecurity status. In component 2, the coping strategy that makes the greatest contribution to the food insecurity index is selling assets to buy food (56%).

Estimation techniques

We employed two empirical techniques for the regression analyses. First, we used the random-effects model to ascertain the effect of the household indicators on overall food insecurity. Second, we applied the random-effects Poisson for count data to assess the effect of the household indicators on the coping strategies, since they are captured as a count. Specific reasons for use of these techniques are explained below.

Fixed effects and random effects models

The random-effects model is used to regress the food insecurity index on the household-level indicators, including income diversification, since the index is a continuous variable. The random-effects model is chosen over the fixed-effects model because the panel data structure is unbalanced (Asteriou and Hall 2011; Nguyen 2010). Use of the random-effects model is also supported by the Breusch-Pagan Lagrange multiplier (LM) test, which is significant and leads to the rejection of the null hypothesis of zero individual- or time-specific variance components (Baltagi 2008; Cameron and Trivedi 2010; Torres-Reyna 2007).

Random-effects Poisson and population-averaged Poisson models

The random-effects Poisson and population-averaged Poisson are used to assess the effects of the household variables on each of the six coping strategies employed to measure food insecurity. Since the coping strategies are captured as a count for the number of days they were adopted, the data follows a Poisson distribution. The fixed-effects Poisson technique was not considered because the number of periods is short ($T=3$) and will suffer from the incidental parameters problem. This means that the individual-specific errors cannot be consistently estimated (Baltagi 2008; Cameron and Trivedi 2010; Greene 2004). The significant likelihood ratio (LR) test indicates that the random-effects model is preferred to the population average model.

The empirical models are shown in equations (7.1) and (7.2).

Empirical models

Random-effects model for the effect of socio-economic variables on food insecurity

$$\begin{aligned} FIn\sec_{it} &= \beta_0 + \beta_1 Loc_{it} + \beta_2 Emp_{it} + \beta_3 \ln Incnf_{it} + \beta_4 Agric_{it} + \\ &\beta_5 Statemp_{it} + \beta_6 \operatorname{Re} mit_{it} + \beta_7 Newmem_{it} + \beta_8 Commeet_{it} + \\ &\beta_9 Chmsq_{it} + \beta_{10} Mkt_{it} + \beta_{11} District_{it} + \upsilon_i + \varepsilon_{it} \end{aligned} \tag{7.1}$$

Random-effects Poisson model for the effect of socio-economic variables on food insecurity

$$\begin{aligned} \Pr[FIn\sec_{it} = 1 \mid X_{it}] &= \alpha_0 + \alpha_1 Loc_{it} + \alpha_2 Emp_{it} + \alpha_3 \ln Incnf_{it} + \\ &\alpha_4 Agric_{it} + \alpha_5 Statemp_{it} + \alpha_6 \operatorname{Re} mit_{it} + \alpha_7 Newmem_{it} + \\ &\alpha_8 Commeet_{it} + \alpha_9 Chmsq_{it} + \alpha_{10} Mkt_{it} + \alpha_{11} District_{it} + \delta_i + \eta_{it} \end{aligned} \tag{7.2}$$

where *FInsec* represents the food insecurity index in (2) and the coping strategies in (3). *Loc* is a categorical variable representing three locations (Freetown, other urban and rural); *Emp* is the employment status of the household head; *lnIncnf* is the natural log of the income from non-farm economic activities and is also a proxy for income diversification; *Agric* is a binary variable for whether the household head is engaged in agriculture or not; and *Statemp* is a four-level categorical variable that describes the head's actual status in employment. *District*, represents the 14 districts in Sierra Leone, while *Remit, Newmem* and *Commeet* are binary variables representing receipt of remittance, additional member joining the household and attendance at community meetings respectively. *Chmsq* and *Mkt* respectively represent continuous variables such as attendance to church/mosque and number of visits to the market. β_0 and α_0 are constants to be determined; υ_i and δ_i are the individual-specific; while ε_{it} and η_{it} are the general error terms.

Analysis and discussion

The analysis is separated into two parts. The first discusses the effects of households' socioeconomic variables on the overall food insecurity (index); the second focuses on the mechanisms of the analyses by looking at the effects of these socioeconomic variables on the specific coping strategies that reflect food insecurity. Note that, we report intensity rate ratio (IRR) for the random-effects Poisson and that this is interpreted just like odds ratio. IRR values greater than one signify an increase, and those less than one a reduction.

We can see from Table 7.8 that during EVD outbreak periods, agricultural households became more food insecure than non-agricultural households. The inference is that agricultural households suffer from EVD-related restrictions in movements, resulting in them being forced to eat the seeds stored for cultivation in the next planting season. Losing such seeds is tantamount to a loss in livelihood, resulting in food insecurity. This resonates with earlier studies that found agricultural households to be more food insecure (WFP and VAM 2015).

In contrast to the food insecurity threat to wholly agricultural households, those that diversified their income portfolios by engaging in non-farm economic activities were less likely to be impacted by the Ebola pandemic. This is because the increase in income generated from non-farm economic activities resulted in a reduction in the level of food insecurity facing the household. The benefit of non-farm economic activities is that they are (mostly) not seasonal. For wholly agricultural households, the impacts of restrictions on movement during the planting season are ongoing, resulting in the households being at higher risk of food insecurity even when the EVD-related restrictions ceased to apply. This finding supports that of the AFDB et al. (2015).

Looking at the other socioeconomic indicators, we can see that in EVD outbreak periods, households in Freetown (major urban centers) were less likely to be food insecure compared to those in rural areas and in other urban areas. Based on this finding, we call for policy-makers to direct more attention to rural populations and those living in satellite communities, as they are at a higher risk of becoming food insecure during pandemics.

It should also be noted that households that received remittances were less likely to be food insecure during the Ebola pandemic. The social inclusion indicators are almost all insignificant in reducing food insecurity. These indicators include attendance at a community meeting, church/mosque or market. The reason behind this outcome is that most households faced similar conditions regarding these indicators given the imposition of restrictions on movement and related socioeconomic activities.

Income diversification and its effect on the intensity of food insecurity

As in the food insecurity analysis, households that engaged in agricultural activities were likely to experience higher levels of intensity in their food insecurity situation than counterparts engaged in other economic activities. Increases in incomes from non-farm economic activities reduced the intensity of food insecurity. The analyses at this point are comparative and the findings as follows.

In specific terms, agricultural households were 48% more likely to sell assets to buy food; 38% more likely to rely on less preferred or expensive food; and 20% more likely to reduce number of meals eaten in a day, than non-agricultural households. Conversely, an increase in non-farm enterprise income by 1.00 Le (leones—the currency of Sierra Leone) reduced intensity of selling assets to buy food by 4.4%. intensity of relying on less preferred or expensive food by 7.1% and intensity of reducing the number of meals eaten in a day by 7.4%. Although the agriculture variable was insignificant in explaining the other coping strategies, a 1.00 Le increase in income from non-farm economic activities reduced households' intensity of limiting portion size at meal times by 8.9%, intensity of

Table 7.8 Random effects model for socio-economic determinants of household food insecurity

		Location		
Food insecurity index	*Full*	*Rural*	*Freetown*	*Other urban*
Location (Base = other)				
Rural	–0.140	—	—	—
	(0.112)	—	—	—
Freetown	–0.277*	—	—	—
	(0.156)	—	—	—
Employed (1 = yes; 0 = no)	–0.262*	–0.520	–0.187	–0.287
	(0.134)	(0.323)	(0.241)	(0.181)
ln(revenue from enterprise)	–0.118***	–0.047	–0.158***	–0.125***
	(0.021)	(0.037)	(0.039)	(0.029)
Agric. activity (1 = yes; 0 = no)	0.355***	0.610***	0.443**	0.290***
	(0.087)	(0.189)	(0.212)	(0.107)
Status in employment (Base = employee)				
– self employed	0.221**	0.597***	0.082	0.228
	(0.104)	(0.213)	(0.176)	(0.152)
– cooperative/Volunteer/ Apprenticeship	0.411**	0.675**	0.400	0.367
	(0.160)	(0.313)	(0.291)	(0.229)
Remittance received (1 = yes; 0 = no)	–0.050	0.356	–0.090	–0.138
	(0.107)	(0.243)	(0.169)	(0.147)
New member joined household (1 = yes; 0 = no)	–0.120	–0.298	–0.421**	0.034
	(0.106)	(0.233)	(0.181)	(0.135)
Attended community meeting (1 = yes; 0 = no)	0.037	0.008	0.290**	–0.022
	(0.073)	(0.153)	(0.141)	(0.100)
Attendance to church/mosque	0.002***	0.004**	0.001	0.002**
	(0.001)	(0.002)	(0.001)	(0.001)
Market visits	0.002	0.005**	–0.001	0.000
	(0.002)	(0.002)	(0.004)	(0.004)
Districts (Base = Kono/Koinadugu)				
Kailahun/Pujehun	0.144	–0.059	—	0.296
	(0.268)	(0.437)	—	(0.353)
Kenema/Bo	–0.250*	–0.288	—	–0.255
	(0.138)	(0.290)	—	(0.156)
Bonthe/Moyamba	–0.305*	–0.423	—	–0.252
	(0.163)	(0.291)	—	(0.204)
Port Loko/Kambia	–0.196	–0.241	—	–0.170
	(0.194)	(0.290)	—	(0.269)
Bombali/Tonkolili	–0.278*	–0.222	—	–0.300*
	(0.150)	(0.289)	—	(0.179)
Western Rural/Urban	–0.099	0.213	1.642***	–0.358
	(0.172)	(0.268)	(0.541)	(0.227)
Constant	1.469***	0.022	—	1.639***
	(0.328)	(0.603)	—	(0.446)
Observations	2,051	376	457	1,218
Number of households	1,153	223	263	681

		Location		
Food insecurity index	*Full*	*Rural*	*Freetown*	*Other urban*
Wald chi2 (F-test)	104.84***	37.68***	28.218**	46.31***
DF	18	16	11	16
R^2	0.066	0.086	0.085	0.056
σu	0.879	0.683	0.450	1.021
σv	1.281	1.301	1.133	1.325
Θ	0.320	0.216	0.137	0.372
Breusch-Pagan LM (chibar2)				

Robust standard errors in parentheses *sigma_u* = $\sigma_{u;}$ *sigma_e* = $\sigma_{v;}$ *Rho* = θ

***p<0.01, **p<0.05, *p<0.1

Source: Authors' estimates using *High Frequency Cell Phone Survey*

restricting adult consumption for small children to eat by 6.9%, and intensity of borrowing food or relying on help from a friend/relative by 13%.

Summary and recommendations

The chapter sheds lights on the Ebola Virus Disease and the attendant food insecurity arising from the disruption of socioeconomic and geopolitical activities in countries affected by the pandemic. The discussion focuses on the coping strategies adopted by households to mitigate food insecurity risks. While some households sell assets to buy food, others switch to less preferred or expensive food. Some households limit portion sizes; others restrict adult consumption so that small children have sufficient food. Some households reduce the number of meals per a day, while others resort to the borrowing food or relying on help from friends and relatives. We constructed a food insecurity index using the six coping strategies while analyzing these strategies independently. Such coping strategies can be said to exhibit the direct elicitation approach to identifying food insecure households.

We applied econometric techniques, including the random-effects model for continuous variables and the random-effects Poisson and population-average Poisson, to panel data generated by appending data from the three rounds of the High Frequency Cell Phone Survey. Evidence from the analyses indicates that during outbreaks of EVD, agricultural households are more food insecure than households engaged in other economic activities. A similar pattern is observed when considering the intensities in food insecurity. However, increases in non-farm income for households that have diversified their income portfolios were found to lead to reductions in food insecurity and intensity of food insecurity during the EVD pandemic. Urban and remittance-receiving households are also less-affected by EVD outbreaks in terms of food insecurity.

Based on the findings above, we recommend that agricultural households diversify their income-generating activities to include non-farm activities. Such

Table 7.9 Poisson random effects model for socio-economic determinants of household intensity of food insecurity

	(1)	*(2)*	*(3)*	*(4)*	*(5)*	*(6)*
	Sell assets to buy food	*Rely on less preferred or expensive food*	*Limit portion size at meal times*	*Reduce number of meals eaten in a day*	*Restrict adult consumption for small children to eat*	*Borrow food or rely on help from a friend/relative*
	IRR	*IRR*	*IRR*	*IRR*	*IRR*	*IRR*
Location (Base = Other urban)						
Rural	1.052	0.992	0.930	0.856	0.920	0.868
	(0.127)	(0.090)	(0.088)	(0.086)	(0.107)	(0.139)
Freetown	0.888	0.903	0.777	0.827	0.780	0.784
	(0.191)	(0.128)	(0.127)	(0.128)	(0.159)	(0.204)
Employed (Yes = 1; No = 0)	0.947	0.808**	0.697***	0.824	0.695***	0.898
	(0.169)	(0.083)	(0.078)	(0.117)	(0.095)	(0.191)
ln(revenue from non-farm enterprise)	0.956	0.929***	0.911***	0.926***	0.931***	0.869***
	(0.027)	(0.017)	(0.018)	(0.022)	(0.026)	(0.032)
Engaged in agricultural Activity (Yes = 1; No = 0)	1.480***	1.376***	1.106	1.195*	1.185	1.088
	(0.168)	(0.096)	(0.089)	(0.112)	(0.123)	(0.152)
Status in employment (Base = employee)						
Self-employed	1.152	1.266**	1.273**	1.047	1.210	0.935
	(0.145)	(0.138)	(0.143)	(0.136)	(0.161)	(0.156)
Cooperative/volunteer/ apprenticeship	1.237	1.469***	1.278*	1.276	1.052	0.759
	(0.238)	(0.197)	(0.185)	(0.208)	(0.205)	(0.167)
Remittance received (Yes = 1; No = 0)	0.996	0.901	1.024	1.063	0.834	1.035
	(0.131)	(0.087)	(0.100)	(0.121)	(0.114)	(0.176)
New member joined household (Yes = 1; No = 0)	0.985	0.836*	0.952	0.948	0.929	0.977
	(0.133)	(0.082)	(0.105)	(0.125)	(0.132)	(0.152)

Attended community meeting (Yes = 1; No = 0)	1.022	0.974	1.003	0.959	1.075	1.137
	(0.095)	(0.059)	(0.068)	(0.080)	(0.089)	(0.126)
Attended church/mosque (Yes = 1; No = 0)	1.000	1.001	1.002***	1.002***	1.001*	1.002**
	(0.001)	(0.001)	(0.001)	(0.001)	(0.001)	(0.001)
Went to the market (Yes = 1; No = 0)	1.002	0.997	1.005*	1.001	1.001	1.006
	(0.003)	(0.002)	(0.002)	(0.003)	(0.003)	(0.004)
Districts (Base = Kono/Koinadugu)						
Kailahun/Pujehun	1.155	0.954	1.043	1.016	1.334	1.255
	(0.250)	(0.152)	(0.176)	(0.186)	(0.270)	(0.321)
Kenema/Bo	0.977	0.857	0.869	0.743**	0.909	0.730
	(0.152)	(0.094)	(0.098)	(0.096)	(0.132)	(0.142)
Bonthe/Moyamba	1.022	0.858	0.726**	0.659**	0.953	0.705
	(0.216)	(0.118)	(0.107)	(0.111)	(0.172)	(0.170)
Port Loko/Kambia	1.198	0.783*	0.801	0.917	0.928	0.915
	(0.208)	(0.114)	(0.119)	(0.151)	(0.173)	(0.196)
Bombali/Tonkolili	0.976	0.812*	0.810	0.735**	0.827	0.775
	(0.179)	(0.097)	(0.107)	(0.104)	(0.124)	(0.141)
Western rural/urban	1.000	0.926	0.918	0.766*	0.974	0.726
	(0.215)	(0.135)	(0.146)	(0.114)	(0.190)	(0.177)
Constant	0.580	2.731***	4.356***	2.975***	1.974*	2.709*
	(0.241)	(0.725)	(1.214)	(0.969)	(0.750)	(1.458)
Alpha	1.430	0.768	1.003	1.281	1.535**	2.488***
	(0.353)	(0.162)	(0.177)	(0.228)	(0.303)	(0.545)

continued

Table 7.9 continued

	(1)	*(2)*	*(3)*	*(4)*	*(5)*	*(6)*
	Sell assets to buy food	*Rely on less preferred or expensive food*	*Limit portion size at meal times*	*Reduce number of meals eaten in a day*	*Restrict adult consumption for small children to eat*	*Borrow food or rely on help from a friend/relative*
	IRR	*IRR*	*IRR*	*IRR*	*IRR*	*IRR*
Observations	2,052	2,052	2,051	2,052	2,052	2,052
Number of households	1,153	1,153	1,153	1,153	1,153	1,153
Wald Test (chi^2)	303.00***	108.03***	106.34***	66.69***	99.08***	312.58***
LR Test (rho = 0): $\chi 2(01)$	266.83***	444.13***	751.90***	762.27***	584.06***	438.68***

Robust *p*-values in parentheses ***$p<0.01$, **$p<0.05$, *$p<0.1$. LR test: likelihood ratio test. IRR: incidence rate ratio

Source: Authors' estimates using *High Frequency Cell Phone Survey*

activities, and the income they generate, function as risk-coping strategies when other socioeconomic activities have been disrupted by the onset of a pandemic. Non-farm economic activities are also unaffected by, or less vulnerable to, the season-dependence of farming activities and therefore offer more resilient income streams. Wholly agricultural households, in contrast, are highly vulnerable to disruption during specific seasons and struggle to recover financially as income-generating activities are season-limited. Another recommendation is that governments and civil society organization direct increased attention—in the form of relief and aid—to rural and satellite communities during pandemics, as these households are at the greatest risk of becoming food during outbreaks of disease such as EVD.

Note

1 African Development Bank (AFDB), Government of Sierra Leone (GoSL), World Bank (WB), World Food Programme (WFP), European Union (EU), Food and Agriculture Organization of the United Nations (FAO).

References

Adem, M., E. Tadele, H. Mossie, and M. Ayenalem. 2018. "Income Diversification and Food Security Situation in Ethiopia: A Review Study." *Cogent Food & Agriculture* 4 (1): 1513354.

African Development Bank (AFDB), Government of Sierra Leone (GSL), World Bank (WB), World Food Programme (WFP), European Union (EU) and UN Food and Agriculture Organization (FAO). 2015. *State of Food Security in Sierra Leone 2015: Comprehensive Food Security and Vulnerability Analysis*. Retrieved from https://reliefweb.int/sites/reliefweb.int/files/resources/wfp288316.pdf.

Agbola, P. O., D. O. Awotide, A. E. Ikpi, P. Kormawa, V. O. Okoruwa, and D. A. Babalola. 2008. *Effect of Income Diversification Strategies on Food Insecurity Status of Farming Households in Africa: Result of Analysis from Nigeria. Result of Analysis from Nigeria* (No. 725-2016-49415).

Agyeman, B. A. S., S. Asuming-Brempong, and E. E. Onumah. 2014. "Determinants of Income Diversification of Farm Households in the Western Region of Ghana." *Quarterly Journal of International Agriculture* 53 (1): 55–72.

Alinovi, L., G. Hemrich, and L. Russo. 2007. *Addressing Food Insecurity in Fragile States: Case Studies from the Democratic Republic of the Congo, Somalia and Sudan.* Rome: Citeseer.

Asteriou, D., and S. G. Hall. 2011. *Applied Econometrics*. New York, NY: Palgrave Macmillan.

Baltagi, B. 2008. *Econometric Analysis of Panel Data*, 4th edn. Chichester: John Wiley & Sons.

Beavers, A. S., J. W. Lounsbury, J. K. Richards, S. W. Huck, G. J. Skolits, and S. L. Esquivel. 2013. "Practical Considerations for Using Exploratory Factor Analysis in Educational Research." *Practical Assessment, Research & Evaluation* 18 (6): 1–13.

Cameron, A. C., and P. K. Trivedi. 2010. *Microeconometrics Using Stata.* Retrieved from www.stata.com/stata-news/statanews.23.4.pdf.

De Waal, A., and A. Whiteside. 2003. "New Variant Famine: AIDS and Food Crisis in Southern Africa." *The Lancet* 362 (9391), 1234–1237.

FAO. 2000. *The State of Food Insecurity in the World 2000*. Rome: Food and Agriculture Organisation. Retrieved from www.fao.org/FOCUS/E/SOFI00/img/sofirep-e.pdf.

FAO. 2017. *Regional Overview of Food Security and Nutrition in Africa 2017. The Food Security and Nutrition–Conflict Nexus: Building Resilience for Food Security, Nutrition and Peace*. Accra: Food and Agriculture Organization of the United Nations. Retrieved from www.fao.org/3/a-i7967e.pdf.

Figuié, M. 2016. *Impact of the Ebola Virus Disease Outbreak on Market Chains and Trade of Agricultural Products in West Africa. Report for FAO REOWA (Resilience, Emergencies and Rehabilitation in West Africa)*. Food and Agriculture Organization of the United Nations.

Greene, W. 2004. "The Behaviour of the Maximum Likelihood Estimator of Limited Dependent Variable Models in the Presence of Fixed Effects." *The Econometrics Journal* 7 (1), 98–119.

Himelein, K., M. Testaverde, A. Turay, and S. Turay. 2015. *The Socio-Economic Impacts of Ebola in Sierra Leone* (Round 3). Retrieved from www.worldbank.org/content/dam/Worldbank/document/Poverty%20documents/Socio-Economic%20Impacts%20of%20Ebola%20in%20Sierra%20Leone,%20April%2015%20(final).pdf

Himmelgreen, D. A., N. Romero-Daza, D. Turkon, S. Watson, I. Okello-Uma, and D. Sellen. 2009. "Addressing the HIV/AIDS—Food Insecurity Syndemic in Sub-Saharan Africa." *African Journal of AIDS Research* 8 (4): 401–412.

Jolliffe, I. T. 2002. "Principal Components in Regression Analysis." *Principal Component Analysis*. Springer Series in Statistics, 167–198.

Kaiser, H. F. 1974. An Index of Factorial Simplicity. *Psychomertrika* 39: 13–36.

Lahai, J. I. 2016. *Gender in Practice: Culture, Politics and Society in Sierra Leone* (Vols. 1–14). Oxford: Peter Lang Ltd.

Lahai, J. I. 2017. *The Ebola Pandemic in Sierra Leone: Representations, Actors, Interventions and the Path to Recovery*. Basingstoke: Palgrave Macmillan.

Maxwell, D. G. 1996. "Measuring Food Insecurity: The Frequency and Severity of 'Coping Strategies'." *Food Policy* 21 (3): 291–303.

Mentamo, M., and N. R. Geda. 2016. "Livelihood Diversification under Severe Food Insecurity Scenario among Smallholder Farmers in Kadida Gamela District, Southern Ethiopia." *Kontakt* 18 (4): e258–e264.

Naysmith, S., A. de Waal, and A. Whiteside. 2009. "Revisiting New Variant Famine: The Case of Swaziland." *Food Security* 1 (3): 251–260.

Nguyen, M. C. 2010. XTSUR: Stata Module to Estimate Seemingly Unrelated Regression Model on Unbalanced Panel Data. *Statistical Software Components*. Retrieved from https://ideas.repec.org/c/boc/bocode/s456953.html.

Oldewage-Theron, W. H., E. G. Dicks, and C. E. Napier. 2006. "Poverty, Household Food Insecurity and Nutrition: Coping Strategies in an Informal Settlement in the Vaal Triangle, South Africa." *Public Health* 120 (9): 795–804.

Richards, P. 1996. *Fighting for the Rainforest: War, Youth and Resources in Sierra Leone*. Oxford: James Currey.

Richards, P. 2005. "To Fight or to Farm? Agrarian Dimensions of the Mano River Conflicts (Liberia and Sierra Leone)." *African Affairs* 104 (417): 571–590.

Shariff, Z. M., and G. L. Khor. 2008. Household Food Insecurity and Coping Strategies in a Poor Rural Community in Malaysia. *Nutrition Research and Practice* 2 (1): 26–34.

Smillie, I., L. Gberie, and R. Hazleton. 2000. *The Heart of the Matter: Sierra Leone Diamonds and Human Security*. Partnership Africa Canada Ottawa. Retrieved from www.pacweb.org/Documents/diamonds_KP/heart_of_the_matter-full-2000-01-eng.doc.

Torres-Reyna, O. 2007. *Panel Data Analysis Fixed and Random Effects Using Stata (v. 4.2).* Data and Statistical Services, Princeton University. Retrieved from https://pdfs.semanticscholar.org/f70f/9754bc51b1eb2e74dc7dc4e47549910730ed.pdf.

UNDP. 2015. *Socio-Economic Impact of Ebola Virus Disease in West Africa: A Call For National and Regional Containment, Recovery and Prevention.* United Nations Development Group. Retrieved from https://reliefweb.int/sites/reliefweb.int/files/resources/ebola-west-africa.pdf.

UNECA. 2014. *The Socio-Economic Impacts of Ebola Virus Disease (EVD) in Africa.* United Nations Economic Commission for Africa. Retrieved from www.uneca.org/sites/default/files/PublicationFiles/eca_ebola_report_final_eng.pdf.

WFP and VAM. 2015. *Food Insecurity on the Rise as Ebola Abates: Application of Shock Impact Simulation Model (SISMod) to Measure Ebola's Economic Impacts on Hunger.* World Food Programme and Food Security Analysis and Trends Service. Retrieved from https://documents.wfp.org/stellent/groups/public/documents/ena/wfp275534.pdf.

Williams, B., A. Onsman and T. Brown. 2010. "Exploratory Factor Analysis: A Five-step Guide for Novices." *Australasian Journal of Paramedicine* 8 (3): 1–13.

World Bank. 2014. *Update on the Economic Impact of the 2014 Ebola Epidemic on Liberia, Sierra Leone, and Guinea.* World Bank Group. Retrieved from www.worldbank.org/content/dam/Worldbank/document/Economic%20Impact%20Ebola%20Update%202%20Dec%202014.pdf.

Zerai, B. and Z. Gebreegziabher. 2011. "Effect of Nonfarm Income on Household Food Security in Eastern Tigrai, Ethiopia: An Entitlement Approach." *Food Science and Quality Management* 1: 1–22.

8 Institutional interventions in the advancement of food security and health

In 2012, the Economist Intelligence Unit (EIU) created a Global Food Security Index (GFSI) to statistically monitor the dynamics of food security, with specific emphasis on food affordability, availability, quality and safety. The affordability category, or the capacity to afford nutritious food without unnecessary stress, is measured across six indicators: (1) food consumption as a share of household expenditure; (2) proportion of the population under the global poverty line (% of population with income under U.S.$3.10/day at 2011 purchasing power parity, or PPP, exchange rates); (3) GDP per capita at PPP exchange rates; (4) agricultural import tariffs; (5) presence of food safety-net programs; and (6) access to financing for farmers. The availability category, which assesses factors that influence the supply of and access to food, is measured across eight indicators: (1) sufficiency of supply; (2) public expenditure on agricultural research and development; (3) agricultural infrastructure; (4) volatility of agricultural production; (5) political stability risk; (6) corruption; (7) urban absorption capacity; and (8) food loss. And the quality and safety category, which moves "beyond traditional welfare metrics, such as poverty and issues of access and supply" to the "nutritional quality of average diets" and the level of political and environmental security, is measured across five indicators. They are (1) diet diversification; (2) nutritional standards; (3) micronutrient availability; (4) protein quality; and (5) food safety (Economist Intelligence Unit 2017, 15).

Across sub-Saharan Africa, the EIU has continually ranked Southern Africa as having higher levels of food security due, in part, to people's incomes (calculated by the levels of employment and PPP), political stability and the diversification of diets and micronutrients (including iron and vitamin A) in the food consumed per household. Next is East Africa; however, despite having relatively higher levels of employment than Central and Western Africa, East Africa is also the region with the highest levels of hunger due, in part, to the problems of drought and famine. Next is West Africa. Despite success stories in terms of food affordability in countries like Ghana, Nigeria and Sierra Leone, the region remains a poor performer overall in terms of food availability, quality and safety. Even so, West Africa is ranked above central Africa, where food supply is very low, agricultural infrastructure appalling and malnutrition alarmingly high.

The central thesis of this chapter is that, while the increasing incidence of food insecurity imposes enormous pressure on governments at the national levels to mitigate against health shocks, it has not prevented them from formulating policies and developing innovative policies to increase crop yield and increase per capita dietary energy supply (DES) in line with the FAO's aggregated estimates of household energy (kcal) consumption per day. In this regard, the primary objectives of this chapter are, first, to evaluate the goals, policy directives and guiding principles of the national food and nutrition policies (NFNP) of sub-Saharan African countries that received a country ranking and overall score in the 2017 GFSI; and, second, to use the identified goals as a baseline to explore some of the key strategies and interventions to contain food insecurity. That said, we begin this chapter with an overview of the causes of food insecurity, before examining the various strategies states have used to end food insecurity. Using the "Ghana model on buffer food stock" as a guide, we examine the magnitude of the transfers between the agricultural sector and the health sector to determine whether this model (attending especially to its best practices and lessons) can be replicated in countries affected by the Ebola Virus Disease outbreaks between 2013 and 2014.

The role and resilience of the state: from food insecurity to food and nutrition security

Some have criticized the EIU for selecting computational indices that can be challenged politically and using complex statistical principles that can be misinterpreted by policy-makers, leading to the development of inadequate policy responses (Thomas et al. 2017, 5). Despite these possibilities, the place of sub-Saharan Africa in the GFSI is self-explanatory. The robustness of country ranking, when tested against the proportion of population under the global poverty line (affordability dimension) and public expenditure on agricultural research and development (availability dimension), and when these outliers are tested against the recurring changes in the aggregate gains of food secure countries (mostly the OECD countries), shows that food insecurity represents a debasement of the relevance of sub-Saharan African governments; an assault on human security, and a disregard for the right to life of those who die prematurely as a result of food unaffordability and unavailability, and the poor quality of what is available, within an already politically volatile and environmentally unsafe lifescape.

While the term food insecurity can be defined simply as a "catastrophic shortfall in food production" in the face of a "rapid decline of the purchasing power of specific social groups," its origins and causes are not straightforward. That notwithstanding, it is an accepted fact that persistent food insecurity undermines prospects for political stability and, hence, the legitimacy of governments. The interconnectedness between food insecurity and poverty (Baro and Deubel 2006); food insecurity and civil wars (Messer and Cohen 2007); food insecurity, climate change (drought, famine and rainfall anomalies) and instability (Fjelde and von Uexkull 2012; Hendrix and Glaser 2007); and food insecurity and high mortality rates, poor health and disease (Abrahams, Mchiza and Steyn 2011) all make food-insecure countries prone to state failure (broadly defined). Indicative of this disturbing reality are the annual reports by the FAO, WHO and the World Bank on the contribution of state weakness to creating the conditions for food insecurity and malnutrition across the sub-region. Notwithstanding this, the conclusions of these reports are that the attainment of food security and the prevention of malnutrition depends on direct government intervention.

The state and the making of food insecurity?

There are many reasons for skepticism over the ability of sub-Saharan African governments to reverse food insecurity. Governmental actions contributed, in part, to the creation of the precursor conditions for persistent food insecurity and the blame has been laid squarely on governments ever since. Generally, governments in sub-Saharan African countries prior to the Millennium Development Goals (MDG) era did not recognize or, rather, refused to accept the right to food as a human right. In the 1960s, when the UN World Food Programme (WFP) was busy putting modalities in place to remove barriers to the transnational flow of food aid, these governments were projecting a postcolonial resistance to neoliberal global market forces; in the 1970s, when food security insurance schemes resulted in surpluses of food in the global North and, with it, the rise of food-based humanitarianism directed to Africa, the neopatrimonial networks and rogue economies created by these governments had set in motion a militarized strategy for nationalization of their private sectors. With the rent-seeking elements of the patron–clientele systems already in control of the state, foreign food aid relieved the governments of responsibility for investment in the agricultural sector. In the 1980s, when the FAO was calling for the broadening of food security, African governments, already facing state failure, did not know how to react; and where they did, the availability of food was actually seen a threat to their survival. These governments saw the lack of food as a mechanism for control of their rebellious populations, who might stand up for their rights if they were adequately fed. In the 1990s, when the UN was reaffirming freedom from hunger and malnutrition as human rights, these governments were busy fighting civil wars that had erupted as a result of inequalities and relative deprivation, including food deprivation.

Even so, some of the 'humanitarian aid' regimes that came to help save the people from food shortages (see Shaw 1991), and even some of the regulators of the cereal pricing systems within the international political economy—before, during and after the 1986 and 1994 General Agreement on Tariffs and Trade (GATT) Uruguay rounds of international trade talks (see, Watkins 1991)—were either extremely touchy about the consequences of sub-Saharan Africa's food insecurity on the volatility (price distortion) of the market in the global North, or were wary of the consequences of the political resistance of governments to their self-interested agendas in the sub-region. Amid all this, African governments, despite their criticism of global inequalities, did little by way of projecting resilient and progressive alternatives—bringing us, again, to the skeptics' view of the role of postcolonial African governments.

Even the interventions of the FAO and the WHO were construed as a threat to governments' militarized understanding of state sovereignty. At the same time, the apparent 'intervention' moves of the private sector in the agro-forestry and cash-crop industries was also suspect. The poor business sector and volatile political environment created by governments played a role in closing off direct foreign investment in the agricultural and healthcare sectors. The outcomes included the loss of billions of (U.S.$) dollars' worth of returns from the private sector, and the destruction of millions of tons of wheat, maize and rice due to inadequate post-harvest technologies that would have been provided by private sector investment. Without private investment it is difficult, if not impossible, to attain crop diversification; and without such diversification, the incidence of malnutrition increased to unprecedented levels.

On the scale of regionally integrated foreign policy of states within the Organization of African Unity (OAU), there was (between the 1960s and the 1990s) a reluctance to consider food insecurity as a humanitarian crisis for fear that it could be generalized beyond the 'provision' of food to the poor and turned into a militarized discourse, one that would create a precedent easily exploited by those wanting to intervene in other countries militarily. Underneath the resistance to making food insecurity a collective security agenda across the region was the anxiety that interventions to end food insecurity and malnutrition had the potential to create a 'state of exception' in the humanitarian aid discourse and, with it, a debasement of the sovereign authority of governments, Such, at least, was the view before the rise of the international responsibility to protect (R_2P) doctrine, which transforms sovereignty from an entitlement to a responsibility; a responsibility that calls on the international community to invoke 'complementarity powers' to intervene where governments are reluctant or unable to align their national interests with the global interests of peace, security and sustainable development (see Bellamy 2010)—including ending global-scale state failures through the reinvention of human security institutions (see Walker et al. 2009).

This state of exception that existed prior to the emergence of the new norm of state sovereignty as responsibility, the arguments suggest, would have opened up additional possibilities for the "well-fed" (mostly those who control GATT) to impose their will on the "hungry" (those on the periphery of the international political economy). The inability of sub-Saharan African countries to change minds within the global north on the negative impact of government-subsidized agricultural sectors in OECD countries on the farmers of sub-Saharan Africa also reinforced the inability of sub-Saharan African cash crops to compete on the world stage. The effect of this, apart from the distortion of prices, can also be seen in the imbalances in countries' balance of trade. With no money left to purchase the surplus produce from their farmers—a move that would have led to the creation and solidification of buffer food stock regimes—the agricultural sector failed; and, in its place, an import-substitution strategy of 'unsustainable' development took root. Before long, sub-Saharan Africa became reliant on imported rice for its daily per capita dietary energy (kcal) supply.

At the sub-continental level (i.e., within the trade and economic blocs of Central, East, Southern and West Africa) there was less emphasis on food security. Amid the lack of a consistent, authoritative measure to determine the exact amount of produce crossing borders, member countries of the Economic Community of West African States (ECOWAS), the Common Market for Eastern and Southern Africa (COMESA), the Southern African Development Community (SADC), the East African Community (EAC) and the Horn of Africa in the Intergovernmental Authority on Development (IGAD), were unable to quantify the impact of sub-regional trade on per capita dietary supply and food security. The same goes for the West African Economic and Monetary Union (WAEMU), the Economic and Monetary Union of Central Africa (CEMAC) and the Southern African Customs Union (SACU) with its associated monetary union (the Common Monetary Area, CMA). They were unable to make a case, in the annual returns, that there was (and still, is) a connection between a common market and food security; and between these common markets and peoples' daily dietary intake of good quality food (see Matthews 2003, 59–69).

This means is that, where these institutions attempted to project the idea of "free movement" of goods (agricultural produce) and services (technology and expert human resources), the intended goal was, in theory, for the benefit of the people; however, in practice, it served the self-seeking interests of the lumpen-bourgeoisie, whose understanding of governance was far-removed from the lived experiences of the poor households. Their strategies to promote income transfers across the different economy-related sectors of member states resulted in suboptimal growth in the agricultural sector.

Their strategies for the agricultural sector were ineffective for two reasons. First, countries within these economic zones had similar comparative advantages in the production of wheat, maize and rice; and for some (especially those within ECOWAS), cassava, palm oil, groundnuts, fish, gari, vegetables and beans. Second, the governments within these zones were victims of the 'loss–loss' and 'loss–win' prisoner's dilemma they had created for themselves. Instead of promoting the development of each other's agricultural sectors, these governments encouraged their people to smuggle what they lacked from neighboring countries within their economic zones. For example, according to the 2009 statistics gathered by the Guinean *Système d'Information sur les Produits Agricoles en Guinée* and reported in the Government of Sierra Leone's *State of Food Security and Nutrition Policy* of 2011, the middle class of Guinea's capital Conakry has a preference for the cereal produced in Sierra Leone's rice-producing districts of Kambia and Port Loko; hence, there has been a constant increase in the tonnage (from 300 tonnes in 2005 to 360 tonnes in 2009) of smuggled rice from Sierra Leone (Government of Sierra Leone and World Food Programme 2012, 23). The authors of these reports also contend that substantial volumes of palm oil were traded in the black market across the West African region and that Sierra

Leone has been benefitting from this trade. And, although it is hard to ascertain, given the multiple crossing points between both counties, Sierra Leonean traders usually offer advances to their counterparts in neighboring countries in order to secure their much-desired goods. While these advances, generally provided during the lean season, provide a cushion for the small-scale businesses of individual traders, it hardly creates a cushion for the whole country against food insecurity.

The institutional interventions of states to achieve food and nutrition security

In the face of the problems created by governments, and while at the same time recognizing that population increases (despite wars and pandemics) were having an impact on the per capita dietary energy supply in the sub-region, the food security initiative that was to have been managed by sub-Saharan governments through the OAU's Millennium Partnership for Africa's Recovery Programme (MAP) and the Omega Plan was also rendered ineffective by a lack of political consensus. This crisis was resolved (or so it seemed) on July 3, 2001, when MAP and the Omega Plan were merged to create the New Africa Initiative (NAI). On July 11, 2001, during the OAU's Assembly of Heads of State and Government, the NAI was approved and, on October 23, 2001, a policy framework for NAI was adopted, thus giving birth to what is known as the New Partner for Africa's Development (NEPAD).

Soon after its formation, NEPAD began to introduce a series of initiatives to support national programs for food security. Examples include the African Development Fund (ADF), which NEPAD created to assist (through loans and grants) government investment in the crop, fisheries, and livestock sectors, as well as to enable governments to manage the agro-forestry sector in line with the ADF's guidelines for procurement under Community-Based Investment Projects (CBIP) and climate change, in line with the agreed international standards set by the regulators of the global emissions trading schemes recognized by NEPAD. Other initiatives aimed to develop a stable and sustainable agricultural sector and bridge the infrastructure gap, especially in the areas of the digital divide, energy, transport, water and sanitation—all essential components of food security.[1]

It has been suggested by NEPAD that these initiatives are to be achieved by the regional economic communities of Africa. What NEPAD requires from them is a commitment to prioritize, among other human security measures, food security; and, in tandem, to accept, as a peremptory obligation, a duty to act as the platforms in whose name NEPAD would fight for Africa's place in the international market and to inject modern technologies into the production and storage of supply cash crops. For this reason, governments are required to create national food security and human nutrition regulatory institutions. Such institutions have been created and are playing an increasingly important role in the promotion of food security. However, as shown in the next section, these national regulatory institutions can function only to the extent their mandate allows, and can operate only to the degree to which their intervention strategies are appreciated both nationally and regionally.

In 2014, NEPAD facilitated the AU consultations that resulted on the adoption of the *Malabo Declaration on Accelerated Agricultural Growth and Transformation for Shared Prosperity and Improved Livelihood* (hereafter the Malabo Declaration) at the AU Assembly of Heads of State and Government meeting in Malabo, Equatorial Guinea, on June 26–27, 2014. The Malabo Declaration contains eight declarative commitments.

1 Governments recommit to the fundamental principles and values that define the Comprehensive Africa Agriculture Development Programme (CAADP) process and NEPAD programs, which are also in line with the following AU decisions and declarations on agriculture, food, and nutrition security: the 2003 Maputo Declaration on Agriculture and Food Security in Africa [Assembly/AU/Decl.7 (II)]; the 2004 Sirte Declaration on the Challenges Of Implementing Integrated and Sustainable Development in Agriculture and Water in Africa [Ex/Assembly/AU/Decl. 1 (II)]; the 2009 Sirte Declaration on Investing in Agriculture for Economic Growth and Food Security [Assembly/AU/12 (VIII)]; the 2007 Decision on Abuja Special Summit of the AU on Fertilizers [Assembly/AU/Dec.117 (VII); and the 2007 Decision on the Abuja Summit on Food Security in Africa [Assembly/AU/Dec.135 (VIII) (African Union 2014, 1).
2 Governments bind themselves to enhance investment finance, both public and private, to agriculture. To this end, governments agree to uphold their earlier commitment to allocate at least 10% of public expenditure to agriculture, and to ensure its efficiency and effectiveness; and to ensure that they enhance or create the "appropriate policy and institutional conditions and support systems for the facilitation of private investment in agriculture, agri-business, and agro-industries, by giving priority to local investors." In line with the AU's Constitutive Act, all governments should work towards the creation of an African Investment Bank (African Union 2014, 3).
3 Governments promise to end hunger in Africa by 2025 and, to this end, resolved to "accelerate agricultural growth by at least doubling current agricultural productivity levels, by the year 2025." To accomplish this, they will also put in place the necessary policy and institutional conditions and support systems to facilitate:

> sustainable and reliable production and access to quality and affordable inputs (for crops, livestock, fisheries, amongst others) through, among other things, provision of 'smart' protection to smallholder agriculture, among others.
>
> (African Union 2014, 4)

Agricultural productivity also called for halving the post-harvest losses (by 2025). This is good move because the 2011 estimates (projected and actual) of the World Bank, the Natural Resource Institute and the FAO put the annual losses for sub-Saharan Africa at U.S.$4 billion—out of an estimated annual value of grain production of U.S.$27 billion (World Bank et al. 2011, xii).

4 Governments resolve to ensure that the agricultural growth and transformation process is inclusive and contributes at least 50% to the overall poverty reduction target. To this end, they agreed to provide sustained budgetary support. The intended outcomes were the sustained increment of the agricultural sectors' contribution of at least 6% to each country's GDP (African Union 2014, 4).
5 Governments commit themselves to create new trade and market opportunities and to fast-track the establishment of a Continental Free Trade Area (CFTA), which should lead to the creation of a continental Common External Tariff (CET) scheme to increase investment in markets and trade infrastructure (African Union 2014, 5).
6 Governments commit to the reduction of vulnerabilities in the livelihoods of Africa's population through building resilient systems, and to make sure that, "by the year 2025, at least 30% of our farm, pastoral, and fisher households are resilient to climate and weather-related risks" (African Union 2014, 5).
7 Governments pledge themselves to create, using the CAADP Results Framework, an independent, systematic, regular review process that involves tracking, monitoring and reporting on the progress of the progress made in implementing the provisions of the Malabo Declaration. To this end, they agreed to "foster alignment, harmonization and coordination among multisectorial efforts and multi-institutional platforms for peer review, mutual learning and mutual accountability" (African Union 2014, 5).
8 Governments also promised to submit a proposal with a view to enhancing the institutional capacity of the AU and NEPAD, whose roles will continue to expand.
9 Governments commit to a practical process of translation of these commitments into results. Towards this end, they called upon NEPAD's Planning and Coordinating Agency (NPCA)

> to develop an implementation strategy and roadmap that facilitates the translation of the 2025 vision and goals of Africa Accelerated Agricultural Growth and Transformation into concrete results and impacts, and report to the January 2015 Ordinary Session of the Executive Council for its consideration.
>
> (African Union 2014, 5)

The goals, policy directives and guiding principles of the national food and nutrition policies across sub-Saharan Africa

There are numerous specific objectives (SOs) mentioned in the national food and nutrition policies (NFNP) of sub-Saharan African countries, the accomplishment of which requires a set of policy directives (PDs); collectively, the SOs and PDs determine the scope and intensity of the government's food security and health interventions in line with the country's commitment, originally, to the MDGs and, now, to achieving the Sustainable Development Goals (SDGs) on food security and nutrition (SGDs 6, 7, 11, 12, 15 and 17) and a number of international conventions on the right to adequate food as fundamental human right, including Article 25 (1) of the Universal Declaration of Human Rights and Article 11(1) and 11(2) of the International Covenant on Economic, Social and Cultural Rights.

Statement of methodology

In order to examine the goals, directives and principles of country-led food and nutrition policies, as well as to understand the magnitude of transfers between the agricultural and public health sectors, a qualitative content analysis research method was employed. We considered the variations in country-level inputs to achieve food security before concluding that a content analysis tool would help us determine the presence of certain words or concepts within the selected international and national food security and nutrition policy texts. It is widely accepted in the literature that content analysis enables researchers to compute and analyze the presence, meanings and relationships of words and concepts, and then make inferences about the messages within the texts (Jolliffe 1993). Content analysis enables the researcher to create codes and classifications of meanings, and break them down for rational and objective analysis without losing sight of the relevance of the influence of the subjective worldviews of the authors of the texts being studied, and the cultural environments, as well as the space-time differences, that shaped the content of the texts (McTavish and Pirro 1990; Downe-Wamboldt 1992).

Discussions: Table 8.1

The key texts we evaluate are (1) the FAO report *Regional Overview of Food Security and Nutrition: The Challenges of Building Resilience to Shock and Stress* (2017); (2) the policy directives (framed in line with NEPAD's guidelines and the Malabo Declaration) of the EAC, ECOWAS and SADC regional economic communities; and (3) the NFNP policies of Ghana, Liberia and Sierra Leone (see Table 8.1, below).

Discussion: Table 8.2

In Table 8.2 (below) we are interested in whether these country-level policies contain specific SOs and PDs to ensure (a) the modernization and transformation of the agricultural sector; (b) the promotion of social protection schemes—such as school-feeding programs—through their social transfer programs; (c) the use of the agricultural sector to reduce poverty; and (d) the establishment of

Table 8.1 Overview of regional-level resilient food security policies to combat food insecurity and malnutrition shock and stress

Regional economic community	*Name of policy, timeline, and source*	*Strategies (in line with the Malabo Declaration and NEPAD Guidelines)*			
		Modernization and transformation of the agriculture sector	*Social protection schemes*	*Poverty reduction*	*Food availability, affordability, quality and safety*
EAC	Vision 2050: Regional Vision for Socio-Economic Transformation and Development (2016–2050) (EAC Secretariat 2016)	Improved mechanization, irrigation, seeds and use of fertilizers. Investment in the construction of modern road and railway networks (along the Namanga, Sumbawanga, Coastal, and Arusha corridors), sea and lake ports, and air transports. Establishment of a regional electricity power market, in collaboration with the United Nations Economic Community for Africa (UNECA).	Human capital development aimed at creating well educated and healthy people in the region.	Increased productivity and regulatory price intervention to ensure that the protection of farmers. Achieve increased socio-economic growth through the following achievable targets: • GDP per capita (US$)—from its 2014 figure of $1014 to $10,000 in 2050. • Average Regional Economic Growth (%)—from its 2014 figure of 5.8 to 9.9 in 2050. • People Living Below Poverty Line, below $1.25/day (%)—by reducing its 2014 figures of 40 to 5% in 2050. • Income Distribution (Gini Co-efficient)—from its 2014 figure of 0.35 to 0.2 in 2050. • Unemployment Rate (%)—by reducing from its 2014 figure of 14 to 5% in 2050. • Gross Capital Formation (as a % of Total Export)—from its 2014 figure of 24.3 to 40.5% in 2050.	Developing early warning systems and technologies can pre-empt disasters and contribute to building the resilience of the community. Strengthening policies and frameworks is imperative for improving food security. EAC commits itself to spend at least 10% of national budgets on agriculture development pursuant to Maputo Declaration.

continued

Table 8.1 continued

Regional economic community	*Name of policy, timeline, and source*	*Strategies (in line with the Malabo Declaration and NEPAD Guidelines)*			
		Modernization and transformation of the agriculture sector	*Social protection schemes*	*Poverty reduction*	*Food availability, affordability, quality and safety*
ECOWAS	2025 Strategic Policy Framework: ECOWAS Agricultural Policy (ECOWAP) (2017–2025) (ECOWAS Department of Agriculture, Environment and Water Resources (DAEWR) 2017)	Improving water management; the increase of agro-forestry-pastoral productions. Establishment of the West Africa Climate-Smart Agriculture Alliance (CSAA) (launched in 2015) to help about 6 million smallholder farming households reduce the impact of climate change and improve their lives. Funding for the CSAA comes from both the private sector and the NEPAD-International Non-Governmental Organisation's Alliance on CSA (NEPAD-iNGO Alliance) initiative. Access to subregional and international markets.	Climate-smart agriculture, and gender-responsive interventions. Including the targeting of interventions, at the level of zones, households and household members (gender-specific approach/ women's task reduction, in particular). Improving livelihoods of the vulnerable households and promoting social safety nets, taking into account the malnutrition of children, pregnant and breastfeeding women.	Created a Development Programme for the Transformation of Agriculture policy (with a timeline of 2017–2025). Increased employment in the agricultural sector.	Development of a "Zero Hunger Index" in 2014. The diversification of food supply in general, particularly in those areas where family self-consumption remains a major food supply modality for rural households (promotion of market gardens, in particular). Implementation of all 15 National Agricultural Investment Plans (NAIPs), and the Regional Agricultural Investment Plan (RAIP). NAIPs and RAIP are focused mainly on productive investments and cover the different sub-sectors, i.e., agriculture, livestock, fisheries and forestry. Increase production of rice above +95%, maize +130%, poultry +48%, cattle +85%, pig herd +59%. Innovative lending programs for farmers. Building strong value chains for crops, livestock and fisheries.

	Development of regional instruments for food safety management. Improvement of nutritional status; Reform of the institutional framework. Agricultural research and technology transfer. Capacity-building; and financing of agriculture. Effective inputs supply systems. Dialogue on the complementarities of national agricultural systems. The ECOWAS Regional Agricultural Investment Plan and Food and Nutrition Security (RAIPFNS) framework has provided the roadmap for a regional dialogue on the forms of specialization and complementarities of agriculture that would transform agricultural sector and increase the per capita dietary energy supply in the region.	Promoting employment, vocational training and securing the status of producers, farm workers, women and young people.		Trade in agricultural products (mainly livestock, cereals, market gardening, roots and tubers) within and outside ECAWAS. Work within the strategic framework of the RAIPFNS (which was launched on 12 December 2016) to achieve the following results by 2025: • Result 1.1. Agro-forestry, pastoral and fisheries productivity and production are increased. • Result 1.2. Production systems and techniques are adapted to climate change, and the management of natural resources for agro-forestry-pastoral and fisheries exploitation purposes is improved and sustainable. • Result 1.3. Post-production losses are reduced. • Result 1.4. Decent employment and incomes are increased. • Result 1.5. Gender inequalities are reduced and women are able to access grants, loans and innovative farming methods.

continued

Table 8.1 continued

Regional economic community	*Name of policy, timeline, and source*	*Strategies (in line with the Malabo Declaration and NEPAD Guidelines)*			
		Modernization and transformation of the agriculture sector	*Social protection schemes*	*Poverty reduction*	*Food availability, affordability, quality and safety*
SADC	The SADC Industrialization Strategy and Roadmap (2015–2063) (SADC Secretariat 2015)	In addition to the macroeconomic convergence efforts of the Committee of Central Bank Governors (CCBG), SADC countries should use macroeconomic policies to foster accelerated industrialization within a developmental state.	Mainstreaming gender and youth issues. Support youth innovation and entrepreneurship, with emphasis on science, technology, engineering and mathematics (STEM) training for youth.	Increase private sector investment and jobs creation in areas like services, manufacturing, horticulture, transport, energy, agricultural and trade industries. To achieve the targeted GDP per capita of US$9,000 by 2050; and to US$17,000 by 2063—an annual income growth of about 5%. Tax generation from the following domestic sources:	Infusion of advanced technology in food production. Ensure the advancement of scientific agricultural research to increase crop yield and resilience in the face of climate change. Improve the national infrastructure of member states and to support and facilitate marketing. Commercialization of agricultural sectors.

	Investment in efficient and affordable infrastructural services (consisting of transport, communications, ICT, energy and water supply)—in line with SADC's Regional Infrastructure Development Master Plan (RIDMP) and Industrial Upgrading and Modernization Programme (IUMP) that were formulated to support program for industrial take-off. The ICT sector will be regulated by the ECOWAS Agriculture Regional Information System (ECOAGRIS). Build legal and institutional capacity for formulating, implementing and enforcing intellectual property rights.	• The internal fiscal system/ taxation. • The financial sector. • Capital markets. • Private equity funds. • Public-private partnerships. • SADC Development Fund. • Sovereign Wealth Funds. • Remittances. • Institutional savings, including Pension Funds.	Develop agro-industrial clusters that would promote agribusiness. Facilitate access to finance, particularly for small-scale female and young farmers. Support smallholder farming to create more quality employment. Promotion of women and youth in agri-business. Building capacity for cooperatives to enhance women.

Source: The table is our construction based on the methodological technique of content analysis

structures to ensure these countries will achieve the GFSI threshold on food availability, affordability, and quality and safety, with the intent of ensuring diet diversification that meets the nutritional standards of the FAO and WHO recommended human energy requirements. The justification for focusing on these four areas is based on our observation that the statist responses to the problems of food insecurity and malnutrition work within the international and regional frameworks; and, therefore, irrespective of the noticeable differences in the language frames of the NFNPs of these select countries, they all share one similarity—namely, that the intended outcome is to end food insecurity and increase their overall ranking in the GFSI and increase their per capita dietary energy supply score in the FAO's ranking.

For the outcomes of national policies, we relied on the longitudinal monitoring and evaluation reports of the Global Database on the Implementation of Nutritional Action (GINA) for Liberia and, for Sierra Leone, the reports of USAID (USAID et al. 2016), the WFP and the Government of Sierra Leone (2012) and the supplementation commentaries discovered within the GINA database. The discussion on Ghana is omitted as it is the case we use in the next section to suggest options for the Ebola-affected countries in the sub-region.

In the case of Liberia, GINA's evaluation is that the success of the country's food security and nutrition strategy should be measured against the food and nutritional needs of young children. Our reviews of reports from Médecin Sans Frontières, WHO, FAO and Liberia's health ministry, and data from the Liberian Institute of Statistics and Geo-information Service, revealed that the needs of young Liberians are yet to be met, despite relative success in area of community-based food and nutrition security interventions. While child nutritional indicators integrate factors relating to food availability, access and utilization, the over reliance on food imports, the incidence of stunting (low height for age), underweight (low weight for age) and wasting (low weight for height) is still very high. Consequently, the GINA authors conclude that the fundamental determinants of child nutrition (including nutritional care for lactating mothers) and food security should be the key indicators for assessing the "likely sustainability of current child nutritional status and any progress achieved under the FSNS [Food Security and Nutrition Strategy]" (Ministry of Agriculture 2008, 4).

With regard to Sierra Leone, the agricultural sector is contributing to the health sector, but the problem is still visible. About 6% of people were malnourished and 1.3% severely malnourished. Of children aged 24–35 months, 21% were acutely stunted; 10% of these acutely stunted children were also suffering from wasting (and of these, about 5% were severely wasted). These reports also suggest that about one-fifth of Sierra Leonean children are underweight, with 7% classified as severely underweight. It was the expectations of many that rice (the most important subsistence crop) and other foods (such as cassava, palm oil, groundnuts, fish, gari, vegetables and beans) being produced at the rate of 60% self-sufficiency (see Table 8.3) would have reduced the pre-Ebola outbreak malnutrition figures. However, this expectation has not been realized. Like Liberia, Sierra Leone's uncontrolled, albeit open-door, policy on food importation has resulted in the importation of more rice than the 40% quota that was required to supplement the 60% of locally produced grains. This has contributed to the dislocation of the locally produced organic cereals in the market, and a reduction in households' intake of diets recommended by FAO's dietary guidelines. To address this, the authors of the USAID report (2016) recommend a shift to the fist sector:

> Increasing fish production—and thus its availability and consumption—may help reduce malnutrition. Fish contains a significant quantity of micronutrients, essential fatty acids and animal protein and is a valuable food to improve diets that lack essential vitamins and minerals. The consumption of fish is particularly important during the first 1000 days of life (from the onset of pregnancy to a child's second birthday), as the fatty acids it provides promote optimal brain and neurological development. The fisheries sector, which is composed of artisanal, inland and industrial fishing, has significant growth potential in Sierra Leone. Growth in the fisheries sector would create opportunities to improve food and nutrition security and increase employment and income generation.
>
> (USAID et al. 2016, 8)

From unpreparedness to food security and emergency preparedness in Ghana: lessons for the transformations of the Ebola pandemic-affected countries in West Africa

After independence in 1957, the Nkrumah government embarked on a Seven-Year Development Plan (1963–1969/70) (Rimmer 1966). While this seven-year plan was intended to transform the Ghanaian economy through physical capital accumulation, its emphasis on an import substitution path to economic development resulted in the adoption of restrictive, unsustainable economic policies (Waterbury 1999). As the imbalances in the import/export ratio continued, the country's GDP was negatively impacted. The export/GDP ratio and export volume index plunged from 18.5% in 1972 to 3.3% in 1985; the agricultural sector also registered a negative growth rate over the years 1975 (12.9%), 1976 (3.5%), 1979 (7.8%) and 1983 (4.6%) (Aryeetey and Fosu 2002, 3–5). Moreover, the 1981–1983 period saw Ghana suffering from a drought that by early 1983 had plunged the whole country into the harshest drought conditions in modern Ghanaian history. In the same year, bushfires swept across the country, destroying about 10,000 hectares of food crops in southern Ghana and vast areas of rice cultivation in the northern parts of the country (Ofori-Sarpong 1986). The effect of these disasters was a famine that affected most households' dietary and calorie intake.

Conditions began to take a positive turn in 1986, when the government adopted a series of measures to encourage the liberalization of the economy. However, the effect of the pre-1986 policies continued to impact the country until 1997. Between 1984 and 1997, there was Ghana's growth performance

Table 8.2 Overview of country-level resilient food security and nutrition policies to combat food insecurity and malnutrition shock and stress

Country	*Name of policy, timeline and source*	*Strategies (in line with the thresholds of the Global Food Security Index, and the Kcal benchmarks of FAO)*		
		Social protection schemes	*Reduction of malnutrition (Specific objectives and policy directives)*	*Food availability, affordability, and quality and safety*
Ghana	National Nutrition Policy for Ghana, 2013–2017 Source: http://extwprlegs1.fao.org/docs/pdf/gha145267.pdf	Political (government) acceptance that adequate nutrition is a universal human right issue. According the policy, the "right for all people living in Ghana to have access to safe and nutritious diets shall be observed in accordance with the fundamental basic human right to be free from malnutrition and related disorders" (see page 26 of the Ghana national nutrition policy).	Policy Objective One: Commitment to promote optimal nutrition as an essential component of health and development among all people living in Ghana. To achieve this, the following policy measures were identified: • Promote optimal infant and young child feeding. • Promote optimal nutrition among women in the fertile age. • Prevent and control micronutrient deficiency disorders, with an emphasis on vitamin A deficiency, anemia, and iodine deficiency disorders. • Strengthen nutrition support for vulnerable groups, including the aged and people in emergencies. • Promote nutritionally adequate and safe diets and nutrition services in institutions. • Promote healthy diets and lifestyle throughout the life cycle. Policy Objective Two: Increase access and create demand for quality and timely interventions, for effective management of priority nutrition problems in Ghana. To achieve these the following policy measures were identified: • Scale-up management of acute malnutrition nationwide.	Improved access to agricultural extension services and markets within regionally and internationally. Enlarged farmers' access to agricultural inputs. Increased government spending on capacity development and the extension of delivery services that would, in turn, create venues for the small holder farmers' adoption to best agricultural practices. Investment in development of technologies that would reduce pre-harvest loss in select commodities: cassava, horticultural crops maize, soy beans, rice cowpea, and fish. Implementation of several phases of a Medium-Term Agriculture Sector Implementation Plan (METASIP) to ensure availability and affordability of rice, maize, sorghum, and millet. On food quality and safety, the government has since 2014 been implementing innovative harvest techniques to reduce chemical residues, fungal toxins, and microbial contamination of large-scale harvested crops.

	• Provide adequate nutrition services as part of the treatment and care of HIV/AIDS, TB, malaria and other infectious disease. • Early case detection and management of overweight/obesity and nutrition-related deficiencies.	Governmental commitment to promote food security and assure food quality and food safety at the individual, household, community, and national levels. To achieve these the following policy measures were identified: • Promote practices that will ensure availability, access, diversity, proper storage (through a Buffer Stock Scheme) and utilization of variety of foods. • Ensure all persons living in Ghana have secure access to adequate amounts of nutritious food, irrespective of their social and vulnerability status. • Modernize and improve crops, livestock, fisheries, and other food commodity production to meet local food needs • Create the collaborations needed to ensure a secure and safe food system in Ghana. • Continuously review, improve and enforce food safety standards and regulations. • Create demand for safety and quality in the food system.

continued

Table 8.2 continued

Country	*Name of policy, timeline and source*	*Strategies (in line with the thresholds of the Global Food Security Index, and the Kcal benchmarks of FAO)*		
		Social protection schemes	*Reduction of malnutrition (Specific objectives and policy directives)*	*Food availability, affordability, and quality and safety*
Liberia	National Food Security and Nutrition Strategy, 2018: A cross-sectoral strategy for the Government of Liberia Source: https://extranet.who.int/nutrition/gina/sites/default/files/LBR%20 2008%20 National%20 Food%20 Security%20 and%20 Nutrition%20 Strategy.pdf	Improve knowledge on household food security. Strengthen community-level action.	Government commits itself to: • Support local production and/or procurement of supplementary and ready-to-use-therapeutic foods. • Diversify diets. • Incorporate information on food safety, food preparation and healthy diet and lifestyles into school curricula and the training of health professionals and agriculture extension workers. • Conduct assessments on the extent and epidemiology of micronutrient deficiencies. • Raise knowledge and awareness on the importance of nutrition during pregnancy and optimal breastfeeding and lactation, at all levels. • Provide nutritional care of the sick child during and after illness to prevent growth failure. • Improve women's nutrition, especially during pregnancy and lactation. • control the incidence of anemia in women and children. • Provide, where possible, vitamin A deficiency control, particularly in young children, and control iodine deficiency. • Protect consumers through improved food quality and safety strategies and enforce food standards. • Increase access to safe water, sanitation, and proper housing.	The political expectation that all concerned sectors (public and private) will walk within the guidelines of the Food Security and Nutrition Strategy (FSNS), whose central aim is to achieve national self-sufficiency in rice production; and create opportunity costs for Liberian farmers to produce rice when it may be more advantageous for them to use their land and apply their labor to produce other crops, using the income realized to purchase rice, whether local or imported. Exploit all opportunities for food production; address production constraints. Maintain predictable and stable food imports. Strengthen strategic food reserve mechanisms, including: • International food aid: Make appropriate use of international food assistance. • Improve people's access to food by advocating for the Liberia's access to the international agricultural markets.

Sierra Leone	Sierra Leone National Food and Nutrition Policy Source: https://extranet.who.int/nutrition/gina/sites/default/files/SLE%20 2009%20 National%20 Food%20 and%20 Nutrition%20 Policy.pdf	Political (government) acceptance that adequate nutrition is a universal human right issue. According the policy, the "Sierra Leone Government is accountable and obligated as set out in national laws and international conventions, treaties and resolutions on the right to food" (see page 20 of the Sierra Leone national food and nutrition policy). Government expresses commitment to explore avenues within its social programs to ensure that the integration of nutrition in household activities takes social nutrition Lens (SNL) approach. the SNL ensure that, political commitment is followed through without 'socially harming' the rural poor.	Ensure governmental intervention to protect, promote and support early and exclusive breastfeeding for infants from birth until six months, followed by introduction of nutritious and appropriate complementary foods with continued breastfeeding for up to two years and beyond. Promote appropriate feeding practices for the family especially pregnant and lactating women at facility and community levels. • Policy measure: Strengthen preventive measures against nutrition related diseases. Ensure antenatal, post-natal and 'family package' services are promoted and introduced at the community level, especially through outreach clinics. • Policy measure: Provide curative services to individuals who are malnourished or present a condition requiring diet therapy. Ensure that all patients in hospitals are provided with optimum dietary services to complement their clinical management; Community-based Management of Acute Malnutrition (CMAM) approach should be integrated into child survival and development initiatives; and supplementary feeding program should be integrated to ensure continuum of care for malnourished children. • Policy measure: Institute nutritional surveillance system for monitoring the food and nutrition situation in the country.	Policy directive 1: All relevant organizations should integrate nutrition considerations in programs and activities. • Policy measures: (a) Undertake advocacy for policy-makers, policy advisors and program designers at national and district levels on nutrition issues and their relationship to development. (b) Actively promote and facilitate adequate household food security (quantity, quality and safety) to satisfy daily dietary needs of the population. Policy directive 2: Small-scale farmers should be provided effective support to improve their access to domestic food production and supplies. • Policy measure: Promote adoption of appropriate feeding practices of households. Policy directive 3: Effective operational research and periodic surveys aimed at improving food security and nutrition should be integrated into programs of relevant research institutions. • Policy measure: Coordinate activities of relevant agencies involved in food and nutrition issues. Government talks about its commitment to increase production and supply of food in the following ways.

continued

Table 8.2 continued

Country	*Name of policy, timeline and source*	*Strategies (in line with the thresholds of the Global Food Security Index, and the Kcal benchmarks of FAO)*		
		Social protection schemes	*Reduction of malnutrition (Specific objectives and policy directives)*	*Food availability, affordability, and quality and safety*
			Government to undertake a regular and coordinated food and nutrition system that assists in long-term health and development planning, program management, timely warning and design of intervention programs should be instituted: • Policy measure: Promote operational research and periodic surveys into food and nutrition issues. The Nutrition Division of the Ministry of Health and Sanitation makes a commitment to ensure that activities to address nutrition issues are reflected in plans of other programs of the Ministry and implemented in a coordinated manner.	• Ensure availability of adequate and appropriate technologies together with improved agricultural inputs at the appropriate time during agricultural season, especially for poorer groups. • Expand 'Operation Feed the Nation' program to cover all vulnerable districts. • Integrate nutrition activities into Farmer Field Schools program, which is designed for decentralized community-based market organizations. • Collaborate with private sector to improve food storage, processing with value addition, marketing and distribution systems for local markets. • Strengthen and implement National Food Standards, and laws including code and guidelines on food hygiene for locally produced and imported foods. • Establish partnerships with consumer protection organizations. • Strengthen and implement community-based agriculture extension services.

Source: The table is our construction based on the methodological technique of content analysis

made most ECOWAS member countries to look for ways to use the 'Ghana model' of economic reform. However, the government was faced with the daunting task of increasing employment levels (Aryeetey, Harrigan and Nissanke 2000). The inability of the state to translate its economic growth into improved rates of employment was due, in part, to the policies it pursued. According to Ernest Aryeetey and William Baah-Boateng, the government focused most of its attention on

> achieving macroeconomic stability and accelerated growth without adequate employment consideration. Growth appears to have emanated from mining. Sectors with high labor absorption rate such as manufacturing, tourism, agriculture, and exports have not attracted the necessary investment to enhance growth and employment performance. The Ghanaian economy, therefore, requires a thorough review of the current national development policies to generate growth that would promote job creation and improve incomes for the realization of its poverty reduction goals.
>
> (Aryeetey and Baah-Boateng 2007, i)

According to Aryeetey and Augustin Fosu, in 1984 Ghana had set several targets for itself with the intention of becoming an upper middle-income country by the turn of the century. Ghana's policy-makers at the time decided to adopt a Harrod-Domar model because they believed it was the model that would best help them achieve the targeted 8% average annual growth. But a lack of political will made it nearly impossible for the five-year (1996–2002) targets to be met. During this period, the "performance of the economy and economic growth" was pigeon-holed by the non-attainment of macroeconomic targets. In particular, while the GDP was expected to grow between 7.1% and 8.3% in the period 1996–2000, actual growth was between 4.2% and 5.0% (Aryeetey and Fosu 2002, 2). With the government falling short of its targets, the GDP growth rate was at the modest 4.4 percentile. Although the agricultural sector grew by 3.9%, and the manufacturing and services sectors by 4.9% and 5% respectively, inflation for the year 2000 was 40.8% (higher than the end-of-year target of < 10% the government had projected) and the Ghana Cedi had depreciated by almost 100% (Aryeetey and Fosu 2002, 3).

This situation began to change for the better after 2002, due, in part, to the economic reforms instituted by President John Kurfour. The economy was repositioned to meet its macroeconomic and agro-industrial targets. By the year 2010, GDP rose by 39.57% (compared to 28.53% in 2008). GDP per capita for 2017 was U.S.$1,813.80, equivalent to 14% of the world average. By way of comparison, the highest GDP per capita, in 1960, was U.S.$1,049.41, and the lowest, in 1983, U.S.$701.50. Also, the agriculture sector began to experience a significant increase in production when the political will embraced both crop (corn, yams, cassava and other root crops) and livestock (cattle, sheep, goats, pigs and poultry) agriculture. Between 1971 and

1983, with the import-substitution industrialization in full swing, the cash-crop yield fell by an average of –2.7%. During this time, the country was self-sufficient only in plantain. Increased use of technical inputs in agriculture, along with change in both political and economic mindsets, brought about a significant increase in productivity and contributions to the country's GDP. For example, the agriculture sector's contribution to GDP in 2007 was GH¢5352 (Ghana cedi million), compared to GH¢6699.52 in 2016 and GH¢8441 in 2017 (Trading Economics 2018). This was a huge boost to the country's GDP when one considers the that the budgetary expenditure allocations to the Ministry of Food and Agriculture were GH¢411.821 million, GH¢501.502 million and GH¢759.680 million for the 2015, 2016 and 2017 financial years respectively (Ministry of Food and Agriculture 2018a, 4).

At the same time, the rise in real income, relative to population growth, meant that local demand for Ghana farm products also increased. The changes brought about by consumer behavior would not have occurred without government investment in technological innovations. The effect of these was a production surplus, which caused a boost in exports of Ghana-made food and farm products to the world markets (mostly in Africa and Western Europe). But the unexpected market shocks caused by the 2008 global financial crisis were a pointer to the volatility of the stock market. In fact, as the IMF senior economist S. Pelin Berkmen and her colleagues observe, sub-Saharan African countries were new to the world market, and had small leveraged domestic financial system, average credit growth, external debt, while lacking a robust exchange-rate market that would have buffered the impact of the shock (Berkmen et al. 2012). The crash in the world market had a ripple effect on Ghana's agro-economic sector. Post-harvest losses were in the millions of U.S. dollars. Faced with other troubles required financial action, the government was unable to procure the over-surplus harvests from farmers for the purpose of keeping some of them in business.

In response to the continued volatility of the price system, relative to the U.S.$, the Ghanaian government introduced a series of short-, medium- and long-term measures to cushion, not just the farmers, but the whole country in the event of another crisis. One of these policies—which is the focus of our analysis—was the *Medium-Term Expenditure Framework (MTEF) for 2018 and 2021*, released by the Ministry of Food and Agriculture (MOFA) in 2018. The MTEF has 15 policy objectives that are relevant to the food and nutrition security sector. They are: promote irrigation development; improve agriculture financing; promote sustainable environment, land and water management; promote the development of selected staple and horticultural crops; promote agriculture mechanization; improve science, technology and innovation application; promote seed and planting material development; increase access to extension services and re-orientation of agriculture education; promote the development of selected cash crops; promote livestock and poultry development for food security and income generation; improve institutional coordination for agriculture development; increase private sector investments in agriculture; improve post-production management; develop an effective domestic market; and expand agriculture exports (Ministry of Food and Agriculture 2018a, 1).

A few years before the MTEF was launched, the MOFA had already scaled-up its interventions to get the people to be the owners of the process of building a resilient food and nutrition security regime. For example, in 2017 it launched a 'Planting for Food and Jobs scheme' (PFJS) with a targeted aim of achieving, by 2020, the following objectives:

- i To ensure immediate and adequate availability of the selected crops in Ghana through improved productivity and intensification of food crops, and extended support to private sector service providers.
- ii To provide job opportunities for the teeming unemployed youth in the agriculture and allied sectors, and,
- iii To create general awareness for all formal workers to either have farms and grow some cereals or vegetables or establish backyard gardens, when enough land is not available and accessible (Ministry of Food and Agriculture 2017, 12).

To increase productivity, the PFJS was narrowed to focus on two main mechanisms:

- i [The] facilitation of adoption of inputs, good agronomic practices and output marketing through an integrated e-agriculture platform, and,
- ii [The] provision of support to private actors who are engaged in delivery of goods and services along the value chains in an efficient manner (Ministry of Food and Agriculture 2017, 13).

While it is still in its early stages, the impact and scale of these food security and emergency preparedness interventions through the MTEF and PFJS can be measured, at least on an interim basis, using governmental budgetary allocation, people-centric implementation strategies, and government commitment. To the private sector, the Ghana government has shown what was needed to restore investor confidence, namely, the political will and action to (1) ensure the availability of start-up capital for setting up cash-crop and livestock firms; (2) create a conducive atmosphere streamlining the legal and bureaucratic procedures for land lease, and business registration; (3) toughen the national agencies responsible for investigating and prosecuting financial and economic crimes; and (4) imposing a tax regime on imports (with exemptions for medicinal and dietary supplements that would help those who are malnourished). This tax regime will not only protect local business from external competition and phase out the import-substitution industrialization complex, but also provide the government with some of the funds it needs to carry out the stated objectives of the MTEF and PFJS.

To the small-scale farming households, government has committed itself to purchase their harvested products at a guaranteed fixed price (this was realized with the launch of the Ghana Commodities Exchange (GCX)[2] by President John Mahama in 2016), to supply them with improved seeds and fertilizer at subsidized prices, to train 1,200 extension services officers and 4,000 extension services assistants (at the five main agricultural studies colleges), and to modernize the farming sector by introducing modern machines,[3] innovative irrigation systems (such as the One Village One Dam Initiative[4]), and e-Agriculture (a "technological platform to monitor and track activities and progress of farmers through a database system" (Ministry of Food and Agriculture 2018c, para 13)). To the people, the government made an unprecedented political commitment to continue in the medium-term to invest in food and nutrition, and to ensure that a guaranteed portion of the 'quality' food procured would be made available to those at risk of malnutrition, including children and lactating mothers.

To achieve these commitments, the government established the National Food Buffer Stock Company (NAFCO) in 2017. This is Ghana's first grain training enterprise (GTE), but not the first in sub-Saharan Africa. Kenya had the National Cereals and Produce Board (NCPB), Zambia the Food Reserve Agency (FRA), Malawi the Agricultural Development and Marketing Corporation (ADMARC), Ethiopia the Ethiopian Grain Trade Enterprise (EGTE), and Tanzania the National Food Research Agency (NFRA). According to the Agricultural Policy Analyst of the OECD Trade and Agriculture Directorate, Annelies Deuss, these eastern and southern Africa GTEs were "in charge of social safety net stocks." While they "lost importance in the late 1980s and 1990s following economic reforms … they re-emerged in the early 2000s and are now again dominant players in African grain markets" (Jayne 2012; Deuss 2014, 11). What makes NAFCO different from these GTEs is its mandate and its activities. These are the issues we evaluate below, with the aim of suggesting two main ways that Ebola-affected countries could adopt the best practices of the NAFCO model to transform their own food and nutrition security and emergency preparedness.

NAFCO: relationships, mandate and interventions

Relationships

NAFCO is a government agency, with a directorate status under the MOFA and operational relationships with other government ministries, departments and agencies (MDA), including the Agricultural Development Bank (ADB), the Animal Production Directorate, the Directorate of Crops Services, the Women in Agricultural Development Directorate, the Agricultural Engineering Services Directorate, the Plant Protection and Regulatory Services Directorate, the Grains and Legumes Development Board, the Metropolitan, Municipal and District Assemblies (MMDAs), and the Veterinary Services Directorate. It also works closely with relevant international development partners, such as the African Development Bank (AfDB), Canadian International Development Agency (CIDA), the FAO, the European Union (EU) and the WFP.

Mandate

NAFCO's mandate is as follows:

> To guarantee an assured income to farmers by providing a minimum guaranteed price and ready market. To mop up excess produce from all farmers in order to reduce post-harvest losses resulting from spoilage due to poor storage, thereby protecting farm incomes. To purchase, sell, preserve and distribute food stuffs. To employ a buffer stock mechanism to ensure stability in demand and supply. To expand the demand for food grown in Ghana by selling to state institutions such as the military, schools, hospitals, prisons etc. To manage governments emergency food security. To carry out such other activities that are incidental to the attainment of above objects or such other duties as may from time to time be assigned by the Minister of Food and Agriculture.
>
> (Ministry of Food and Agriculture 2018b, para 7)

Activities

NAFCO's activities are determined, in part, by seven foundational objectives, the success of which depends on the participation of small-holding farming communities, the large-scale private sector, MDAs and the international donor community. The activity-setting objectives are as follows.

First, to work towards the stabilization of food grain supply and price. Under this objective, NAFCO's activities have extended to include a broad-based engagement to store a surplus of at least 422,600 tonnes of maize annually. This, of course, excludes (a) the replenished start-up operational stock the government provided at the start of NAFCO's work in 2017, and (b) the emergency stock of government, which is reserved in NAFCO's silos to be used in times of complex

Table 8.3 NAFCO's start-up operational stock and emergency government stocks

Commodity		*Metric tonnes*
Start-up stock		
Maize	White maize	15,000
	Yellow maize	15,000
Rice		15,000
Soya beans		10,000
Emergency government stocks		
Maize		10,000
Rice		10,000
Soya beans		1,000

Source: Authors' construction based on the data provided by the MOFA. 2008. http://mofa.gov.gh/site/?page_id=705

political and humanitarian emergencies like environmental disasters and pandemic outbreaks (see Table 8.3, below).

That said, to achieve its target without drawing on its operational stock, NAFCO has created a model to help it determine the when, where and of ensuring a continued unprocessed food supply, and when to distribute (to hospitals, prisons and schools) the processed food supply.

Second, to create employment for the youth. Under this objective, NAFCO works closely with community-based organizations like the Youth in Agriculture Program (YIAP) to develop what it calls a "Block Farm Concept" (BFC). This BFC, which is linked to the government Poverty Reduction Strategy Paper (PRSP), was developed to assist the youth in poor, rural communities to use the limited resources to they have to develop basic infrastructure that would enable them to commercialize their garden plots, diversify what they produce in those plots, and sell a portion of the harvest to NAFCO (under its 'T+1' clearing and settlement system) while still being able to reserve enough for household consumption and re-planting the next season.

Third, to ensure a continued increase in the 'emergency food reserve bank' (EFRB). Under this objective, NAFCO's activities includes creating a stabilization plan for a "build-up of food stocks at the time of buying." This plan is continually evaluated (and, where necessary, amended) for the purposes of increasing public awareness of the benefits of the EFRB, and to study changes to the climate and the trends and patterns of the dreaded crop-eating fall army worm (a maize crop-eating pest), the Bamisia tabaci (a roots and tuber crop insect pest), the Crambidae, Busseola fusca and Chilo partellus (rice, wheat and sorghum eating pests), and leafhoppers (a bean-crop pest).

Fourth, to work towards ensuring that there is macroeconomic stability despite season-to-season variations in food grain production. Under this objective, NAFCO is working in partnership with the relevant government ministry and the banking sector to either prevent or limit the level of inflation. Moreover, to maintain its guaranteed buyers' price, NAFCO and its licensed sub-agents and companies must see to it that each seller makes at least a 10% profit margin. To achieve this, they (NAFCO and the farmers) have reached an agreement on the following price: GH¢45 for 100kg maize, GH¢35 for 85kg paddy rice, and GH¢75 for 100kg soya beans (Ministry of Food and Agriculture 2018b, para 20).

Fifth, to act as Ghana's foreign exchange earner. Under this objective, NAFCO's activities employ best practices to make monetary gains from goods (agricultural products) and services (expertise) in global markets.

Sixth, to promote the consumption of locally grown rice, maize and soya beans. Under this objective, NAFCO, in partnership with the ministries of health and education, is engaged in mass public education to change public perceptions. One of the most successful methods of public awareness-raising is supplying this produce to hospitals and schools (under the school feeding program).

And, finally, to do everything within its mandate to boost agro-processing factories. Under this objective, NAFCO has transformed itself into a key supplier of raw produce (especially that which is are more than the surplus and reverse threshold) to licensed buying factories[5] for processing into a variety of nutritionally balanced food.

Recommendations for the Ebola pandemic-affected countries

There are various ways adoption of the Ghana model could help transform the food and nutrition situation in Sierra Leone, Guinea and Liberia. These could include investment in the following areas.

1 Moving from an endless process of planning to encourage the agriculture and health sectors to actually adopt coherent policies and scale up their investment in agriculture through government–private sector partnerships.
2 Governments and the private sector, especially the banks, should increase investment in rice production, processing and marketing. Here the focus should be on the procurement, management and transportation of modern technology and fertilizer, and selecting, with the help of global positioning systems (GPS), designated arable land where the government and the private sector could cultivate new varieties of crops and livestock.
3 Making youth and women a catalyst for agribusiness development and growth. To achieve this, government should allocate at least 10% of annual budgets as recommended by the *Malabo Declaration on Accelerated Agricultural Growth and Transformation for Shared Prosperity and Improved Livelihood* of 2014.
4 Government should also invest in catalytic technology, e.g., mechanization, irrigation and efficient water-management machinery.
5 The government should invest in livestock development and commit to increasing the annual yield of livestock with high source of protein, e.g., guinea fowl, ducks, grasscutters, rabbits and fish. These livestock are already readily available in the Mano River basin region (Sierra Leone, Guinea and Liberia). What is needed is the establishment of buffer stock companies to reach out to small-scale farming communities that have such livestock. That way, communities that lack these livestock can access them through the central agents, the buffer companies.
6 Strengthen sustainable biodiversity conservation and management including forest and tree crop development.
7 Increase production of other crops to ensure diversification.
8 Establish a multi-country consortium to develop a regional nutrition and food program.

Notes

1 For more on these initiatives see the website of NEPAD. www.nepad.org/content/about-nepad (accessed: July 23, 2018).

2 However, for this exchange to operate effectively, it has been suggested by experts that the country would need "about 10,000 metric tonne capacity warehouses in strategic locations across the country"; and for participating farmers, they will receive the funds for their commodities a day after the exchange in line with what the GCX model, the "'T+1' clearing and settlement system" (Ashiadey 2016, paras. 8, 16).

3 According to the MOFA,

> To promote agricultural mechanization, 220 tractors and accessories comprising 141 Maize shellers, 77 Multicrop threshers were distributed to farmers and service providers. In 2018, the Ministry will distribute 200 tractors and matching implements; 1,000 power tillers and walking tractors; 30 tractor mounted rippers; 10 tractor drawn rear blade; 10 tractor mounted slasher; 60 boom and orchard sprayers; 4,000 motorized sprayers; 60 mechanical and pneumatic planters; 50 cereal harvesters; 200 multi-crop threshers; 400 irrigation kits (engine and solar powered sprinklers sets); and 100 green house technology for horticulture production.
>
> (Ministry of Food and Agriculture 2018a, 5)

4 The 'One Village One Dam' initiative is aimed at "facilitating the provision of community-owned and managed small-scale irrigation facilities across the country, especially in northern Ghana." Towards this end, the MOFA has, between 2017 and 2018, identified 192 small dams and dugouts in 64 districts for development (Ministry of Food and Agriculture 2018a, 6).

5 As of June 2018, NAFCO has 73 Licensed Buying factions. According to the MOFA, these licensed buying factories also have the mandate to reach out to farmers at their farm gates. They can also buy

> cereals from the farmers on behalf of NAFCO. Most of the farms in Ghana are located in remote areas and it would be difficult for NAFCO to reach them all, which is the reason why NAFCO has employed the services of these LBCs to work on their behalf. A margin is added to the farm gate prices for the LBCs prices. The committee takes into consideration factors like transportation, sacks, drying, bagging, sewing and handling to come up with this margin. The LBC prices are as follows; Maize (100kg)—Gh¢70 Paddy Rice (85kg)—Gh¢45 and Soya (10kg)—Gh¢85.

References

Abrahams, Zulfa, Zandile Mchiza, and Nelia P. Steyn. 2011. "Diet and Mortality Rates in Sub-Saharan Africa: Stages in the Nutrition Transition." *BMC Public Health* 11 (1): 801.

African Union, The. 2014. *Malabo Declaration on Accelerated Agricultural Growth and Transformation for Shared Prosperity and Improved Livelihoods (Malabo, Equatorial Guinea, June 26–27)*. The African Union Secretariat. https://au.int/sites/default/files/documents/31006-doc-malabo_declaration_2014_11_26-.pdf.

Aryeetey, Ernest, and Baah-Boateng. 2007. *Growth, Investment and Employment in Ghana*. Policy Integration Department, International Labour Office, Geneva. www.oit.org/wcmsp5/groups/public/-dgreports/-integration/documents/publication/wcms_085043.pdf.

Aryeetey, Ernest, and Augustin Fosu. 2002. *Explaining African Economic Growth Performance: The Case of Ghana*. Growth Working Paper No. 7. African Economic Research Consortium Research Project on "Explaining African Economic Growth

Performance. Nairobi, Kenya: African Economic Research Consortium. www.africaportal.org/publications/explaining-african-economic-growth-performance-the-case-of-ghana/.

Aryeetey, Ernest, Jane Harrigan, and Machiko Nissanke, eds. 2000. *Economic Reforms in Ghana: The Miracle and Mirage*. Oxford, UK: James Currey Publishers.

Ashiadey, Bernard Yaw. 2016. "Ghana's Commodities Exchange to Begin Trading 2017." *Tralac Trade Law Centre*, 2016. www.tralac.org/news/article/9936-ghana-s-commodities-exchange-to-begin-trading-2017.html.

Baro, Mamadou, and Tara F. Deubel. 2006. "Persistent Hunger: Perspectives on Vulnerability, Famine, and Food Security in Sub-Saharan Africa." *Annual Review of Anthropology* 35: 521–538.

Bellamy, Alex J. 2010. *Global Politics and the Responsibility to Protect: From Words to Deeds*. Routledge.

Berkmen, S. Pelin, Gaston Gelos, Robert Rennhack, and James P. Walsh. 2012. "The Global Financial Crisis: Explaining Cross-Country Differences in the Output Impact." *Journal of International Money and Finance* 31 (1): 42–59.

Deuss, Annelies. 2014. *Review of Stockholding Policies [Paper Prepared for the OECD Global Forum on Agriculture: Issues in Agricultural Trade Policy]*. Paris: Trade and Agriculture Directorate, OECD.

Downe-Wamboldt, Barbara. 1992. "Content Analysis: Method, Applications, and Issues." *Health Care for Women International* 13 (3): 313–321.

Economist Intelligence Unit, The. 2017. *Global Food Security Index, 2017: Measuring Food Security and the Impact of Resource Risks*. New York, NY: The Economist Intelligence Unit'. https://foodsecurityindex.eiu.com/Home/DownloadResource?fileName=EIU%20Global%20Food%20Security%20Index%20-%202017%20Findings%20%26%20Methodology.pdf.

Fjelde, Hanne, and Nina von Uexkull. 2012. "Climate Triggers: Rainfall Anomalies, Vulnerability and Communal Conflict in Sub-Saharan Africa." *Political Geography* 31 (7): 444–453.

Government of Sierra Leone, and World Food Programme. 2012. *The State of Food Security and Nutrition in Sierra Leone, 2011*.

Hendrix, Cullen S. and Sarah M. Glaser. 2007. "Trends and Triggers: Climate, Climate Change and Civil Conflict in Sub-Saharan Africa." *Political Geography* 26 (6): 695–715.

Jayne, T. S. 2012. "Managing Food Price Instability in East and Southern Africa." *Global Food Security* 1 (2): 143–149.

Jolliffe, Lee. 1993. "Yes! More Content Analyses!" *Newspaper Research Journal* 14 (3–4): 93–98.

Matthews, Alan. 2003. *Regional Integration and Food Security in Developing Countries (Prepared for the Agricultural Policy Support Service, Policy Assistance Division)*. Vol. 45. Rome: Food and Agriculture Organization of the United Nations.

McTavish, Donald G. and Ellen B. Pirro. 1990. "Contextual Content Analysis." *Quality and Quantity* 24 (3): 245–265.

Messer, Ellen, and Marc J. Cohen. 2007. "Conflict, Food Insecurity and Globalization." *Food, Culture & Society* 10 (2): 297–315.

Ministry of Agriculture. 2008. National Food Security and Nutrition Strategy: A Cross-sectoral Strategy for the Government of Liberia. Ministry of Agriculture, Monrovia, Republic of Liberia. Retrieved from www.foodsecurityportal.org/sites/default/files/National%20Food%20Security%20and%20Nutrition%20Strategy_Mar08_0.pdf

Ministry of Food and Agriculture, Government of Ghana. 2017. Planting for Food and Jobs: Strategic Plan for Implementation (2017–2020). Accra: Ministry of Food and Agriculture, Government of Ghana. http://mofa.gov.gh/site/wp-content/uploads/2018/03/PFJ%20document%20New%20New.pdf.

Ministry of Food and Agriculture, Government of Ghana. 2018a. *Medium-Term Expenditure Framework (MTEF) for 2018–2021: Programme Based Budget Estimate*. Accra: Ministry of Food and Agriculture. www.mofep.gov.gh/sites/default/files/pbb-estimates/2018/2018-PBB-MoI.pdf.

Ministry of Food and Agriculture, Government of Ghana. 2018b. *National Food Buffer Stock Company (NAFCO): Background, Mandate, Objectives, and Price Determination.* 2018. http://mofa.gov.gh/site/?page_id=705.

Ministry of Food and Agriculture, Government of Ghana. 2018c. *Planting for Food and Jobs (PFJ): Frequently Asked Questions (FAQs)*. 2018. http://mofa.gov.gh/site/?page_id=15114.

Ofori-Sarpong, E. 1986. "The 1981–1983 Drought in Ghana." *Singapore Journal of Tropical Geography* 7 (2): 108–127.

Rimmer, Douglas. 1966. "The Crisis in the Ghana Economy." *The Journal of Modern African Studies* 4 (1): 17–32.

Shaw, Daniel John. 1991. "Food Aid for Africa in the 1990s." *Food Policy* 16 (6): 431–435.

Thomas, A.-C., B. D'Hombres, C. Casubolo, F. Kayitakire, and M. Saisana. 2017. *The Use of the Global Food Security Index to Inform the Situation in Food Insecure Countries.* EUR 28885 EN. Luxembourg: Publications Office of the European Union. http://publications.jrc.ec.europa.eu/repository/bitstream/JRC108638/jrc108638-revised_version.pdf.

Trading Economics. 2018. "Ghana Gross Domestic Product: 1960–2018." 2018. https://tradingeconomics.com/ghana/gdp.

USAID, M. M. Pasqualino, S. H. Thilsted, M. J. Phillips, and A. S. Koroma. 2016. *Food and Nutrition Security in Sierra Leone with a Focus on Fish in Tonkolili District.* Washington, DC: http://pubs.iclarm.net/resource_centre/2016-23.pdf.

Walker, Brian, Scott Barrett, Stephen Polasky, Victor Galaz, Carl Folke, Gustav Engström, Frank Ackerman, Ken Arrow, Stephen Carpenter, and Kanchan Chopra. 2009. "Looming Global-Scale Failures and Missing Institutions." *Science* 325 (5946): 1345–1346.

Waterbury, John. 1999. "The Long Gestation and Brief Triumph of Import-Substituting Industrialization." *World Development* 27 (2): 323–341.

Watkins, Kevin. 1991. "Agriculture and Food Security in the GATT Uruguay Round." *Review of African Political Economy* 18 (50): 38–50.

World Bank, The, The Natural Resource Institute, and Food and Agricultural Organisation (FAO). 2011. *Missing Food: The Case of Postharvest Grain Losses in Sub-Saharan Africa.* Report Number 60371-AFR. Economic and Sector Work. Washington, DC: The World Bank. https://siteresources.worldbank.org/INTARD/Resources/MissingFoods10_web.pdf.

9 Conclusion

In the sub-Saharan African (SSA) context, the fundamental issues underlying state fragility have been erroneously theorized by some authors as being mere reoccurrences of life which do not deserve global recognition, while the role of governments in the making of fragile states has been downplayed. Historical discourses have acknowledged the impact of fragility (broadly defined) in SSA as a series of complex phenomena. However, this acknowledgement is often followed by reservations about the ability of African states to build resilient socio-politico-economic structures that can efficiently and effectively address the myriad of problems facing the sub-region. Fragility in the context of African institutions is conceptualized as dysfunctional state structures. Some of the definitions discussed in Chapter 2 illustrate how the African Development Bank (AfDB), for instance, considers fragility as a phenomena that emanate from the internal and external challenges facing states and the inability of their governments to manage them. This 'inability,' the AfDB notes, stems from the lack of effective institutions and processes whose legitimacy is as questionable as their inability to maintain societal cohesion. (AfDB 2014, quoted in Ferreira 2015, 34). In fact, the organization called 'G7+ of Fragile States,' is also of the view that state fragility began in SSA when government institutions failed to prioritize sustainable socio-economic development, inclusive political interaction, security, justice, jobs, good management of resources, and accountable and fair service delivery after independence from European imperial control (G7+ 2013, 1). These perspectives—presented by the AfDB and the G7+—clearly positioned the state and its institutions at the center of the making of fragility.

In this book, we presented a state-centric approach to examine the role of the state in the making of fragility; and, through what we termed, 'fragility-as-resilience methodology', we positioned the state as a key driver in the unmaking of fragile spaces within SSA. The centralization of the state in the fragility and resilience discourse in SSA is important. It sought to, and succeeded in, projecting the performative function of the state in the fight to reverse the problem of state fragility; and with it, to change the trajectory of the definitions of fragility (like those presented by the AfDB and the G7+) that have downplayed the role of the government institutions of African states in addressing the problem of state fragility. Closely connected to the centrality of the state, Chapter 3 presents the framing of impact to identify the correlates of armed conflicts on state fragility. The discussion points to the fact that the concept of conflict is a relative term and on the basis of this acknowledges that its impact on state fragility should be examined contextually. Similarly, Chapter 4 examines the behavioral language used in framing state-led Peace Accords and how that are linked to battle-related deaths in a year or two following the conclusions of peace negotiations. Having identified the state as a strategic contributor in the making of fragile states (from Chapters 1 and 4), it is prudent to position the state as having a major role to play in the unmaking of fragility. These issues are presented in the next section by focusing on topical issues that were discussed in Chapters 5 and 7.

That said, the state-centric and 'fragility-as-resilience' approaches were employed to position the state as the key policy maker instrumental in the adoption or design and implementation of policies necessary to end child labor and to advance food security and health. In Chapter 6, governments interventions towards the elimination of child labor is largely depicted in actions required for the protection, prevention and reaction campaign to reduce child labor. The states across SSA have mainly bought into the policies of international organizations resulting in more similarities than variations in anti-child labor intervention strategies across countries (see USDOL 2017). These similarities in policy formulation are approached from the vulnerability framework that is built on five frames including social (cultural), medical, educational, economic and legal. Among these, education has been the main strategy that has been employed across countries to pull child laborers into schools and away from the farms, but empirical evidence has shown some potential pitfalls. This is because, farm households, faced with climate change conditions, are increasingly engaging in non-farm economic activities as income diversification strategies and continue to demand child labor. They are especially used after school and whole days over the weekend, sometimes in both on-farm and non-farm activities (Koomson and Asongu 2016). The legality framework also strikes some semblance across countries but although they are adopted by national parliaments of SSA countries, their applications are informed by international and regional conventions and norms that underpin them (USDOL 2017). These similarities of frames could serve as a platform for the construction of a secure regional child protection database for the exchange of ideas and the development of a regional child offender registry system.

Beyond the general policy of using education, there are country-specific interventions that are tailored to address the child labor menace within particular economic sectors and within countries in general. This is where the local ownership of the institutional framework is emphasized. In the Ghanaian case, policies such as Livelihood Empowerment Against Poverty (LEAP); and Mobilizing Community Action and Promoting Opportunities for Youth in Ghana's Cocoa-Growing Communities (MOCA) have been implemented to provide and supplement incomes of poorer households so that child labor hours will be reduced considerably (USDOL 2017). MOCA especially is aimed at eliminating the use of children in cocoa production through research, monitoring, and enforcement of the anti-child labor laws of Ghana. In Cameroon, Project 559 and Country Program Action Plan (2013–2017; 2017–2021) which have the state's involvement have been designed mainly to combat the street children phenomenon and to provide health and psychosocial care besides the provision of education (USDOL 2017). Similar country-specific interventions can be found across SSA.

In Chapter 8, the state-centric and 'fragility-as-resilience' approaches were again employed to provide an evidential report of some interventions that can be adopted by the state to advance food security and health. In identifying the key strategies and interventions to contain food insecurity, we acknowledge that the Ebola-affected countries have national food security and nutrition strategies, but emphasis is placed on the Ghana model to serve as a blue-print for other fragile states in SSA. In essence, the ways in which adoption of the Ghana model can help to transform the insecurity situation among the Ebola-affected countries were found to include but not limited to: (i) engaging in government–private sector partnerships to encourage stakeholders in the health and agricultural sectors to adopt coherent policies and to scale-up investment; (ii) heighten public-private sector partnership (especially with banks) to increase investment in the production, processing and marketing of rice; (iii) governments taking steps to achieve both the Maputo and Malabo declarations of allocating at least 10% of annual budgets to the agricultural sector; (iv) governments must invest in mechanization, irrigation and efficient water-management machinery; (v) increase production of other crops to ensure diversification; and (vi) establish a multi-country consortium to develop a regional nutrition and food program (Ministry of Food and Agriculture 2018).

The possibilities of Africanizing future research on the state, fragility and resilience in SSA

The aforementioned issues provide a picturesque view of a need for a paradigm shift in research regarding the conceptualization and analytical approaches adopted to understand the issues of statehood and conflicts; poverty and child labor; and food insecurity and health among other fragility-related topics in SSA. Of course, asymmetric knowledge differentials should continue to exist in the production of scholarship about the role of African states in the making and unmaking of fragility (Lahai and Lyons 2016). For this reason, and in acknowledging the relevance of the varying perspectives, Lahai and Lyons (2016) contend that any approach that seeks to centralize the state is likely to be challenged with quandaries and queries of when and where to start the process of framing a positive role for the state through research. Nonetheless, some solution to this challenge can be found in Blake's analysis of knowledge-framing of the continents in archaeology and politics (Blake 2010), where he calls for a transformation of dysfunctional values into platforms for the reconfiguration of the discourse of self, place and identity (Blake 2010; Lahai and Lyons 2016). Blake (2010) emphasizes the need to reconceptualize the postcolonial states of

Africa using the logical narratives that are embedded in the material, structural and constitutive knowledge about the continent's past. Lahai and Lyons (2016) also add that, without an Africanized policy aimed at making SSA resilient, the much anticipated governance and peacebuilding for the postcolonial states will remain an illusion.

Concerning the role of research in the formulation of sustainable Africanized policies, Lahai and Lyons (2016) stress the need for a hybrid approach to peace, security, and governance and development in the continent. This simply calls for policies that incorporate both strategic Eurocentric and Africanized policies that place emphasis on the African identity and the role of the state. The hybrid approach formed the underlining principle throughout the process of inquiry and validation of existing ideas to formulate the content of this book. The hybrid approach, with emphasis on statehood, has unequivocally resulted in the application of a state-centric approach to the conceptualization and proposed design of interventions to address the fragility menace in SSA.

On the question of design: the use of a multidisciplinary approach and application of mixed method in the analysis has resulted in a myriad of theoretical, conceptual and empirical revelations. In specific terms, we conducted a review of over 270 scholarly documents (including books, articles and others) on statehood, fragility and resilience in SSA. Methodological frameworks were drawn from mathematical and applied linguistics, securitization theory, political theory, legal theory (and international labor law), applied child development theories and applied econometric techniques to analyze statehood, fragility and resilience in the socio-political economy of SSA. Based on this, we recommend, that studies on fragility within SSA should begin to centralize the state as the unmaker of fragility so that outcomes and findings get to reflect the true experiences of the African people. Also, it is imperative that scholars begin to have relook at the fragility indicators to incorporate a stand-alone indicator on women and children as part of the fragility indicators.

In Chapter 4, we employed a novel methodology to analyze the link between conflict de-escalation and battle-related deaths (BRDs) within the context of behavioral language frames. By counting the number of times conflict de-escalation words (CDWs) were used in 49 Peace Accords (PAs) signed across countries in SSA from 1990 to 2003, we were able to empirically ascertain that, in general, CDWs are inversely related to BRDs. In specific terms, the link between reconciliatory words and BRDs is non-linear, in that at lower numbers of reconciliatory words in PAs, BRDs continue to increase but once these words increase beyond the threshold of 35 reconciliatory words, BRDs begin to reduce marginally. The analysis revealed that CDWs often grant state/non-state actors an opportunity to cooperate. Words that imply peace are also negatively linked to BRDs. This has resulted in the emergence of a new theory known as "theory of conflict de-escalating words (CDWs)." We recommend that future studies that aim at studying PAs and fragility should employ the "theory of conflict de-escalating words" so as position the study within the scope of being able to empirically test hypotheses using statistically robust techniques. It will also help in identifying which words to prioritize when framing PAs to yield their intended outcomes.

In Chapter 5, this book partially responded to the missing stand-alone fragility indicator on women and children by drawing a link between poverty, child labor and fragility. Employing the ordinary least squares technique on survey data from Ghana and Tanzania, the empirical analysis confirmed the widely acknowledged theoretical notion that poverty is a major driver of the incidence of child labor within and across households and nations. By linking the synthesis of the literature to the empirical findings, further deductions were drawn to show that: (i) child labor is directly related to fragility in general and to all the separate fragility indicators; and (ii) poverty-driven child labor can perpetuate a country's long-term underdevelopment which may fuel the mechanisms that further drive countries into a state of fragility. The centrality of the state in this discourse is depicted in the payment of low adult incomes by the state which compels households to engage in early introduction of children into the labor market in order to smoothen overall household consumption. Future studies can be designed to provide deeper insights into the links between poverty, fragility and child labor.

In Chapter 6, it was identified that, over the years, governments' formulation of anti-child labor intervention strategies have been shaped by child development theories. Some of the child development theories that were identified include: (i) Freudian psychosexual development theory; (ii) Erik Erikson's psychosocial development theory; (iii) Jean Piaget's cognitive development theory; (iv) Bowlby's attachment theory; and (v) Vygotsky's sociocultural theory. It is worthy to note that these theories have not been the only underlying factors that have shaped anti-child labor policies, but these have also been influenced by biases in the form of current trends of child labor activities. For example, if child labor in exploitative commercial sex is the most prevalent within a country, the framing of the anti-child labor policy will be biased towards the elimination of vulnerable children from that commercial sex industry or sector with less emphasis on child labor in other sectors. These revelations notwithstanding, future studies on child labor intervention policies should examine these with a state-centric approach and should also consider studying them along with child development theories to determine which one works best for the study area. That will help to make future child labor policies more effective.

On another sparsely researched topic in the fragility literature, we examined the Ebola pandemic and household food insecurity in Chapter 7 since the nature of the pandemic and the resultant deaths have socioeconomic and food insecurity implications. Focusing on Sierra Leone, we used the three rounds of the High Frequency Cell Phone Survey data and employed Random-effects Poisson and population-averaged Poisson models in the analytical process. Revelations from the analysis showed that households that engage in agriculture only and those located in rural areas are more vulnerable to food insecurity while income-diversified households are more resilient towards food insecurity during an Ebola pandemic. The recommendation here is for governments to promote while households take the necessary steps to embrace income diversification so as to remain resilient to food insecurity during an Ebola pandemic. Future research can use panel data from different Ebola-affected countries to produce more robust estimates.

References

Blake, Cecil. 2010. *The African Origins of Rhetoric*. London: Routledge.

Ferreira, Ines Afonso Roque. 2015. "Defining and Measuring State Fragility: A New Proposal." In, 39. Berkeley, CA. http://cega.berkeley.edu/assets/miscellaneous_files/109_-_ABCA_2015_Ines_Ferreira_Defining_and_measuring_state_fragility__A_new_proposal_May15.pdf.

G7+. 2013. "Note on the Fragility Spectrum." G7+. www.g7plus.org/sites/default/files/resources/g7%2B%2BEnglish%2BFS%2BNote%2BDesign.pdf.

Koomson, Isaac, and Simplice A. Asongu. 2016. "Relative Contribution of Child Labour to Household Farm and Non-Farm Income in Ghana: Simulation with Child's Education." *African Development Review* 28 (1): 104–115.

Lahai, John Idriss, and Tanya Lyons. 2016. *African Frontiers: Insurgency, Governance and Peacebuilding in Postcolonial States*. London: Routledge.

Ministry of Food and Agriculture, Government of Ghana. 2018. "National Food Buffer Stock Company (NAFCO): Background, Mandate, Objectives, and Price Determination." 2018. http://mofa.gov.gh/site/?page_id=705.

USDOL. 2017. "2016 Findings on the Worst Forms of Child Labour." Bureau of International Labour Affairs, U.S. Department of Labour, https://businessandhumanrights.uconn.edu/wp-content/uploads/sites/1850/2017/11/US-Dept-of-Labor-2016-Worst-Forms-of-Child-Labor.pdf.

Index

For Product Safety Concerns and Information please contact our EU representative GPSR@taylorandfrancis.com
Taylor & Francis Verlag GmbH, Kaufingerstraße 24, 80331 München, Germany

www.ingramcontent.com/pod-product-compliance
Lightning Source LLC
LaVergne TN
LVHW011127300926
849160LV00008B/547

9781032174181